FALLING BACKWARDS

JANN ARDEN

FALLING BACKWARDS

a memoir

Alfred A. Knopf Canada

PUBLISHED BY ALFRED A. KNOPF CANADA

Copyright © 2011 Jann Arden

www.randomhouse.ca

Knopf Canada and colophon are registered trademarks.

Grateful acknowledgement is made for permission to quote from "Snowbird."

Library and Archives Canada Cataloguing in Publication

Arden, Jann
Falling backwards : a memoir / Jann Arden.

Issued also in electronic format.

ISBN 978-0-307-39984-7

1. Arden, Jann. 2. Singers—Canada—Biography. 3. Composers—Canada—Biography.
4. Lyricists—Canada—Biography. I. Title.

ML420.A676A3 2011   782.42164092   C2011-901969-8

Text and cover design by Jennifer Lum

Cover photograph by Andrew MacNaughtan

Printed and bound in the United States of America

9 7 5 3 1 2 4 6 8

*With much love do I dedicate this book to
my parents, Joan and Derrel Richards,
and to my dear brothers, Patrick and Duray.*

And to Bb—three little numbers you know to be true.

Great spirits have always encountered violent opposition from mediocre minds. —ALBERT EINSTEIN

INTRODUCTION

look across my yard every morning at my parents' little house. They live fifty feet from me now. I can see their lights go on in the morning and shut off at night. I can see them moving about in the yard when they're watering plants or cutting wood or when my mother is digging up her flower beds. I watch them and I smile. Sometimes I catch myself wondering what in the world I will do when they are not there anymore. I drink cold water and tell myself to stop being so selfish. I close my eyes tightly and open them again, hoping that my thoughts will be cleared away. They never are completely.

I have fourteen acres of land west of Calgary, not far from where I grew up. Not far from where this story begins. My mother and father met on a blind date in the late fifties, before there were colour TVs and cellphones and CDs and computers and even Spanx, for that matter. My mom's old friend Freda, who's now deceased, was determined to set my mother up with her boyfriend's pal, convincing her that this blind date would be different. Freda told my mom that *this* guy was funny and smart and had a job, for Pete's sake! What else could a girl possibly want? Freda didn't seem to care that my mother *kind of* already had a boyfriend (though my mother says she never really liked him all that much anyway), and asked what would one little date on a Saturday night hurt anybody? My mother reluctantly agreed to go out with my dad. The rest, as they say . . .

It's hard to believe that my parents are still together and going strong some fifty-three years later. They have survived things that would have crushed most couples. They persevered where others would have cracked in half. I don't think I could have done what my mother and father did, and that was to go ever forward with their shoulders back and their jaws set straight and their faith unwavering. Both my parents *lasted*. They beat the odds. They survived each other, for starters, and that was—and is—no small feat. I don't know if something was in the water, but not a single one of my friends' parents divorced either. I thought about that one day and just shook my head. It says a lot about the company I kept and continue to keep all these years later.

My parents are my treasures. They are my secret weapon, my shield, my strength and my faith. Whenever I went off the rails, and that was fairly often as I was figuring out how to be a person, I turned to them for comfort and solace and direction and forgiveness. They were always there for me, always.

I sometimes see my dad standing in the yard. He's perfectly still and quiet, with his arms resting on his rake, and he's looking off over the fields. I wonder what he's thinking about. I wonder if he's thinking what I am thinking.

I asked him once what it was like getting older, and he told me that he couldn't feel it and he couldn't see it in the mirror either. He said he just saw himself the same way he always was. I think about that conversation a lot.

So many things have changed around me, but I still see the same face when I look in the mirror. I know what my dad meant.

Living is a process. You plod along and hope you're on the right road and if you're not, well, that's okay too. I know that from experience now.

When I was in my early twenties, I moved out to Vancouver for a few years and managed to get myself into a lot of trouble. Not legal trouble, but emotional and spiritual trouble. I felt so lost and so down and out. I made one mistake after another. I was on some kind of self-destruct mode. Eventually I picked myself up and hosed myself down and ended up, as my mother often says, making something of myself, despite myself. She also says to me, "Thank God you could sing, or who knows where you'd have ended up." I don't like to think about that.

Years later I returned to Vancouver for a series of sold-out concerts. It was a giant contrast to the days when I was busking on the streets for a buck or two to buy cigarettes and wine. I couldn't believe I was there, standing on a beautiful, brightly lit stage, singing my songs for people who had paid to see me. I felt vindicated somehow. I'd survived the stupidity of my youth.

After one of the shows I had the limo driver take me across the Lions Gate Bridge to the North Shore, where I'd gotten myself into so much trouble. I had him drive by my old apartment building on Third Street, where I had lived twenty-five years earlier. It was boarded up, to no one's surprise—least of all mine. It stood there like a tombstone. The pouring rain added nicely to the movie I was creating in my head. I saw my young self, staggering in drunk through the beat-up front door. I closed my eyes and clearly pictured the old mattress on the floor, the ironing board I used as a kitchen table, my beloved cassette deck. I sat in the car for ten or fifteen minutes with the window down, looking out at the street. The cold rain was spitting at my face.

I won, I thought to myself. I won. I felt a weight lift off my heart. I said a prayer in my head about gratitude and forgiveness, and then I had the driver take me back across the big bridge to my hotel. I lay in my bed that night and thought about how I'd gotten to where I was that day. I fell asleep smiling.

chapter one

THE GRAND OPENING

I was reluctant, to say the least, to get here. My mother tells the story on pretty much every birthday I have ever had. She most often smiles—a laugh lurking inside of her little bird-like chest—and says, "When you were born, I said, 'Let me die, let me die.'" She really isn't kidding.

For some reason, that line always made me laugh too. Not that it was a prelude to a happy tale, but it was a funny one nonetheless. She'd go on to say that the doctor just let her suffer through two long days of pushing and pushing and pushing to no avail. I guess I was backwards or feet first or probably just refusing to come out of her at all. Why would I want to fly out into the abyss without really knowing what in God's name I was getting myself into? I'd still be in there now if I'd had my way.

One thing about being born: it's hard for everybody involved. You learn within a few seconds that it's not going to be easy being a person. That first breath must really be something. I am kind of glad I don't remember it. The human body is an extraordinary thing. What it is capable of doing is, quite simply, miraculous.

I can't even begin to figure out how an eight- or nine- or, God forbid, twelve-pound body inches its way out of something that seems to be smaller than the slot in a slot machine. And never mind that, after the twelve-pound body has fought its way out of the womb, the whole bloody layer-upon-layer works suddenly just folds itself back together like a book with a few ripped-up pages. Like nothing ever happened. Kind of like a Slinky.

My mother would disagree with me, I'm sure, as something did indeed happen. I am in pain just thinking about childbirth. In fact, I suddenly have to fold my legs together and hum "Happy Birthday." My poor mother; all that suffering, and for what?

Oh yeah, me.

My mom said that back in those days they didn't just give women C-sections like they do now. I mean, now women *pick* the day they'd like to have their baby.

"Ah yes, Doctor, I have March 27th open after 4 p.m. after my pedicure." I can just picture that in my head. In 1962, they made you push until you thought you couldn't push anymore. Epidurals weren't even that common. It was natural childbirth or bust. She almost did bust.

"I thought it was either going to be you or me," she'll often say. I tell mom that I am really very glad that it wasn't either of us.

I always ask the same questions. Where was dad? Wasn't he in the room? Didn't they let men in the birthing room?

"He didn't want to come in," she says. "He went home and went to bed while I was lying there thinking I would die."

My mom was apparently just about to throw in the towel on the both of us when the doctor appeared. They were finally, after two days, going to do a C-section. They had to call him at home to come in to do the operation and, according to my mother, he took his sweet time getting there. You'd think they could maybe have found another doctor who was *in* the hospital? To top things off, I think he got caught in a snowstorm. Yes, a snowstorm in March, which is fairly typical for Alberta. It can snow in Calgary in July.

Fortunately for my mother and for me, we didn't end up needing him after all—not for a C-section, anyway—because I decided to come out into this complicated world all on my own. I think all the doctor ended up doing was grabbing my legs and turning me around. I mean, turning a person around? In a womb? My dear mother said it was nothing short of agony. I have given her the odd sympathy card on my birthday. It seems fitting, somehow. The card simply reads, "I am sorry about your vagina. Love, Jann."

The nurse at the hospital told my parents that they wouldn't be able to bring me home until they had a name for me. Velvet was an early contender. My mother was an Elizabeth Taylor fan, and she loved the movie *National Velvet*. Thank God that never stuck. My parents didn't even smoke pot, so that's not an excuse. I ended up being named after a cartoon strip called *Jane Arden* that ran from 1927 to 1968. My mother loved that cartoon strip. Jane was a reporter *and* a crime fighter and a force to be reckoned with, and I guess mom thought I would be too. But mom didn't like the name Jane, so she substituted an *n* and called me Jann—Jann Arden Richards. Maybe they were just desperate to get the hell out of the Calgary General Hospital, but that was their final answer. Final answer: Jann Arden.

I could have been called "Baby Girl Richards," which kind of has a stripper ring to it. (My real stripper name would have been Louise Bentley, if you were to base it on the first street you lived on and your mother's maiden name. Or is it your first dog's name and your mother's maiden name? If it had been my first dog's name, I would have been Aquarius Bentley.)

As much as my mom teases me about how hard it was getting me out of her body and onto the planet, I don't actually try to imagine the pain she endured. I have a bad period and I'm ready to call in a midwife with a morphine drip. They could at least have given my mother a big glass of vodka. Forty-eight hours is a long time to be stuck in a canal of any kind. The Panama Canal only takes a day to float through and that involves a giant ship. (There's not a goddamn thing to look at going through the Panama Canal, according to my dad. I sent them through there once on a cruise.) Two days in a birth canal? That's beyond cruel and unusual.

My mother told me that my head was so pointed that she kept a hat on me for a year, but that I had a cute face—like that was supposed to make me feel good about the pointed head bit? I've seen a few pictures that were taken of me in those first few months of my life, but I've never been able to ascertain whether I indeed had a pointed head or not. Maybe it's because I was always wearing a hat.

She should have known I would be difficult, considering that my older brother Duray nearly killed her while he was being born three years earlier—he was a lot fatter than I was. I guess it's true what they say about forgetting the pain of childbirth, because that's what my mother did. She forgot all about the misery and went ahead and tried it again. I guess she figured things would be all stretched out, and I would just drop onto the ground after one push.

My parents adopted my little brother Patrick five years after I was born, which made a lot of sense. They wanted another baby, and mom couldn't put herself through the whole almost dying by giving birth thing again. My mom was not childbearing material, although she does get an A for effort from my older brother and me. Her thing-a-ma-dingy had seen enough pain for one lifetime. (I just want to say "vagina" instead of all these other ridiculous euphemisms, but my friend Nigel said he did *not* want me to write down the word "vagina" in this book. He said his mother wouldn't read a book with the word "vagina" in it and *he* did not want to read the word "vagina" either. He said it would make him feel really uncomfortable, so I promised him I would neither write or use the word "vagina," and a promise is a promise.)

A few years after we were blessed with Patrick, my mom had a hysterectomy. Right about now she will be saying, "Why would you write that in your book? Maybe I don't want anybody to know that I had a hysterectomy." She was thirty-seven years old when she had her uterus out, and I would be very happy to give her mine if she'd like to have another one put in. I am not using mine for anything special. I don't see why my mother couldn't bear me a child, since she is home more than I am. If she wants grandchildren from my branch of the family tree, she's going to have to have them herself. (I don't know how to record that on the family tree; I will have to consult some of my Mormon relatives, if they're still willing to talk to me after they read this.)

Not every life starts with a giant bang like mine. Some people just slip into the world, seemingly unnoticed by anyone or anything. They fall into the cracks that nobody seems to see but God. Thank God for God is all I have to say about that. From the beginning of my life, from what I have pieced together, I have somehow felt noticed. I don't know how to explain it other than it feels like the Universe has one eye following me around no matter where I go or what I do. It's creepy but comforting at the same time.

I have always felt observed by something or someone. Something catches my eye and I turn to see what it is, but it's just shadows or dust floating through the air. I may just have a multiple personality disorder, which could mean that I have just been following myself around all this time. If that's the case, I am a nice bunch of girls.

My mother said that when they finally did take me home, I refused to eat. I wouldn't breast-feed or bottle-feed or any kind of feed. Not milk, not cereal, not formula, not even KFC. Well, I am sure they didn't try KFC, but if they had I bet I would have eaten that. At least the popcorn chicken, for crying out loud; it's smaller. I would have eaten popcorn chicken for sure.

My parents had to have a nurse visit our home and stuff food down my throat. She waltzed in—the nurse, that is—and, according to my mother, took out her own special spoon, loaded it up with some horrible concoction and crammed it down my throat. Our family doctor told my parents that I was very anemic, and that if that nurse didn't get me to eat he was going to send me to Africa to live with the Masai people. Maybe the Masai people could get me to eat goat meat and white corn and curdled milk from a gourd. (Well, the doctor never said that, but I'm telling the story, so I'll say what I want).

My mother said she couldn't bear to watch the nurse holding me down and shoving that spoon into my head. She had to leave the room. I guess I bawled the entire time, very loudly, like I was being killed rather than saved. Didn't this woman know I was destined to be one of the greatest singers the world has ever known? Okay, that Canada has ever known? Okay, that the Canadian prairies have ever known? Okay, that my local community centre has ever known? Didn't she realize that my voice would one day become a golden tool for all things musical and melodic and, from time to time, depressing? She could have damaged my precious vocal cords. I guess she didn't realize this because that nurse came back time after time until my tiny body pulled itself out of an iron-depleted slump. I find it amazing that they even had nurses who made house calls back then, but then again they had people who delivered milk and ice cream and eggs and diapers and Fuller brushes and Avon and newspapers and mail and pretty much anything else you wanted to have delivered.

They even had folks who came to your house to give you accordion lessons. I am not sure what happened to all those home delivery people. They died, I assume. Those were the days. Customer service was the rule, not the exception. That sounds exactly like something my mother would say. Good grief. Each and every moment I sit here, my mother slowly takes over each and every one of my cells. I will wake up and be her and the circle will be complete. Kind of like in *The Lion King* . . . (I am hearing African drumming in my head.)

The home-visiting nurse did get me to eat on my own eventually. My mother will often talk about how terrible that woman was. But not once in my life since have I ever had trouble eating. She must have cured me. It's a miracle.

I grew up on a quiet little street in southwest Calgary. We lived in a very modest house with a cracked concrete driveway that my mother scrubbed on her hands and knees with soap and water and I am not kidding. My mom is the cleanest person in Canada, if not the world. This is a woman who used to vacuum the dog. (The dog loved it.) She has worn out vacuum attachments with simple friction. Metal against rug. Rug always wins. I am surprised any of us kids had skin on our bodies. We were scrubbed into bright pink beings every night of our young lives. My mother was very proud of how clean our house was. You could seriously make Jell-O in any toilet in our house on any day of the week, and then eat it out of there. She was clean and we were all grateful for it.

We lived in the perfect neighbourhood. We had good neighbours and there were lots of other kids racing around on any given day, so I was in my glory. I was social, to say the least. My mom said I was like the Pied Piper. I sought out new people to charm at every possible opportunity and brought them home with me. I always wanted to be liked. Not much has changed in that way—being liked is important to me. I wish I didn't care what people thought, but I always have and I always will. I didn't even know who or what the Pied Piper was when my mother said that to me. She also told me that I was just like a whirling dervish. I didn't have a clue what that was, either. I finally saw a whirling dervish on TV about ten years ago. They are men in lengthy white outfits who certainly do whirl around like crazy people, but I am definitely not like a whirling dervish. I don't know what my mother was thinking. Yes, maybe I was like a Pied Piper, but that's as far as I am willing to go. Anyway . . .

The neighbourhood looked like a spread in *Better Homes and Gardens*. I don't remember anybody on our block ever being robbed or shot. Kids could walk to school in the sixties and not have to have a parent drive them the two blocks there (in their giant SUVs, no less). There were lovely trees and flowers everywhere, and people waved at you from their front lawns. Sprinklers waved back and forth over perfectly groomed lawns while the proud owner stood with his hands on his hips admiring his mowing job. Everybody looked out for everybody, or maybe they were just completely nosy. Either way, Neighbourhood Watch was in full swing on our street. People didn't lock their doors every hour of the day. They actually left them wide open with just the screen door shut. No one was scared of being mugged in the middle of a Tuesday afternoon. The world wasn't quite the paranoid mess it is now.

I just remember being happy. I didn't have a worry in the world. Nobody ever died in that world. No one got sick. *Everybody* had a job they went to, and they seemed to love every minute of it. (Little did I know.) If you've ever seen the movie *Pleasantville*, that was us. Houses all lined up and painted perfectly. Bicycles lying out in the front yards with pink baskets attached. Swing sets and monkey bars in the backyards with eight kids hanging off them. I was healthy and sun-kissed and innocent. I was beyond lucky. My childhood memories are like panes of glass, sunlit and clear.

It's amazing to me how life eventually begins to wear you down, but in a good way. There is such value in loss. There is so much to learn from failure. You just don't realize it at the time. Every blow you take makes you that much taller and stronger. Like I've said before, it's hard being a person, and I was a busy little person. I can't remember a time when I wasn't thinking about things: big things, grown-up things. I wondered why I was here at all, and where I came from and how my hands knew to move when my brain told them to. I had so many questions running around in my head. Nothing seemed simple to me. Sometimes I made myself physically dizzy from thinking too hard. Everything I thought had some cosmic attachment to it. I had been briefed briefly about God by the church we went to, that he loved me and that he knew everything that I was thinking about, good or bad. That was a bit disconcerting to me. I didn't like to think that God could see me in the bathroom wiping my little white bum. I didn't like to think that God was able to see me picking my nose on the rare occasion I did it. I didn't want God to know one single thing that I was thinking. He would think I was crazy. I was told that God was everywhere, and that he was a very good God, and that if a person were good, they would be rewarded in heaven. How about rewarding me now, I thought to myself? I was pretty darn good today, God! You find out early on that life is not based on a system of punishment and reward. Bad people often get ahead and good people can and will die of cancer. There is no sense to be made of any of it. You just have to get up and deal with the day.

When I was six or seven one of our neighbours died of a heart attack. I wondered how a heart could attack anybody. My mother said that it was a shame that a good person had to die so young. It would have been easier had he been a bad person, I guess. That makes more sense to all of us. I felt sorry for God having to make all those hard decisions. I knew for sure I would never want to be God. I could mark that off my to-do list. Whew.

I was a short, small person, always the smallest in the class, but I was a big thinker. I preferred thinking to pretty much doing anything else. When I was really young, like six or seven, I did love being social, but as I got a little bit older, I was more or less happy being on my own whenever possible. My mother always said that I could entertain myself for hours on end. I am sure I could. I could doodle on a piece of paper for three or four hours and not notice a single second going by. I didn't mind being by myself at all, although my mother tells me that I was seldom, if ever, alone. I think you can be alone even when you're with someone else—you can be alone together. Even when I was playing with other kids, I was in some far-off place making up my own version of things. Daydreaming was my specialty.

My parents were very practical. They are still very no-nonsense people. They always told me that things happen to you in life and you just throw your shoulders back and keep going. I have learned so much from them over the years, invaluable things that have saved me a hundred times over. Persistence is more important than any-thing else—that's one of the lessons. Another one: the harder you work, the luckier you get. Both of them have served me well count-less times.

Things at 6307 Louise Road were easy and breezy and pretty much devoid of any kind of worry. The days were simple and organized. My family seemed to be really very normal. We fit in with every-body else. My parents were very present to me then, and they always seemed to be around. My dad worked hard at his job and I didn't see much of him during the day, but the lot of us always had dinner together in the evening. Dad was usually home on weekends and his specialty was Saturday morning breakfasts. Eggs over easy and crunchy dark-brown bacon that was cooked beyond recognition and—my personal favourite—his home-fried potatoes. They were so crispy and salty. No one could make them they way he did. The nearly black pieces of potato were worth fighting over. We sat at our round white table with the white plastic swivel chairs in the kitchen with the sheer yellow curtains that my mom had made with her very own hands, and always fought over the last piece of burnt bacon and the last crispy potato. If I were to go to my parents' house, right this very minute, they would have a side plate covered with a paper towel on the counter with leftover bacon sitting on it. They would also be having potatoes of some kind, no matter what meal of the day it was, breakfast, lunch or dinner. I think we ate more potatoes than the country of Ireland before the great famine.

I know we were very blessed. I realize that more now than ever. The sixties seemed abundant. In our house, no one ever really talked about people being poor. I'm sure there were lots of people struggling to make ends meet, but my parents protected me from anything unsavoury or sad. They were my magic dome, the two of them. They seemed to let only the good in. I never even remember them raising their voices to each other—which I know is hard to believe—but they didn't . . . until some time later.

One of the most interesting features of our small white house on Louise Road was the milk chute. It was built right into the wall of our house, right by the back door. Everybody in our neighbourhood had one. Nobody bought milk at a store, they had it delivered by the milkman.

The milk chute was like a really fancy dog door, complete with handles. It was about four feet off the ground with the milkman's little door on the outside of the house and our little door on the inside. The doors were slightly askew, so he'd have to slide the bottles of milk over to our side, and then we'd grab them out of there like it was a pop machine. You never even had to step outside, which was great in the winter. I am sure that's why people had milk chutes; the milk would have frozen sitting out on a front step in about two minutes. After all, it is winter in Alberta eleven and a half months out of the year. It feels that way, anyway.

I can remember one day waiting for our milkman to come with the homo milk and our whipping cream and, I hoped, our chocolate milk. We didn't get chocolate milk that often, but when we did it was like Christmas and Halloween and Easter and May Day all at the same time, whatever May Day is.

I listened for the milk truck to pull up in front of our little white house and then I stuck my head into the milk chute and held my breath. I imagined he would open the milk chute and see my adorable freckled face grinning at him like the Cheshire cat and exclaim how desperately cute I was. Unfortunately, because the milk chute doors weren't aligned, he actually couldn't see me sitting there with my head in the tiny door grinning at him wildly, and so he began shoving the milk bottles into my invisible, now somewhat shocked, face. I tried pulling my head out of the milk chute, but it had become quite stuck. I mean *really* stuck. It was wedged in there like a marshmallow in a piggy bank, like a bowling ball in a frog's mouth. Like thong underwear on a gymnast doing backflips. My dad had to come home from work to saw me out of that milk chute. Okay, that may be a bit dramatic, but he did have to break off some of the moulding around the opening to get access to my head. My mother reminds me that he had to get some Vaseline, smear it all over my face and pull me out of there like you would a fat finger out of a wedding ring. I remember being very scared and very embarrassed by the whole thing. I never did get to surprise that milkman.

I never saw him at all. And I am really glad now that he didn't see me. I didn't stick my head in the milk chute ever again, although I did look into it from time to time for no reason whatsoever.

The things a person remembers are so random and somehow so particular. Some events quite simply stick to your heart and never come loose. I obviously don't recall all that much about my life until I started school, but I do recall many fragments, little Polaroids that drop out of some mysterious camera in my mind and get waved in front of my face while I'm thinking about something else entirely. Remember this? That's what the Polaroids seem to say. They prompt me for some reason to recall, recall, recall. I can just be sitting quietly in a chair and some vivid picture of my past will shoot through my mind like a bullet, causing me to actually draw a breath between my teeth. What is that? I don't know what it is until I can actually place the memory. Things I haven't thought of in forty years sit themselves on my lap and look up at me like a tired dog. Some of the Polaroids are good and some of them are terrifying.

Flash. Flash. Flash.

The things I remember from before I went to school always seem to involve me crashing into or falling off or wedging myself in things. Nothing frightened me. Everything seemed possible. I was always moving in some direction, but never backwards. What I choose to remember shapes who I am every day. I know that. For the most part I control that. Every day I wake up and feel ever so slightly changed, and I can't go back to who I was the day before. It's simply not possible. The universe makes you fall constantly forward and I am glad that it does. We are renewed over and over again. But memories shape us all. My memories shape and reshape who I am. I draw on them all the time to help me go forward in my life. They somehow guide me through what would otherwise be a very difficult maze. It could be a guiding principle as simple as "remember when you did this and it was really bad? Don't do that again."

Whenever I get together with old friends, we always end up talking about the past, and about things we did together. Places we went, things that happened. It never ceases to amaze me how differently we all recall the very same event. Our minds form our own versions of our lives that will never be the same as anybody else's. I have had so many friends say to me, "Don't you remember that?" No, I don't remember that, or at least I don't remember it the way they do. Maybe that's why witnesses to crimes are considered very unreliable. He was tall; no, he was short; no, wait, he was a purple dog.

I think the universe knows what it's doing in the memory department. Some things we forget out of self-defence, or I do anyway. I find it quite easy to put things into jars, screw on the "not now" lid and set them on a shelf in my brain. You can't possibly carry an entire life around with you all the time. You have to look at it in sections so your mind doesn't implode. I have certain days where I'll take the jars down and have a good look around in them, but those days have become fewer and further in between as I get older. I don't mind glancing in the rear-view mirror now and then, but I don't want to stare.

You are not what you did, but what you will do.

Yes, memories are funny things. Do they make you up, or do you make them up? When I was a kid, I would feel sorry for God. I used to worry about how many of our thoughts he had to store in his own head. I pictured him sitting in his screened-in porch and watching the thoughts pouring in through the tiny squares of the screen and him swatting at them like flies. I pictured him hanging fly strips by the thousands from the pale white ceiling to catch all the prayers that were streaming through every possible opening, trying to make their way to him. It made me feel so heavy hearted. I worried about God. I wondered who he prayed to. It made my little head hurt. I understood for a moment how "impossible" felt.

It's good to remember, but you can't let memories hurt you. Human beings are the only animals on the planet that punish themselves over and over again for something they've done in the past. A dog doesn't punish himself for something he did an hour ago, but people? If we can beat ourselves up about something, we usually do. I try not to do that, but like most other people, I slam myself into a wall every now and then.

The things we choose to remember say a heck of a lot about us.

As far as I can remember as a kid, I always seemed to be crashing, falling, being wedged into or pulled out of one thing or another. There was the milk chute. Then one summer I had to be pulled out of a barbecue. I know you're picturing a gas grill with a lid on it, but the barbecue that I was pulled out of when I was six was one that my dad had built himself from a kit. That in and of itself was probably the problem. It stood about eight feet high and was made out of concrete Lego-style blocks, stacked one on top of the other to form a fairly tall chimney. It seemed like it was a hundred feet tall but I am quite certain it was actually more like eight. There were shelves or wings off to each side where one could put plates and pots of beans or set down a cold beer. This was the barbecue to end all barbecues and I don't know what possessed me to scale up to the very top and look down into that chimney, but I did. And I don't know what possessed me to actually stick my head into the chimney and then wiggle down into it, but I did that too. So now I was upside-down inside an eight-foot barbecue, looking down at the grill and wondering how I was going to get out. I did try to get out for some time, but I couldn't reach to push myself off the bottom and I had no space in which to turn myself around. I hung there for a very long time. I don't know if I was screaming or laughing, but our neighbour Betty Evans heard me from her kitchen window—or heard something, rather—and came out of her house to check. She obviously couldn't see anything at first, because I was obscured in the barbecue, but she kept searching for where the sounds were coming from. She found me eventually and somehow managed to pull me out. Thank you, Betty. I might well still be in there if it weren't for you. I haven't crawled into a barbecue since, you'll be happy to know, although I have really wanted to.

I was always climbing on things: on countertops to get into cupboards or on top of the refrigerator to get at a bag of cookies or onto retaining walls just to get up onto a retaining wall. I just wanted to climb; there was no purpose in it at all. Of course I fell off everything I climbed on. My mother says I was forever covered in bruises. I suffered one or two concussions and various split chins from numerous falls to the earth, and of course mom was mortified about what our family doctor, Dr. Turner, would think. Was I being beaten on a somewhat regular basis? Not at all, but you know how doctors can be—suspicious—and I don't blame them.

I wasn't afraid of anything. I should have been, but I wasn't. Fearlessness wears off as you get older. Reality takes over eventually and replaces fearlessness with doubt. You start doubting everything you do. But in your youth? Ah, youth, teeming with bravado! There actually was a time in my life, albeit a short one, when I truly believed that I would never die and nothing terrible would ever happen to me or my family. I miss that feeling. Now it's a constant fight to defend yourself from succumbing to the dark side. (I can hear Darth Vader breathing inside that black helmet of his.)

Yes, falling, always falling. I fell off bikes (always keep your hands on the handlebars) and dressers and countertops and swing sets and merry-go-rounds. I fell into things like garbage cans. Well, I liked to play in garbage cans, for some strange reason, and I was in them a *lot*. There were hundreds of garbage cans lining the alley behind our white house, and I made sure that I stuck my head into every single one of them. No rotten apple core went unturned! There were treasures to be had, by gum! And probably gum to be had. I apparently didn't know that garbage was garbage yet. Good thing, too.

I got worms from playing in the garbage cans with my friend from across the alley, Davey Hayes. I am sure he talked me into it. I would never have thought something that terrible up by myself. Never! My mother said that Davey's mother was a bit crazy and that Davey was a bit crazy too. That seemed like it would be a good thing to be, considering how hard life could be from time to time.

My mom told me she'd take me into the bathroom in the middle of the night, wrap Scotch tape around her fingers and then stick the tape onto my wee bum hole. Then she'd throw the light switch on to see if she'd caught any worms. She said she caught many a worm poking out of my arse. True story—I swear on my mother's life. The doctor actually told her to do the Scotch tape thing. (Thank God for universal health care.) I am sure that's not something the Scotch tape people tout as one of the many handy uses for their product. De-worming? I should let the Scotch tape people know that it really works. My mother could be the spokesmodel. That whole experience with the worms was much worse for her than it was for me. You'd think a person could feel worms coming and going out of their bum hole. Disgusting, really. That's what you get for eating garbage.

I was also known to eat the odd dead fly off a windowsill, but that could just be an out-and-out lie. I can't imagine that even at six years old I would have found that at all appetizing. I hate flies. I hate moths even more.

There is a picture of me when I was two or three years old, next to my little pal Shelly. My shins are covered in bruises and Shelly doesn't have a mark on her anywhere. I still bruise easily. All I have to do is bump ever so slightly into the corner of a table and I have a bruise the size of a small dog. I had a bruise once on my inner thigh that looked very much like the Virgin Mary and all the neighbours paid me a buck and a quarter to come and look at it. I am kidding—I never charged a red cent.

I don't know how I survived childhood. I don't know how my parents survived my childhood, but we all did. Thinking back now, it was magical. It seemed like one long summer. It never ended. When you start counting your time on the planet by how many summers you have left, you realize how short life really is. My friend Jean said to me once that she hoped she had twenty summers left. It made me stop and think harder than usual. When the summers start feeling shorter, you know you're over that middle of your life hump and well into becoming a senior with a pension and not a single tooth of your own in your head. I can honestly tell you that I don't mind the thought of getting older at all. I am not thrilled about the tooth part, but I am quite relieved that I have the chance to get old, period. Youth can be vicious. I find that the older I get, the shorter my neck becomes, but the more I like myself.

I think my mother was very relieved when I finally started school. She'd have at least four hours in a day in which to fix everything I'd broken. When I did break something, I'd always admit to it. I was a very honest child. She'd march into a room and say to us all, "Who broke this lamp?" And I'd say, "I did." I guess it kind of took the steam out of her being mad at me. She says that I didn't start telling lies until

I was eighteen years old. (It was more like seventeen). She told me that when I turned eighteen I went bonkers; maybe I did go bonkers.

I never had children that I am aware of and I think I am the reason why. I was my own really good reason to never, ever become pregnant. The thought of trying to raise a small version of myself is daunting, to say the least. Well, that and the fact that I am a spinster. Don't worry, I am not the least bit worried about it except when I am awake or sleeping; then it kind of bothers me.

chapter two

FINGER ON A SPINNING GLOBE

started at Jennie Elliott Elementary School in 1967. My first grade teacher, Mrs. May, told my parents at their very first parent-teacher interview that I could very well be somewhat retarded. Political correctness did not exist then. Teachers could say things like that to a parent and not end up in jail. I obviously was *not* retarded, but, rather, a genius. I kid, but not really; no, seriously. Well, I was certainly somewhere between the two.

I just couldn't bear to sit at a desk. Is that retarded? I couldn't stand the little metal bar that attached the chair to the desk. Why would anybody do that? Did they think that a first grade student could and would steal the chairs? And do what with them? They were the most uncomfortable chairs in the history of chairs. Imagine having your dining room chairs attached to your dining room table with a thick metal bar. I rest my case. I just could not sit in that desk with the chair attached. It made me feel so confined. I have never, ever liked being boxed in, although I did also crawl into very small spaces at various points in my childhood. Looking back, I realize what a polarized kid I was.

My parents were horrified that Mrs. May thought
problems of any kind. What parent wants to hear that
cially on their very first parent-teacher interview? I a
mother thought it must have been all the falling off tl
done. Maybe I was brain damaged. My parents were nervc
about my future. I mean, I was a handful at the best of tin

After much discussion of my mental state with Mrs. N
decided that I would be allowed to stand beside my desk ra
sit in it. And that was the end of the retardation problem.
beside my desk seemed to solve most of my issues. I found it
write sitting down. The giant red HB pencils were six in
diameter and I had hands the size of walnuts; sitting down,
hardly hold on to a pencil. On my feet, I was able to at least
gravity. I still have one of those pencils in a trunk in my bedro
looks like a giant red and black suppository. Not that I would
what a suppository looks like, because I don't.

I was very happy to be standing beside my desk. I felt nor
Mrs. May kept a close eye on me from there on out, or is it in
any rate, she kept me at the very front of the classroom, just to
sure I didn't "go off." I loved school. I couldn't wait to get up a
walk the two blocks to the elementary school. It was an adventu
for sure. I loved all the chattering and the visiting. I wanted t
be friends with everybody, and all the activity was intoxicating
I really did have fun, despite Mrs. May's attempts at thwarting my
creativity. One day she even thought it necessary to confiscate a
plastic black spider that I had stuck onto the end of my pencil.
She marched up to my desk, pulled it off without a word and
threw it into a drawer in her desk that I am sure was filled with a
bunch of other wonderful things she had taken from her students
for hundreds of years. What I wouldn't have done to get into that
treasure drawer.

I think she was the first "not nice" person I ever knew. She seemed grumpy and she acted like she hated us. Maybe she was in a terrible relationship, or just depressed. My mom says, "Mrs. May just did not like you, and I don't know why." I think she'd be almost seventy years old now. Well, at *least* sixty-five . . . It is weird to think about that. I hope to God she found a pound of happiness between then and now.

Many years after I had completed grade one I wound up babysitting Mrs. May's children. Well, my friend Sue was the actual babysitter, and I was just along for the snacks, but still. I didn't know it was *her* and she didn't know it was *me*, but I figured it out before she did. I think she must have been remarried because her name wasn't Mrs. May anymore. I don't think she would have let me co-babysit her beloved children had she known that I was the troubled little girl who stood by her desk at the front of the class in 1967.

I had been a babysitter very few times in my teenage life. I knew that whenever anyone called me to look after their kids I was their *last* resort. If they were calling me, there was nobody on the planet left to call. They were beyond desperate and I was in a position to make certain demands. Oh, the splendour of it all! *Must have grape pop* and *must have Old Dutch salt and vinegar chips. Must have cable TV and a remote control.* It was good to be the last resort. A colour TV set would be best, if possible.

Sue and I both thought Mrs. May's kids were little bastards, but perhaps I had been carrying around a grudge from my first grade mental illness debacle. All is forgiven now, and besides, Mrs. May, or whatever her name was, and her new husband had a bunch of beer stashed in their basement that we happily drank while on the job. (No children were harmed, I can assure you.) Beer was almost as good as—if not better than—grape pop, salt and vinegar chips *and* a remote control for a colour TV. If you drank the beer really fast it

could create a feeling that was quite goofy. I thought it was really great to feel goofy from time to time. Who wouldn't?

My mother told me very early on that life was going to be hard. She also told me that we were all going to die eventually. My dad told me the universe was ever expanding.

I had a lot on my mind, as you can well imagine. I found out that I would learn much more from failing than I would from succeeding. But I am jumping ahead . . .

I liked elementary school even though the academic part of it often left me scratching my head. I really thought that I was just there in the classroom to meet people and have fun and play marbles and run around the schoolyard bruising every inch of every limb on our bodies. I loved recess. I would have been happy if school was nothing but recess. I know I wasn't alone in this thought.

I was glad and relieved to move out of Mrs. May's miserable grade one class into the much happier, carefree second grade classroom of Ms. Hurst. She was a huge improvement. I began to think that I would survive elementary school after all.

Ms. Hurst had big, brown eyes, giant piles of brunette hair stacked onto her head, and wore orange lipstick! Mrs. May just had a mess of iron-like red hair pinned like a magpie's nest onto the top of her head. It was scary, to tell you the truth. I am sure there were things trapped in there. Things like first graders and plastic spiders and disgruntled parents of children she didn't like.

Ms. Hurst, on the other hand, seemed to glide to the chalkboard six inches off the ground. It was like she was made of pure magic and fairy sprinkles. It was, after all, the sixties, and Ms. Hurst was very groovy and far out. She talked to all of us like we were actual people, which was unbelievable at first because Mrs. May had yelled at us like we were the spawn of the Devil himself. Every single kid in my second grade class had a crush on Ms. Hurst. All the girls wanted to be just like her and all the boys wanted to hug her leg. (I don't think humping legs had dawned on them at this point.)

I looked forward to getting out of bed and running to school as fast as I could go, just to sit at the front of Ms. Hurst's classroom to learn something. Learning how to print was beyond exciting, and subtraction—well, there was nothing like it! It didn't feel like we were learning, it felt like we were *being*. It's amazing what a caring, interested teacher can inspire in a young mind. For some strange reason I was able to sit at my desk in Ms. Hurst's class without feeling like my own skin was eating me.

Just waiting to see what she was going to wear on any given day was exciting. She had fabulous bell-bottomed jeans and macramé belts and tie-dyed T-shirts and head scarves made out of every imaginable colour and fabric. She also had lovely tailored two-piece suits with matching earrings and sheer pantyhose. I mean, pantyhose? I had never seen anybody wearing pantyhose. (At first I thought she had *really* brown legs and then I figured out that she just had very long, stretchy socks on.) She wore long, beaded necklaces and flower rings on her fingers and open-toed shoes and she always smelled good. A trail of her perfume followed her around the classroom and down the hallway.

The second grade saved me from my previously diagnosed "mental problems" and brought me back into the light of childhood. I felt normal from the moment I entered Ms. Hurst's classroom. And even when I didn't feel normal in Ms. Hurst's class, that was fine too. Mrs. May had kind of knocked the wind out of my personality sails but I also realized in the first grade how tenacious I was going to be, how determined, how steadfast. Elementary school was a battlefield, and I was ready to battle!

I have such fond memories of Ms. Hurst reading to us in the mornings. We all sat in a big, happy circle and she'd pull out a pile of books and ask us what we wanted to hear that day. We each took turns picking our favourite books, although it didn't matter what she read because it all sounded like candy to our little ears. Words poured out of her mouth like ice cream, each one of them fresh and cool and sweet.

I think that's where words took hold of my heart. I had never heard a poem before second grade. I didn't even know that poems existed. Ms. Hurst read us a poem about rows of poppies in a field, and I never forgot it. I have heard that poem many times since then, and it always brings me back to her classroom, sitting in a circle with my arms folded. She'd also tell us stories about her life and her family. I felt like I had been given a glimpse of what it might be like to be a grown-up person. I suddenly wanted to get growing up immediately. A great teacher becomes part of the person you're going to become. I wanted to be a teacher more than anything else in the world. I never quite got there. Sometimes the universe has very different plans for us.

I can picture the faces of my teachers as plain as the watch on my wrist. I can picture myself at a little desk that I could now actually sit in and not have to stand beside, even though the chair was still attached to the desk with a bar. I can picture Ms. Hurst's desk up at the front of the classroom, with her calendar propped up on it and her books piled up on either side and, of course, her beautiful green-and-blue globe of the world.

I loved looking at all the different places on that globe. All those places I had never even heard of. All of the kids loved turning it about. We used to spin it around and try to pronounce the country that our sticky fingers would land on, Finland and Botswana and Turkey and Latvia and hundreds of other exotic, mysterious places.

Canada seemed so small in my mind compared to everywhere else, but looking at the globe made me realize for the first time what a giant country I lived in.

I remember my finger landing on Africa. It seemed the biggest continent of them all, and had the perfect shape of a strawberry. I can remember tracing its outline with the tip of my finger. The globe had bumps on it, the mountain ranges all built up and the coastlines slightly raised as well. It was a beautiful globe. When I started making a little bit of money, I bought one for myself. I look at it every day in my office. (I spin it around on occasion and land my finger on some far-off place and imagine going there.)

I have been to Africa twice now. I have taken two trips to that giant red continent, indelible experiences which have reshaped my life. It seems so funny. A finger on a spinning globe and later you find yourself standing right there on the very spot where your finger landed forty-odd years before. You find yourself spinning as fast as that globe. You can't even begin to understand where all the time has gone.

I loved Ms. Hurst's second grade class. She gave me the first glimpse of myself as a person. I don't know how else to describe it. She was a wonderful teacher: inspiring and interesting and unendingly kind. I remember her, although I doubt very much that she remembers me. It doesn't matter. She probably taught twenty thousand kids in her career and we're all grateful; at least I am.

Life is a series of flashes.

Flash. Flash. Flash. And then you evaporate.

I think we're given glimpses of our futures all the time; we just never bother to pay attention. We're too busy being busy. We're too busy worrying about all the things we'll never get done. We're too busy looking into the mirror and counting the lines that are beginning to surround our mouths and eyes. So many people talk about just being in the moment. I don't know if most of us can even begin to know how to do that. I am still learning. I think I am in the moment and then I realize that I am worrying about what I am going to be doing tomorrow. I haven't mastered the art of now yet. I am still searching for the point.

My mother told me early on that she didn't know if there even was a point. I think you have to keep looking for the point—that's the point. Everybody knows that. My dad has never really said all that much about the point. I think he is on to something.

Flash. Flash. Flash.

Leaving Ms. Hurst's second grade class and moving ten feet down the hall to Mrs. McCrae's third grade class was another giant leap forward for my newly developing character.

Mrs. McCrae introduced me to the beautiful world of art and creativity. She was the teacher who expanded my soul into every corner of the universe. Yes, the ever-expanding one my dad had warned me about. That may sound a bit dramatic, but when you're eight and you stumble onto something you didn't even know existed, it's *big*. I loved art. All of it! I loved drawing and painting and colouring and moulding and building. To this point, the most creative things about me were my climbing skills and being able to chew up pieces of Mr. Potato Head without choking to death.

Mrs. McCrae seemed really old to me, but I am sure that probably means she was in her late thirties. I thought she looked to be a hundred. But I had just spent second grade with the coolest, most beautiful teacher in Jennie Elliott Elementary's entire history of teachers. Ms. Hurst was barely twenty, I am sure, which made Mrs. McCrae seem even older. Ms. Hurst was not an easy act to follow, unless of course you were Farrah Fawcett or Olivia Newton-John. (Neither of whom existed for me yet, so I guess that's not really worth mentioning.) It would have been so great having Olivia Newton-John as your music teacher, and Farrah Fawcett would have been a most excellent gym instructor. But Anne Murray could have kicked both of their arses in gym and music—that goes without saying.

Mrs. McCrae had big shoes to fill, but it didn't take her long to fill them. She was different from Ms. Hurst, but equally inspiring. She had a really curly perm—on the verge of being an Afro—with a touch of grey sneaking in around her temples. Not a great look for a late thirtysomething Caucasian woman from Canada. She was stout and square and had a deep voice that was commanding. She kind of sounded like John Wayne, to tell you the truth. If you closed your eyes and listened to her speak, you would swear you were on the back of a horse riding somewhere in the Wild West with Mr. Wayne himself.

Everything she wore seemed to be either brown or grey or beige. She didn't wear scarves or lipstick and her shoes looked like the ones my dad's mom, my grandmother Richards, wore: sturdy, comfortable, thick-soled shoes with laces on the side. I vividly remember those laces running up the side of her beige shoes. It looked like somebody had made a mistake when they sewed them up. They were perfectly polished shoes, though, so polished you could look up her dress if you were so inclined. Nobody was. She didn't wear perfume; in fact, she kind of smelled like Vicks VapoRub all the time. Maybe she had a bad shoulder or something? She was lovely, though. She had a kind, trusting face. She looked you in the eye, put her hand gently on your shoulder and made you feel like you were the only person on the planet.

Mrs. McCrae was different from any teacher I had had in my very long educational career. (All three years of it so far.) Every student was very attentive and orderly around her. She maintained the quietest of classrooms. There were no spitballs flinging about or graffiti being plastered all over the chalkboard; no children shouting or acting out. No wrestling or gonch pulling. ("Gonch" is what we prairie people call underwear. Out east they call them "ginch.") We all just sat there and listened to Mrs. McCrae teach. If she told us to do something, we did it. She didn't yell at us or talk down to us, she talked to us like we were people, real honest-to-God people and not a bunch of snotty dummies who didn't know whether to sneeze or squeeze an orange. She'd find something good to say to you every day. She'd tell you she liked your shirt or your glasses or your printing. Compliments were better than any old gold star stuck on the top corner of a page. Compliments made your heart grow bigger. Stickers were just shiny. Encouragement is the best drug on the planet. It makes you taller, somehow, and braver.

There was a little boy named Carson in my grade three class who was in a wheelchair. I am not sure why he was in a wheelchair but he was parked beside a desk right in the middle of the room, just like one of us. I was always in awe of how Mrs. McCrae made Carson feel so special and so normal all at the same time. Carson was always smiling madly at her, and she at him. Encouragement and compassion for another human being is something she showed us every day. I forgot about Carson's wheelchair about a week after school started. We all did.

I remember an art project I had been working on for weeks—a clay Eskimo. Every student was given the simple task of transforming a giant lump of clay into some sort of an Eskimo theme, whether that was a whale or an igloo or a dogsled team or, in one little girl named Laurie's case, a rather large candy cane that had nothing to do with anything. She just decided to make a giant candy cane and call it a day. It is possible that Santa's sleigh could have been pulled by a team of husky dogs with candy-cane runners.

I wasn't sure of what I was doing either or if what I was creating was going to look at all like an Eskimo anything. I hadn't seen a lot of Eskimos at that point in my life, so I had very little to go on. I had had an Eskimo Pie, and although it would have been really easy to shape the clay into an ice cream sandwich, it would have been an instant fail, I think. What I did end up doing was this sort of 3-D portrait of a man in his big parka holding his spear. I stuck it onto a piece of cardboard made to look like a picture frame. He had a real fake-fur collar that I must have stolen from one of my mother's old coats and glass eyeballs that I pulled out of an old doll.

Mrs. McCrae went down each row of desks and said something very quietly and privately to each child about their own particular project. She finally came up beside my desk, put her hand on my shoulder, as she often did, looked down at my questionable work of art and simply said, "Jann, that is just a beautiful Eskimo person." I think I blushed to the point of needing a blood transfusion. I honestly believed she meant every single syllable that fell out of her mouth and onto my Eskimo masterpiece. I wish I still had that thing, but I am pretty sure it disintegrated in 1975, despite my mom's best efforts to keep every piece of art any of her three kids brought home. I have a file full of various works of art in my basement that makes me laugh hysterically every time I pull it out. I have a dozen or so scribblers filled with musings from my English classes. Some of my short stories were nothing short of comedic genius, though I was trying really hard to be serious. I have a number of drawings and a few paintings. I am so glad my mom saved all of that stuff for me. I never thought it would turn out to hold such sentimental value. No clay Eskimo, though. It's vaporized into the Great White North itself.

—

About halfway through the year, Mrs. McCrae announced to our class that Jennie Elliott Elementary School would be putting on a musical about Jiminy Cricket. I knew exactly who Jiminy Cricket was because I watched *The Wonderful World of Disney* faithfully every single Sunday night. Our whole family did. That and *The Ed Sullivan Show* and *The Carol Burnett Show*, without fail. (I do need to mention that we were the last people on our block to get a colour television set, and I still blame my parents for that.)

There were going to be auditions for the various parts in the play, but for some reason I didn't end up auditioning. I was just kind of handed the part of Jiminy. The school principal, Mrs. McKill (I kid you not), called me to her office, sat me down and told me I was going to be Jiminy in the play. She didn't even ask me, she told me. She and Mrs. McCrae thought I would be a perfect little cricket. Maybe it was because I was the smallest kid in the class and I'd fit the little, green outfit; who knows? All I know is that I had to sing two or three songs and had a lot of lines to learn, but they were sure I could do it. I was glad somebody was sure, because I couldn't even remember where I hung my coat most days. My own mother said that I very conveniently forgot to put a brush through my hair at least four days of the week. I wasn't a victim of fashion, I can tell you that. I didn't care how I looked, what I wore, or whether or not I fit in with the other kids. Thank God, because no kid should be worrying about that crap in grade three.

To this day I don't know why they thought I could act and sing in a play. I could talk a lot; everybody was quite aware of that. Every report card I ever had said that I basically could not and would not shut up. Whatever it was that those two teachers saw in me, I will never know. I was a funny kid, but that is no indication of any musical talent.

Singing? I would be singing? I don't think I had sung a note in my life up to this point. I really don't. I may have hummed an

Anne Murray song or two. Who didn't do that? "Snowbird" was the only song on Canadian radio for eleven years. Things I *do* remember:

- The giant papier mâché whale that our class took weeks to build for the set.

- Slathering millions of paper strips dipped in goo onto the whale's chicken-wire frame. Painting it an edible-looking blue.

- Eating the goo whenever possible. Feeling sick because of it. It tasted like rotten marshmallow, but I liked it.

- The curtains sweeping open and all the parents sitting in the crowd looking like they had all swallowed canaries, they were so proud. (I know my parents must have been relieved that I didn't faint and fall off the stage.)

I also clearly remember flashbulbs (real ones) going off and Mrs. McCrae mouthing words to me from the side of the stage, like she was willing me through my entire performance. Whenever I forgot a word or two (or twenty-seven), I was relieved to have her there. She was my very own conductor in the wings, with her arms flapping and her eyes widening, her brows rising and falling. I am sure I completely wore her out. She probably drank a bottle of wine all by herself when she got home from that play, and perhaps even puffed away on a menthol cigarette. That would explain the Vicks VapoRub smell. They may have made boxes of wine in those days, and if they did, I am sure Mrs. McCrae would have been drinking from one. Mrs. McCrae and I survived Jiminy Cricket, and we still liked each other.

I don't remember being afraid at all during the performance. I can't recall a single nerve or hesitation, just an unfailing boldness that would become my saving grace over and over as my life continued to unfold.

Life will shoot you out of a cannon whether you want it or not. The universe is the cannon and we are the balls . . .

chapter three

A LITTLE BIT COUNTRY

Grade three would be my last year at Jennie Elliott Elementary School. My parents had decided to move the family out to an acreage west of Calgary, which meant I would be changing schools. When we found out we were going to live out in the sticks, it was devastating. It was for me, anyway. I have no idea what my brothers were thinking.

I mean, the country? Like, farmers with cows and chickens, for crying out loud? Any kind of change when you're eight years old comes as a shock. You don't see anything outside of your mundane, wonderfully banal routine. I worried about all the simple things. Where would I ride my bike and what about my stuff and what would we eat and what would happen to my friends and what would the new school be like and how would I ever meet anybody ever again and what if the kids didn't like me? It's hard meeting new people when you're eight. You have extremely high expectations of other people. (I'm kidding.)

Besides, by the time you're eight you've already made friends, dammit, and you don't want to start all over again. I worried

constantly for weeks leading up to the actual move away from the city. I had never worried before about anything in my life. Worry felt like a weight that poured over me when I was trying to sleep. I thought that this was a direct effect of getting older and turning into a grown-up person. If that was the case, I didn't want to grow up at all. I had to figure out some way to stop worrying and stop growing up—and the sooner, the better.

I wasn't sure how one went about finding and making new companions. I felt like I had just always known the ones I already had, that making friends required no effort whatsoever. You were born and, shortly thereafter, your "forever friends" were handed to you by God himself. End of story. I think making good friends is the easiest and the hardest thing you'll ever do in your life. My friendships are my greatest accomplishments. My friends to this day are my greatest treasures. They represent the truest part of my character and the best part of my soul.

I'd be leaving behind my dear pal Gary. His family lived next door to us on Louise Road, we had gone to kindergarten together, and our parents were fairly good friends as well. He and I were inseparable. When your houses are three feet apart, you get to know your neighbours and just hope that they are God-fearing, decent people who don't have strange things in their basements. You hope that they aren't worshipping the Dark One and that they don't have an elderly, sickly relative hooked up to a feeding tube and an oxygen tank in the back bedroom. They didn't seem to have any of those things. Gary's grandmother lived with them but she was very short and harmless, and smelled good and could cook anything under the sun. She always told me I was full of sass and that I was cheeky. I happened to like "sass." It must have been an English thing because Gary's gram was from overseas and they said things differently than we did in Canada. She probably meant to say that I was full of shit,

but sass sounded a lot better to me and to her, I am sure. Yes, I could very well have been full of sass.

Every day after school either I was at Gary's house or he was at mine. He was the best colourer I had ever seen in my life. I am sure "colourer" is not a word but I am using it anyway. His colouring skills were epic. I often wondered if it was his short, sweet English granny doing all that colouring for him late at night and Gary was just claiming colouring victory when we all laid eyes on the pictures the next day. I never actually saw him colour anything in front of me. (Sorry, Gary, but I didn't. You can come clean about it anytime you want. Nobody can stay in the lines that well. Nobody! And that colour palette? Come on! Your skin tones were legendary!)

I still like colouring to this day. Give me a box of crayons and a big old *Snow White* colouring book and I am a happy girl. And maybe a box of wine. Yeah, crayons and a box of wine. That's the ticket.

Gary and I played with John and Jane West dolls for hours on end. They were plastic western figures that had these really detailed boots and hats and accessories. (I guess boots and a hat *are* accessories). They came with their own horses, Thunderbolt and Cherokee, who in turn had their own perfect miniature saddles and bridles. John and Jane even had their own ranch house, complete with a cast-iron stove in the kitchen; it was beyond awesome. Martha Stewart would have been happy in that kitchen!

They had little vests and chaps and cowboy shirts. I *loved* playing with my John and Jane West dolls. They had bendy arms and legs so you could hang them off lamps and drawers and coat hangers and toilets, if need be. As I recall, they were very hard to melt, but I won't get into that. John and Jane were happily married, or so Gary and I made them out to be. We would muck about with those figurines for hours. Time evaporated in our imaginary world. Eventually we'd be faced with having to go for dinner. My mother would holler my

name and that meant it was time to go home. Her voice could literally penetrate a concrete bunker. I could hear her call my name if
I was sixty miles away. It was a good skill to have.

I have no idea what Gary and I ever talked about. Maybe we
didn't talk at all. Maybe we talked to each other through our John
and Jane West dolls? Once in awhile we included my older brother's
G.I. Joes in our make-believe world. G.I. Joes were plastic army guys
with five o'clock shadows and big guns. G.I. Joe often shot at John
and Jane West, but thankfully John and Jane had their own western
rifles and pistols, so they shot back.

G.I. Joe was always the first to die. I made sure of that. I don't
know why, but G.I Joe seemed like a bad guy to me. As I recall, the
makers of G.I. Joe gave him a fairly big package, if you know what
I mean. John West didn't seem to have wieners or beans. He was a
much more modest doll.

My brother Duray hated me playing with his stuff, and G.I. Joe
was his doll, after all. I mean, he would get really, really mad and
threaten to kick all the spokes out of my precious bike or something
equally horrifying, like hiding all of my marbles or pulling my underpants up to my waist. I can't tell you how much I hated having my
underpants pulled up to my waist. It was a terribly uncomfortable
feeling. The underpants never survived the attack, but I knew how
to get back at Duray.

I threatened to tell my mother that he was stealing her maxi-
pads to make G.I. Joe's bunk beds—which he was—and that put
an end to all his threats. Maxi-pads apparently made perfect little
mattresses for G.I Joes. The old maxi-pads even had straps on
them that you could tie to trees like little hammocks. The new
ones had adhesive strips which weren't really good for anything.
(I remember the first time I used an adhesive-strip maxi-pad like
it was this morning. I put in on upside down, which meant the

adhesive strip was stuck on me and not my underpants, but I digress.)

When we weren't colouring or playing John and Jane West, Gary and I rode our tricycles around and around and around the block. (At this point we hadn't clued in to the fact that riding bikes was exercise, and that we would one day hate every second of cardiovascular activity.) I knew where every crack was in every single inch of sidewalk. I knew where every kid lived and what their names were and what kind of swing set they had in their backyard. I knew what cars would be parked in the front driveways and when they came and went. My neighbourhood was mapped out in my heart and I never wanted anything about it to change.

I had put a pet turtle into my pocket on one of those bike trips around the block with Gary, and sadly I discovered it quite dead after a few hours of pedalling. Why I thought a turtle would survive inside my pants for hours is beyond me, but live and learn, I suppose. I cried rivers and oceans of tears over that dead turtle. I am sure Gary cried too. I hadn't seen many dead things by that point in my life. We conducted a funeral for the turtle, said a few words to Jesus about "his only something-or-other son" and then proceeded to flush him/her down the toilet. John and Jane West also attended the funeral and were very straight-faced through the ceremony. Life, it seemed, was going to be getting harder.

After the funeral, Gary and I took our twenty-five-cent allowances and walked down to the only convenience store in town and bought a bag of salt and vinegar chips and a cream soda, respectively. That would leave us with enough money to buy five pieces of Dubble Bubble gum. If I forwent the Dubble Bubble, I could buy a box of Eddylite Easy Strike matches. It was a hard decision to make. Gum or matches? Thank God they didn't have flammable chewing gum.

First the gum . . . I would chew all five pieces at the same time, almost causing my jaw to lock and my saliva to overtake my head.

The pain was unbearable but necessary. You can't chew just one piece of Dubble Bubble—that's nuts. You have to have at least three pieces in your mouth to make it worth your while. You have to blow out a bubble at least as big as your head to make it any fun at all. You then have to pop the bubble so the gum sticks to your hair and perhaps end up cutting off some of your bangs. I never had to cut my bangs, unless you count the time I fell asleep with the wad of gum in my mouth and woke up with my whole head stuck to my pillow. The gum was the least of my problems. My parents could deal with the odd chunk of hair being cut off of my head. But when I opted not to buy gum, I bought wooden matches.

For some reason there were a few months where all I wanted to do was burn things up. I just liked striking the matches and seeing them burn. You could strike them on anything: a zipper, your two front teeth, your Levi's jeans back pocket, the wall, the floor, your forehead. Any surface could light an Eddylite match. Except for the side of the toilet bowl. I tried that several times and it was too smooth. One morning I crouched in my parents' half-bathroom off their master bedroom and dropped about five hundred *lit* wooden matches down the heating vent one at a time. I didn't think about where they were going. I thought they just dropped into nothing. I knew China was down there somewhere because my gram had told me it was. I don't know why I did it. It just felt good to me. The fact that no one had seen me for two hours and that the pungent smell of sulphur was crawling down the hallway was a dead giveaway that something was amiss.

When he found me, my dad became absolutely out-of-his-mind mad and I do remember getting a really good spanking. We had an old worn-out sort of thick canvas-and-rubber strap that hung in one of the kitchen cupboards, and that's what we'd get whacked with. My dad could be a very frightening man when he was angry.

His face would change and he'd look like a completely different person. He had a temper like a bull in a ring. In this particular case, though, I don't blame him for being angry. I could have burned our house down.

I still love wooden matches. I always feel compelled to buy them when I am in Home Depot. What the cavemen wouldn't have done for a box of wooden matches. They probably would have torched the planet and I wouldn't be here writing this.

Me + fire = the end of the world = arse welts

You'd think I would have learned from the vent incident and the subsequent spanking that I shouldn't be playing with fire, but oh no, not me. My arson phase was just getting under way. I proceeded to burn down a very large hedge at a house around the corner from where we lived, and almost lit their garage on fire. I remember the woman who lived there came screaming out of her back door wrestling with the garden hose and dousing the rather large flames that were now burning with great gusto. It was really scary.

All I could think of was how mad my dad was going to be and that I had better put a phone book between my dad and my bum. I don't think I could sit down for a week after that spanking. My parents didn't know quite what to do with me. I was officially an arsonist. I have to give it to my mom, though, because she always managed to disarm terrible situations for me. She told me that the big fat woman who came charging out of her back door wielding a water hose was horrible and mean and a lousy babysitter, and that at least it was her garage that I almost burned down and not some nice person's. My mom made me feel vindicated somehow, though she didn't tell me that in front of my dad . . .

I am sure I would not be alive to write these words had I burned that large woman's garage down. My father would surely have killed me or at least pulled the arms from my body so I couldn't strike matches anymore. He'd send them to the Masai people in Africa to feed to their goats. I really don't blame him for being mad. Burning down my own house was one thing, but burning down the large lady's house was another thing entirely.

The whole crazy relationship with the matches didn't last long, thankfully. I am glad I didn't become Drew Barrymore in *Firestarter*, but I came pretty close. I have no idea what got into me those weird few weeks. I was just obsessed with watching the sulphur end burst into a little ball of fire. It was instant gratification at its best. I am now one of those people who plays with candle wax in restaurants, although I am trying to curb my enthusiasm for that. Thank God they hadn't invented disposable Bic lighters in the sixties or the whole city of Calgary would have been long gone by 1970. Perhaps even the entire country of Canada. My dad had a Zippo lighter, but he was smart enough to keep it in a safety deposit box buried somewhere in the backyard.

My friend Gary was such a good boy that he didn't come anywhere near me during my *Firestarter* phase. I didn't want to incriminate him anyway. I don't think he even knew that I had been buying matches and burning things down. He was still an angel in my parents' eyes, and I was encouraged at every turn to colour with him. Davey, the boy who made me play in garbage cans, thereby contracting the worms that required the Scotch tape bum worm removal, was my accomplice during the Eddylite Easy Strike period of my childhood. In fact, Davey was the one who thought that the burning of the hedge would be very controllable and that we would not be caught, never, ever! Yeah, sure.

One thing I learned very early on is that boys can be dumb liars, so don't believe a thing they tell you. Davey was quite the character. We should have had our own reality show, if only we had known what those were back then. Our show would have been called *Jann and Davey Plus Crazy*. I might have to contact him to see if he has any interest in that concept. We could recreate the worm scene in the bathroom with my mother. We could burn things up. The Scotch tape people could sponsor us.

Davey is my age, so I am sure he's still somewhere out there in the world. Maybe he became a fire warden or a zookeeper. I highly doubt it, though. As you know, according to my mother he had a crazy mother, so that was half of his problem. I don't know what the other half was. Well, Davey was the other half of the problem, and I think my influence was mixed up in there somewhere too.

When I feared losing touch with my friends after we moved, mom told me that Gary could come to visit us. She didn't mention Davey. I think where we were going had way too many trees to risk allowing Davey and me to spend any kind of quality time together there. As it turned out, Gary ended up coming out to our new house only once or twice. I learned early on that people come and go in your life—and most often they go.

I don't know how my parents managed to buy land in the country in the first place, because they didn't have any money to speak of. My mom said it took them a whole year to pay off their Bay card after they maxed it out buying Christmas presents for us. This went on every year for about fifteen years. They never seemed to be able to get ahead. "We would just get the credit card paid off and it would be Christmas again," she'd say.

My mom has always been very matter of fact. I have never had the sense that she felt sorry for herself about anything. Even though her young life was very hard and often lonesome, she never complained about the hand the universe had dealt her. My mom's dad was a miserable drunk who verbally and physically went after his wife whenever he came home plastered after a bender. Mom would always say that her dad drank all their money away and left them with nothing. They often had to scrape together meals and they seldom, if ever, bought new clothes or treats of any kind. Mom's dad worked in logging camps way up north, and he dragged his family with him, literally to the middle of nowhere. In fact, they were even farther away from civilization than that!

There weren't many other kids for my mom to play with in the camps. She told me that one of her favourite games when she was little was "funeral." She'd wrap a stick up with some old cloth and deliver sermons. That always makes me feel so sad for her. I can picture her there, mumbling humble words over a little grave for a dead stick doll. My mom was witness to a very abusive relationship between her mother and father, but she simply refuses to dwell in the past. She throws her shoulders back and always faces forward.

I am the same way. Life is life. You just get on with it. You do what you have to do to make it work. My dad always said, "The harder you work, the luckier you get," and I believe that with all my heart. My parents are the salt (and the pepper) of the earth.

I didn't have a clue about how much money we didn't have. They sold the house on Louise Road for $24,900 in 1971, which was a whopping $14,900 profit. I spend more than that on feminine protection every month. (Would someone please take my uterus from me and give me a new liver? My uterus is costing me a small fortune that could be going into buying wine.) I can't even get my head around the fact that they bought an entire house for ten thousand dollars in the sixties. It doesn't seem possible.

My parents purchased five acres of land just a few miles west of Calgary with the few thousand dollars they'd made on the sale of the house. Then they had to figure out how to pay for the new house they were going to be building. Interest rates were beyond out of control, and getting a mortgage from a bank was literally signing your life away. You'd be looking at a document that would basically say that you'd have your house paid off in sixty years. My parents remind themselves of just how lucky they were whenever possible.

"If we'd waited even a few more years, we would never have been able to afford to move out here," my mother often said, as she looked out her kitchen window.

I know it was a huge leap of faith for them, moving us all out to Springbank. I know they wanted us to have fresh air and a chance to go to a smaller school. (That is an understatement—there were only forty-two kids in my high school graduating class.) I think they just wanted to invest in something that would make their lives easier forty years down the road. They knew the house and the land would someday be their nest egg, and it has turned out to be just that.

My mom and dad were very excited to be building a brand new house and at the same time scared to death. I hadn't discovered that my parents were real people yet, so I didn't know they had a worry in the world. I thought that my parents were there to look after me: drive me around, feed me, give me pocket money, listen to my problems and solve them. I thought they were there to save me from a hostile world and mean people and diseases of every imaginable kind. I thought they were there to make sure I never got sick or died, period. I didn't know they were actual people with feelings and troubles of their own. Someone should have clued me in. Parents are people. Who knew?

I am sure they lay in bed at night and wondered how in heaven's name they were going to build a house with what little they had. In many ways it was like *Little House on the Prairie*. They bought a giant, grassy field with nothing on it but trees and brush and dirt and they had to make something out of it. We had a lot of work ahead of us.

When we moved, our house wasn't yet built and we had sold our other one. My dad, God love him, bought a small white holiday trailer for a pittance and parked it a few hundred feet away from the building site. He hooked it up to water and power and we were off on our very lengthy camping adventure. (I think we ended up living in the trailer for about a year, which was about ten months longer than my mother would have liked.) And it was camping, there's no doubt about that. It seemed like a lot of fun for the first six months, and then it kind of wore off as the Canadian winter sank its teeth into us. You can freeze your nose off in about three minutes if you're not careful. I know a lot of people without a nose—they just have the nostril holes. (Okay, no I don't.)

We hadn't lived in the trailer long before the weather turned terribly cold. The water line running into the trailer froze almost immediately. My dad tried everything to keep it from blocking up, but we were more or less at the mercy of Mother Nature. My dad said it was a goddamn pain in the ass not having water. We all agreed. It was next to impossible to shower or bathe or wash dishes without it. We drove to my gram's place a lot to take baths and do laundry, but other than that, we were just out there fighting the elements.

My gram was my mom's mom. She lived in Calgary with her second husband, Charlie. It was about a thirty-five- or forty-minute drive for us to get to their house. She was always glad to see us tumble in through her back door with all our plastic bags full of dirty laundry. She and my mom always had a good visit. The coffee pot would go on and some kind of cake would appear on the kitchen table. My mom and my gram could talk the leg off the lamb of God if they had half the chance. They were extremely close (and I could write an entire book about the two of them and the struggles they faced and the hardships they overcame). My gram would prove to be our life-line on many occasions.

My mom and dad slept in the only bedroom in the back of the trailer. Duray and I were in bunk beds off to one side, and my little brother, Patrick, was small enough to sleep on the fold-out kitchen table, which conveniently converted into a little bed. I think our breathing in and out kept us warm at night. My mother is cold at the best of times, never mind in a paper-thin trailer in the middle of winter. It must have been hellish for her. I, on the other hand, loved every minute of being in our home on wheels. I didn't mind seeing my breath hang in the air like a cloud. I thought it was completely fun. I felt like Jane West on a real country adventure. I started to think that perhaps I had found my true calling as an outdoor adventure guide. I would never have to brush my hair again—or my teeth, for that matter. The country life was definitely for me.

At a very early point in our adventure, my parents thought that it would be nice to get us a kitten. Actually, the kitten was part of the bribe we accepted when they moved us out of the city. They promised us a variety of pets, although my father denies that to this day. We were in the country now, after all, and country people had animals! We had room in the trailer for something furry and small, and a kitten would be perfect. We found free kittens advertised in the local newspaper and drove to pick our furry little buddy up. My mom named the tiny grey kitty Smokey or Spanky or Chunky; well, she called it something, I just can't remember what. And there's a reason for that.

We didn't have Smokey very long, I am sorry to say. We had her just long enough to fall in love with her before disaster struck. Mom had let the kitten out onto the steps of the trailer for a little sun and some fresh air and a pee when out of the woods came the neighbour's giant, white husky. My mother was standing right there beside the kitten on the metal steps, when the dog grabbed Smokey, or whatever her name was, by her tiny, fuzzy neck, and ran over the hill with her screeching wildly. We just stood there, watching it happen like a slow-motion car accident. It was so awful. The neighbours were upset, to say the least, when their husky dropped the dead, mangled kitten off at their front door like a trophy. We all sobbed for days.

I decided then and there that I hated that white husky. I threw something at it whenever I had the chance. I yelled and swore at it. That dog soon figured out never to come anywhere near me. The whole thing makes me sad to this day. My mother can hardly even talk about it—though we still somehow always manage to bring it up on the weirdest of occasions, like Christmas or Thanksgiving. You know, the happy holidays. She'll say, "Remember the Sodmonts' big white dog grabbing our little kitten off the steps of that trailer? Wasn't that terrible?" And I always say, "Yes, it was terrible." It's one of those horrible things that sticks to the inside of your eyeballs.

After the kitten was tragically taken from us, I realized that we were not in the city anymore. This was a whole new level of horrible that was much more horrible than the death of my pocket turtle.

The house slowly started growing up out of the earth. Every time my folks got a little extra money, another phase of the construction would begin. We did have builders shuffling around doing things, but it was very apparent that my dad was doing a *lot* of the work himself. My mother was becoming a builder too. They were always busy constructing something. Dad was always swinging a hammer or sawing a floorboard or installing a cupboard hinge or putting in windows or nailing shingles on the roof. And this was after he'd spent an entire day at his real job. He left the trailer early and came home late. Whatever spare or not spare moments he had were spent working on the house.

My dad's entire life had somehow revolved around construction and concrete. He knew every possible thing there was to know about concrete. He knew about quarter-inch and half-inch and two-inch gravel. He knew about crushed gravel and rebar and exposed aggregate and finishing and framing and forming and everything else in between. He knew how long the concrete needed to set and what temperature it needed to be. He knew how much it would cost to pour an eight-foot by ten-foot by four-inch slab and how much concrete you'd need to make a garage pad or a sidewalk or a retaining wall just right. He knew how much concrete—to the very ounce—it would take to make it all work out perfectly. He was the go-to guy for anything made out of limestone, water, sand and gravel.

My dad had his own language when it came to concrete. I'd hear him on the phone talking to somebody about something to do with a job, and it made no sense to me at all. He'd have a cigarette hanging out of his mouth, and I always marvelled at how he could talk and smoke at the same time. He'd hold the phone between his shoulder and his neck, and he'd puff away without missing a beat. The smoke would often billow out of his nose. I thought it looked wonderful. I wondered how in the world he managed to do that. I wanted to blow smoke out of my nose too. It seemed to me like my dad could do anything, and that's because he *could*. He was such a talented man in so many ways.

He pretty much knew all there was to know about plumbing and carpentry and fixing cars and building bird feeders and mending clocks and rebuilding antique furniture of any description. (I have so many of his pieces in my house today and they are all gorgeous.) He knew how to build sheds and change brake pads and plant potatoes and fly kites and make tree forts. He knew how to pull heads out of milk chutes and how to build giant barbecues. My dad's hands were scarred from thumb to pinky with hundreds of punctures and gouges and blisters. He'd lost more fingernails than anybody I'd ever known. He always had a black nail, always. I remember him sitting down for supper, tired and covered in sweat, with at least one black fingernail. He'd have a giant new gouge or an old cut that hadn't healed yet. I would watch him sitting there at the table thinking about whatever it was he was thinking. He'd look at his hands, folding and refolding them. He'd run them through his strawberry hair and look pensive. I wondered what he was thinking about. It must have been something heavy, because around the time I was twelve or thirteen he started drinking a little bit more just to make all the heaviness go away. He always said that he'd drink anything back then, but what I remember him drinking most often was dark rum. The smell of it to this day takes me back through a twisting and turning time-tunnel. My dad sitting there at the table with a dark rum and Coke in his fist and a lit cigarette hanging out of his head. It's a good memory—it could be bad, but it's not. He worked hard all the time, but he was starting to drink hard all the time too.

If I have any kind of work ethic at all, I get it from my parents. They were always so steadfast and determined. They never quit working on things. They worked so hard on the house and the yard and at their jobs, and they never quit working on themselves. They were constantly moving and doing and creating. It was a luxury for them to sit and read the paper at the end of a long day. They are in their seventies now, and they still don't sit down. I swear they're doing cocaine over at their house. Either that or they're inhaling vitamins or they're just really healthy and eager to get things done. I would rather think of the cocaine scenario as it would make me feel a little less lazy.

We usually had dinner together as a family, the five of us sitting around the small pull-out table that was Patrick's bed come nightfall. Our meals were simple and hearty and, well, interesting. My mom was an interesting cook—she had to be because we were still living in the trailer, getting used to all sorts of adventures, culinary and otherwise. She's the first person to admit that when she was first married she did not have a clue about what she was doing. She'd call my gram pretty much every night of the week to ask her at what temperature to cook a roast or how to make a pie crust or how long to boil spaghetti. She didn't know how to do anything. We had some very well-done spaghetti over the years. A single noodle was usually about an inch in diameter. Italian folks would have lit themselves on fire if they'd had to eat my mother's pasta.

My dad didn't talk to us much at the table or any other place, for that matter. He mostly kept to himself. When he did talk, it was often in the form of yelling. He always seemed to be mad about something. He always seemed to be at the end of his rope. He would say, "I'm at the end of my goddamn rope with you kids." So I guess that's how I knew he was at the end of his rope. I have very few memories of him laughing back then. There weren't a lot of things for him to laugh about, I guess.

I thought that's how all dads were—swearing, grouchy bastards. My new friend Theresa's dad yelled a lot too. We talked about that from time to time. I had a kindred spirit in Theresa. We compared grumpy dad stories whenever possible. We still do after thirty-five years. I met Theresa the first day of grade four as we stood outside the elementary school waiting to go into our homerooms. She was so tall compared to me, and shy. I found out a few weeks later that she lived just up the road from us but was assigned to a different bus. I was excited to learn she was within walking distance.

My dad ate with us less and less as the years went by; it was rare to have him home. And when Duray was about fourteen he tended to turn up at the dinner table less and less as well. Then it was just mom and Patrick and me sitting there sawing through pork chops because my mother believed that pork should be cooked to the point where you could make shoes out of it and walk on hot coals without feeling a thing. They always say you should chew your food at least thirty times before you swallow; that was never a problem for anyone in our family. We *had* to chew our food thirty times in order to swallow it without choking to death. We all had really over-developed jaw and temple muscles.

Every time she cooked meat, my mother insisted it had to be cooked thoroughly or you could and would get very sick.

"That chicken has to be very well done or we'll all be sick," she'd lament. Beef, pork, chicken, any kind of animal flesh at all, had to be cooked until it was a fifth of its original size. She'd put a roast the size of a bowling ball in the oven, and four hours later she'd take it out and it'd be the size and colour of a hockey puck. She had had one bad incident with undercooked chicken that prompted her to fry the hell out of everything. We all got terribly sick from it, apparently. (There is no concrete proof that it was indeed the chicken.)

I am very happy to say that I don't remember having food poisoning. I just remember chewing chunks of well-done meat until my temples ached like I had been gnawing on twenty-three pieces of Dubble Bubble for days on end. My dad would often make us sit in front of our plates until we had cleared every morsel off them. I am not sure what that was all about. There was always one of us sitting there in front of our plate staring at a pile of Brussels sprouts or green beans or boiled cabbage. I hated Brussels sprouts more than any vegetable in the world. They tasted like dog farts and copper pennies.

I have a feeling those were the nights that my dad had had more rum than usual. He'd be extra cranky and that meant we'd be watching the clock on the wall and missing *I Dream of Jeannie*. If it was Brussels sprouts we had to sit in front of, we could be there for hours. My dad would usually forget about us sweating it out in front of our warm glasses of milk. My mom would finally come and take our plates away and tell us we were off the hook. He'd go off and have a cigarette or work on some project he had on the go. My mom would release us from our dinner purgatory. If someone had of told me when I was sitting at that dinner table all those years ago that I would someday love Brussels sprouts, I would have shot them on the spot.

My mom has since become a much better cook, although she can still whip up some pretty interesting dishes. I happen to love her liquid version of cheesecake. So what if she forgot one little ingredient? It tasted like cheesecake and that was all that mattered. My Lord, did we laugh that Christmas we were all slurping cheesecake out of bowls.

Our new house was shaping up to be the biggest I had ever seen, and I couldn't wait to move out of the white trailer and get into my own bedroom. In our old house in town I had shared a bedroom with my little brother, Patrick, which wasn't terrible except for the fact that he had severe asthma and I thought he was going to die every night. Other than that it was fine. The poor kid was allergic to his own skin. His little shoulders were always hiked up to his ears just trying to take in a decent breath. In the spring, my parents would have to rush him to the hospital for a two- or three-week stay because he just couldn't breathe. Every summer holiday we ever went on until he was about fifteen years old ended with us taking him to the emergency ward in some little British Columbia town. It must have been terrible for him and scary not knowing where he was, and for him to be away from his parents for who knows how long. Mom and dad couldn't stay with him in the hospital because they had Duray and me to look after back at the summer cottage. So there Patrick would be at night, alone in a giant plastic tent, surrounded by strange nurses and doctors and feeling more homesick than it's possible to imagine.

Living out in the country made his asthma symptoms worse.

All the trees and the pollen and the fields of wild grass and the animal hair were too much for his lungs to take. It was sad seeing him sitting on the sidelines while everybody else ran around playing. His whole body showed his disappointment. Thank God he eventually outgrew his asthma. It just went away one summer and never came back.

Watching someone trying to breathe is horrible. My friend Danielle, who has cystic fibrosis, says it's like drowning on dry land. I always thought that was so profound. Danielle has also always told me that she'd rather be hit than dragged. I think about that when I am alone at night.

I remember the first time I became aware that I had something beating in my chest. I had never thought about my heart or what it did up until that point. My heart never crossed my mind.

One summer when I was nine or ten, my family stopped for the night at a motel on our way to Wood Lake, where my parents took us on vacation every year. To our delight, there was a heated outdoor pool. We were in heaven.

Children + water = happy

Duray and I went diving in the pool for my dad's car keys. We'd been swimming for a few hours and my hands and feet were a wrinkled, waterlogged mess. I looked like an eighty-pound raisin. One more time down to the bottom of the pool, I thought, before we quit for dinner. On my way down to fetch the keys, I felt something go pop.

I thought it was because I had gone down too fast into the deep end of the pool. Maybe my ears had done something weird. I came up to the surface and felt like I was more out of breath than usual. I felt a heavy weight on my chest and my heart was fluttering when it should have been beating. I had no strength in my legs and I was

barely able to drag myself out of the water. I told my mom that I felt funny, but there wasn't much she could do. I didn't say that my heart felt funny, I just said that *I* felt funny. She told me that I'd overdone it, and I thought she was probably right. A good night's sleep cured everything.

My heart felt fluttery for days after the pool incident, though, and I felt weak and breathless. The wild beating was all I could think about. I was a wreck and my mom was getting annoyed with me, I could tell. She thought I was being silly and I really, truly wanted to believe that I was just being silly. Maybe it was all in my head. Maybe I had pulled a muscle?

When my heart finally felt normal again, I was relieved, to say the least. I wouldn't dive so far under the water next time, I thought to myself; that was what had done it. I figured that would be the end of it. But my heart was never the same after that. For years it did strange things. It would suddenly start to speed out of control for no reason at all. I would raise my arm up to get a glass out of the cupboard and my heart would start beating like crazy. It always scared me. I'd lie down and put my feet up and pinch my nose shut to try to get it to slow down. It usually worked, but that still didn't explain why it was happening in the first place. I tried explaining what it felt like to my mother, but I couldn't quite find the right words. I never felt any sort of pain; it was like I had a frightened bird caught underneath my rib cage. Whatever it was, it was stealing my confidence.

My mom took me to our family doctor and he said that, in his professional opinion, it was all in my mind, which was maddening. He told my mom that it was quite normal for adolescents to experience odd cardiovascular behaviour, and that it was part of puberty as far as he was concerned. He told us that it would get better as I got older. As he butted his cigarette out in the ashtray on his desk, he told me not to think about it so much. I thought he was completely

nuts, and so did my mother. I badly wanted to believe that it would go away eventually and that nothing was wrong with me, but somewhere deep down I knew something wasn't right.

My cardiovascular problems didn't go away; in fact, they started getting worse. My heart took off like a rocket on a much more regular basis. The weird part was that at night, when I lay down to go to sleep, it was just the opposite. My heart felt like it was going to stop. It would beat so slowly that I found myself taking giant gasps of air to try and keep it going. Sometimes I thought that if I went to sleep I'd never wake up, so I had to stay up to keep my heart pumping. I was too young to be an insomniac, but that's what I was becoming.

If I had thought I could drink coffee and not end up with the runs like my dad, I would have started drinking three pots of the stuff a day. People were always saying that coffee kept them up at night; I needed some of that. I would wake up in the middle of the night to make sure I was alive. I usually was. Good thing I woke myself up, I'd think to myself. It was all a bit crazy, but I really felt like I had to will my heart to beat at night, that I had to think about it every second or else it would stop. I was exhausted most mornings. I sat on the heat vent while my mom braided my hair and worried about having to go to sleep again that night.

My mom dragged me around to all kinds of cardiologists, none of whom could tell me what was going on with me. My mom was so good about all the doctors' appointments. She never doubted that I had a problem, and that kept me sane most days. She never once told me I was making my heart problems up. She knew me better than that.

One cardiologist told me that I had something called tachycardia, and that it was a condition caused by the sports I was doing. He told me that perhaps it would be best if I were to forgo any athletic endeavours. I wasn't about to do that. I remember my mother telling him that she thought it important that I get as much exercise as possible, all things considered. She thought I should be keeping my heart as strong as possible. He looked at her like she was a filing cabinet.

This whole doctor thing went on for six or seven years. I had basically resigned myself to the fact that I had a weird heart and nobody knew what to do about it. My friends were getting used to me lying down in the middle of the gym floor at a basketball game or on the popcorn-strewn aisle of a movie theatre or on the bathroom tile at a party. I'd lie down and put my feet up against a wall, plug my nose and blow to slow my heart down. It was par for the course now. I wished somebody knew what it was that I had.

I had a funny heart, but my funny heart has always served me well.

chapter four

LEONARD AND DALE

t's hard to write about Leonard and Dale. They were such a big part of my life growing up. The impression the two of them left on my heart is indelible. They were simple, down-to-earth farm boys but they were as crazy as the day is long. There was nothing they couldn't get me to try. They didn't care much about school or anything academic. They just wanted to be outside, running around like tribal nomad people, shooting at anything that moved (and they shot a lot of things). One day they just appeared out of a clearing in the trees. That's what it seemed like, anyway. There they were, standing by our trailer with their dogs in tow, ready to drag me off right then and there. I don't think they even asked me what my name was, they just asked me if I wanted to play and off we went. I think I fell in love with both of them the very first second we met.

Leonard and Dale were cousins. That was one of the first things they told me, like it was a big announcement.

"We're cousins, you know," Leonard said, with his hands on his hips. Leonard could fold his ears in half and make them stick with the help of a little spit, and Dale could turn his eyelids inside out, which he did for hours at a time. I was mesmerized by everything they did, no matter how strange it was. I had never seen anybody turn their own eyelids inside out. Gary would have sooner died than to stick his ears together with spit. I thought boys like these only existed in the movies. I had seen a matinee of Tom Sawyer and Huckleberry Finn, and these two were as close to that in real life as I was ever going to meet.

Dale constantly had a bleeding nose, but he seemed completely unfazed by the blood bubbling out of his nostrils. He'd just wipe his face on his sleeve or snort the blood up into his mouth and spit it out onto the ground in a grotesque pile. I thought that his spitting was wonderful. He could lob a giant glob of spit and blood twenty feet through the air. Leonard spit a lot too. I don't know what it was about spitting, but it was certainly all the rage with those two.

They seemed to have the ability to pee at will. They'd whip out their little wieners (which I had never seen before in my life) and pee on anything and everything. They'd even try to pee their names into the snow. I couldn't quite get over that one. After a few short months in their company, I just peed anywhere I wanted to, too. I never thought twice about pulling my cords down and peeing over the side of a fallen tree. I knew I would never be able to pee my name into the snow, but that didn't matter. It was fun to pee outside. Liberating, actually. It beat having to go all the way back home. I couldn't imagine peeing right in the middle of the yard at our old house in the city. I would have been hauled off by the cops. Gary would have had a heart attack if he'd had to pee outside. He was very proper. Leonard and Dale definitely did not like colouring or playing with dolls of any kind. I think they would have eaten poor Gary alive.

The cousins lived next door to each other, just up the road from us. It was a five-minute run or a thirty-second bike ride. Their grandparents lived behind them at the end of a winding dirt road that looked like it had been ripped right out of the pages of *The Grapes of Wrath*. My gram and Charlie had a little garden in town, but Leonard and Dale's grandparents had a real honest-to-God pig farm right there down the road from where my parents were building our new house. (Pigs, if you don't know, are really mean when provoked. Never throw rotting, baseball-sized onions at a pig in a pen. They will chase you to your yellow school bus if they ever get the chance.)

Leonard and Dale's mothers were sisters and had been given land by their parents when they were married in the fifties, so the whole lot of them had been living in Springbank for a long time. Looking back, I realize how much like hillbillies they were. And I mean that in the best possible charming, down-home, banjo-picking, country way. But Dale's dad would pull out his own rotten teeth with pliers! They didn't believe in going to the dentist, I guess. And I thought the string attached to the door routine was hard-core.

They referred to people like us as "city slickers." I didn't mind being called that—it sounded kind of like an endearment. After we'd lived in Springbank for a few years, I was the one calling anybody who didn't live in the country a city slicker. It always felt good to say it and feel like I owned it.

It didn't matter if it was pouring rain or smack dab in the middle of a winter blizzard, we would be outside running around. We knew every single hill for miles. We climbed every single tree. Snared every single gopher. Shot every single magpie. I became a new version of myself, and it felt like that was who I was meant to be. I was a tomboy and a vagabond and a gypsy and a girl who would never have to have a proper bath again.

After about two weeks, I'd forgotten we'd ever lived in town. I didn't miss Calgary for one second. I think I wore the same pair of

Levi's jeans for two years, until I finally outgrew them. I had a braid down the back of my head that I swear held my eyeballs in place when I rode my bike up and down those pothole-marked country roads. Every morning, my mom braided my hair as tightly as she could, and when she was done my eyebrows had a hard time moving in any direction. She knew my hair would be undone by the time I came home eight hours later; I think that's why she braided it so tight.

In the winter I'd sit on the heat vent when she did my hair and watch *Romper Room*. I loved that show. There was a segment at the end of every episode where the lady host would look through a magic mirror (a tennis racket with no strings) and call out children's names. I always prayed that she'd say mine but she never did. I don't think Jann was a very common name. She'd always say Janice or Janet or Janine, but never Jann. I was always disappointed. I liked watching *The Friendly Giant* too, but I found Rusty, the little rooster who lived in the canvas bag, kind of creepy. He hung on the wall and I always felt bad that he had to live in that bag. Knowing he was a puppet didn't seem to ease my mind.

I have to say that I am haunted by the number of living things Leonard and Dale and I shot or snared. Actually, I am mortified. When you're young you have no reverence for life. You don't realize, or I didn't at least, the value of every living thing. I was just kind of hypnotized by Leonard and Dale and I did whatever they told me to do. The first time I ever saw them kill a gopher, I felt sick. I cried and they both looked at me like I was from another planet. I learned quickly not to cry about anything. If I was going to be part of the gang, I had to acquire a much thicker skin.

Leonard and Dale were very skilled young hunters and crack shots. I am pretty sure they had been shooting .22-calibre rifles from the time they were four years old. I had never seen a real gun before, never mind a functioning bow and arrow. Dale could kill a magpie sitting on a branch with a bow and arrow from fifty feet away. I wanted to learn how to shoot just like he did. I wanted to be like both of them. I wanted to be able to shoot at things from fifty feet away and actually hit them. I just didn't fancy the idea of killing anything.

Leonard and Dale started me out by shooting cans off a fence post. They had a BB gun that you'd have to pump a number of times to build up enough pressure for it to fire the pellet. By "a number of times," I mean at least a hundred. You were exhausted trying to fire off a single shot. As you can imagine, the BB gun was not all that powerful. Even if you had enough energy to pump it a thousand times, you could still follow the shot with the naked eye and see it arc. We'd quite often shoot at each other with it. I always had several disc-like bruises on my arms and legs. It hurt, but we'd always laugh. We actually aimed that little gun at each other's bums and pulled the trigger. We could have lost an eye but it never dawned on any of us that we could blind each other. I am surprised we didn't end up with anything but a few bruises. We were nuts.

I got pretty good at knocking cans off the fence. The bow and arrow was a bit trickier. It was hard for me to pull the arrow back far enough to get any power behind the shot. Eventually, though, practice turned me into a bona fide archer. We killed thousands of magpies and an equal number of gophers. Every summer we had mounds of dead gophers piled up in our field. Leonard's dad gave us a nickel a tail, not that we needed any incentive. We'd combine our money so we could go to the Killarney pool, which was about a three-hour walk into Calgary. Leonard and Dale's dogs would come with us too. They would sit outside the pool on the lawn. They never went anywhere, they just waited there patiently for us to reappear. I always found that amazing. Off we'd go, walking the four or five miles to the Killarney swimming pool on 17th Avenue, with our towels tucked underneath our arms. We thought nothing of going all that way. We would wear our bathing suits under our clothes, put a few apples and some Dad's oatmeal cookies into a bag and start out on our *long* walk into town. I loved every single step of our adventure. I wonder how we must have looked when cars drove by, the three of us marching along with the dogs in tow. I am surprised no one ever stopped to ask us if we were okay or where we were going.

If we had any money left over, we'd sometimes go to the Glamorgan 10-pin bowling alley. That was another two miles west, but hey, who was counting? That would really be a perfect Saturday outing. We'd walk back home with wet bums and wet hair and bloodshot eyes. Who knew you could keep your eyes open in chlorinated water for hours on end? It felt like somebody poured salt right underneath your eyelids. I am surprised we didn't burn our eyeballs out of their sockets. We were as happy as pigs eating onions. Nobody's parents seemed to mind us going all that way. It's not like anybody was the least bit concerned about any of us being abducted. It just didn't happen back then. I know I sound like I am a hundred years old, but the seventies were so much different from how things are today. No parents these days would send three ten-year-olds off on a three-hour walk to a swimming pool. They probably wouldn't send their kids three blocks by themselves, even if they were walking to a police station.

I was so tired by the time I got home after a long, wonderful day of swimming and bowling that I'd just collapse through the back door. I practically fell asleep with a pork chop hanging out of my head on those days. The next day we'd be out there again, running around and playing, among other things, a rousing game of "housewife and husbands." The game would go like this: I would pretend to be the wife in the fort we made out of plywood sheets and chicken wire, pretending to make pancakes and coffee, while Leonard and

Dale would drive the go-cart around Leonard's yard, pretending to be going to their welding jobs. Not much of a game, really. I wanted to drive the go-cart, as being a wife was very uneventful. Eventually they did let me, but I was closely monitored.

Leonard's dad actually was a welder in real life and he made us this awesome go-cart out of an old washing machine engine. I didn't know that washing machines had engines. It could go about twenty-five miles an hour, which is super bloody fast when you're four feet tall, eighty-five pounds and three inches off the ground on a lawn chair gaff-taped to a piece of plywood with four wheels on it. Sometimes I wondered why in the world I had two husbands. Oh well, these were modern times, after all.

We also played a sinister little game called "put Dicky in the dryer." Dicky was a boy from up the road whom Leonard and Dale tormented from time to time. I don't know what it is with young boys, but they are part dirt and part devil. The game was simple: they put Dicky in Leonard's mom's dryer and turned it on. Dicky would fling around like a rag doll, hollering, and then they'd let him out. It seemed like Dicky was in there for an entire fluff cycle, but it was only seconds. He came out a bit stunned. I didn't care much for that game. Poor Dicky. I don't know what wasn't right about Dicky, but he was a troubled little soul. He seemed a little off, and that was before we put him in the dryer. He was one of those kids that everybody picked on. He was constantly taunted and prodded and humiliated. I was friendly with his older sister, Ley, so I knew Dicky fairly well. Ley and I always let him tag along with us when we did things, even if it was just a walk through the field to look for ditch strawberries or Saskatoon berries.

Once, my little brother, Patrick, invited Dicky to one of his birthday parties. My mom made a cake and went to the trouble of icing it all fancy-like, with Pat's name scrawled across the top of it. It was time for my brother to make a wish and blow out the candles and Dicky was so excited that he forgot he had a mouthful of hot dog stuffing his cheeks. You can imagine what happened next. Dicky decided to blow out the candles too and the cake got covered in chunks of wet bun and bits of half-chewed wiener. Patrick bawled his head off, and Dicky just looked around like he didn't know what everybody was so upset about. Mom ended up scraping all the icing off and salvaging the cake as best she could. My little brother still talks about the wiener and the birthday cake incident.

I think God was taking notes on the "put Dicky in the dryer" game. God was writing my name down beside it with a big black marker. I was slowly working my way to hell. At least Leonard and Dale were going to be there to keep me company.

One of the most wonderful things about living in the country was being exposed to so many different kinds of animals. When we had lived in town, the only animals I ever saw were cats and dogs and the odd bird that flitted about in the backyard. I hadn't seen any wild animal that had any girth to it.

Leonard had a giant red horse named Snoopy. It was the biggest and, well, the only horse I had seen in my life. It was some kind of Clydesdale. It had a huge head and huge feet. It was as wide as it was high, and all three of us could ride on Snoopy with room to spare.

It was quite complicated to get on that horse's back. Not even Leonard or Dale could jump up on him, although they tried repeatedly without success. We'd finally have to put Snoopy beside a fence or use an overturned bucket to climb up on him. You'd almost have to do the Russian splits to ride him. Our legs would stick straight out to the side. Leonard would always be in the front, I'd be in the middle and Dale would bring up the rear.

Snoopy didn't seem to mind having three pint-sized passengers.

He'd turn his head around and assess us once we'd gotten aboard, and then just snort a blast of hot, wet air out of his nose, as if to say, "What now? Where are we going, you little twerps?" Leonard would cluck his tongue and snap the reins and we'd start off out down the road. We'd go for hours on Snoopy's back. We'd just plod along, not saying a word to each other. We'd watch the fields unfold, the long wheat pulling at our bare feet, and I do mean pulling. Dale was pulled right off by long, sticky grass once or twice, as I recall. All of a sudden I'd feel his arms rip away from my waist, and there he would be, lying on the ground, winded. I was always afraid he might never breathe again. But Dale would brush himself off and we'd pull him back up on the horse and carry on. He was a really tough little boy. No amount of pain ever fazed him. Leonard, on the other hand, could be a real baby. He would cry at the drop of pretty much anything. I liked him well enough, though, and he did own a go-cart and a horse . . .

Horseback riding was such a lovely way to spend an afternoon. Birds would dart out of the grass to get out from underneath Snoopy's massive hooves. If Leonard dared break him into a trot, the farting would start almost immediately. The gas exploding out of Snoopy's bum sounded like a tuba submerged in water. It was loud and it stank to high heaven. We'd all start to laugh as we bumped along to the sound of one fart after another. I could never quite believe the amount of air that that horse had in its arse. If Snoopy was walking, he was all was calm and quiet, but if we broke into a trot or, God forbid, a canter, he could fart for miles. When Snoopy took a poo (and he *always* took a poo), he'd keep walking like nothing was happening. He could leave a poo trail for a quarter mile. We could always find our way home by following the nuggets of crap he left behind him. Kind of like Hansel and Gretel, only much more disgusting.

Snoopy knew where we wanted to go without Leonard even having to touch the reins. All we had to do was sit on his back doing the Russian splits and enjoying the view. There was a whimsical place called Twin Bridges, where a giant arm of the Elbow River was funnelled through a steel culvert twenty feet in diameter. The water shot through it like a cannon and was a constant, ferocious flow of noisy whitecaps. It was an oasis to us. Snoopy would wade out into the river with us on his back. He'd suck in a long, slow drink and then stand there like a red, hairy statue. No amount of prodding would move him an inch. We just sat there and waited for Snoopy to finish his drink. He'd look over his shoulder at us and wonder why we were still there. He was a funny horse. He had so much personality.

There was a pool about a hundred yards down from the culvert's mouth that was at least ten feet deep at its centre. It was bright blue and green and the water swirled around like paint on a wheel. Leonard would flick the reins and kick his heels and steer Snoopy out into the deep water. We'd giggle like mad as the water rose up over our thighs, inching towards our waists. I'd scream at Leonard to turn us back around. I was so afraid that Snoopy would sink, but he never did. (Maybe it was all the air he had in his body.) Snoopy loved to swim. I was amazed at how agile he was, and how graceful. Snoopy would paddle like a dog and sometimes, for a brief moment, the three of us would be suspended above his back in the water. I'd hang on to Leonard's waist and Dale would hang on to mine. It felt like I was flying. I don't know how we didn't float away.

The summer days we spent barefoot and bareback on Snoopy were some of my favourites.

Leonard and Dale and I would lie on our stomachs in a field for hours at a time, hoping to snare a gopher. They'd place the loop of a string around the gopher hole, cover it with dirt, and then take the end of the string and walk it back to a bluff and wait for the poor little gopher to pop his head up. The boys were patient. They could wait for a long, long time. Then suddenly, *wham!* Dale would jerk the string as the gopher tried to go back down its hole. Sadly, it wouldn't make it. That would be the end of life as the gopher had known it. Leonard and Dale could be cruel. Killing things was just not a big deal to them. They had done it all their young lives. The gopher was usually paraded around on its string for a minute or two, looking beyond terrified, and then slammed into the side of a tree or the top of a big rock. That same thing would happen about ten or fifteen times in a single afternoon. My heart hurts thinking about the hundreds of gophers that died on those hot summer days.

The magpies were an entirely different story. The boys would climb up a tree to get into their nests and take the babies out and set them all on the ground. The chicks didn't know what to do; they just sat there with their mouths opening and closing. The parents would swoop down on us with every bit of courage they had, trying to thwart our evil plans. They'd scream at the top of their magpie lungs and fly at our heads. Leonard and Dale would laugh and swing at them with sticks, and I would usually just scream and duck. Magpies are big birds. Their black–and–white wing span can be up to two feet across. They were cruel scavengers themselves, not that that justified the boys' actions. Magpies eat all the pretty birds' eggs. That's what mom would tell me: the robins' and the blue jays' and the sparrows'. The magpies would go into their nests and eat all the eggs or the little chicks that were waiting for their mothers. Cruel birds indeed. The magpie chicks were usually featherless and pink, depending on how old they were, and as round as a baseball. Leonard and Dale would just smash them with rocks or hit them with old tree branches like they were swinging at baseballs. I did it too, not often, but I certainly would participate on occasion. I buried two magpie chicks in a ditch once, and I have never forgotten it. I buried them alive and I feel sick about it to this day. I felt God watching me and shaking his head. I felt like God had his big notepad out and he was writing my name down again.

You get those flashes of memories in front of your face that steal your breath from your chest. I see piles of dead birds and gophers. I see their little faces, I really do, and am instantly ashamed. Youth and its boundless, heartless atrocities.

As cruel as the boys could be, they often showed mercy and empathy. I saw them many times try to nurse a baby gopher back to health with an eye dropper when the wee thing had been separated from its mother (probably because we killed her). I saw them from time to time rescue a stunned bird after it had hit a window. I'd seen them gently hold kittens and ooh and aah about how cute they were. They always surprised me. They had so many layers to them. They were never cruel to their dogs; they always looked after them, making sure they were always well fed, with fresh water to drink. I came to understand that to them some animals were expendable. I would not have wanted to be a gopher or a magpie between 1971 and 1976 in Springbank, Alberta.

Leonard and Dale's grandparents had a whole bunch of pigs in pens and chickens running about without a care in the world on their farm. (They used to raise minks in the fifties and sixties during the big mink coat fad, I was told. I remember my gram having a mink stole complete with the head still on it. I loved to play with it. Thank God they don't have those anymore.) Their chickens had huts but they weren't put into them very often. It was every chicken for himself, I guess you could say.

Before we moved out there, I had seen pictures of pigs, but I had never actually seen one up close and personal. It was shocking, to tell you the truth. These were *huge* pigs! They were the size of small ponies and they were filthy and fat and they wanted nothing more than to get out of their pens and eat us alive. They had huge teeth. You wouldn't think a pig would have huge teeth, but these did! And they had long, coarse hair. The hair looked more like quills than hair. Pigs have little beady eyes that follow you around like one of those creepy paintings. No matter where you go, the pigs' eyes are glued to you, following every move you make. We loved going down to the farm and climbing up onto the pens to throw old onions at them, or rotten eggs. There were dozens of eggs all over the place. The grandparents both liked nothing more than to sit and drink their generic beer and puff away on their hand-rolled cigarettes, so things were kind of going to pot around there. Thank God they weren't smoking pot, because that would have been the end for the pigs and the chickens.

We spent hours pestering those pigs. They'd rush at the fence and smash into the side of it so hard that the ground would shake. We'd laugh hysterically and then lob a couple dozen more eggs at their heads. The funny part was that they ate everything we threw at them. They couldn't swallow those onions fast enough. As soon as we pelted them with a giant rotten onion, one pig would rush over to pick it up, throw its head madly back and eat it in one fell swoop. The pigs made the weirdest sounds. They certainly didn't go "oink, oink." They sounded more like angry dinosaurs than anything else. They can squeal if they want to, too—it can be high-pitched and completely horrifying, like a baby being thrown down a well. (Not that I know what that sounds like.)

Duray and I were walking up our gravel road to catch the bus one morning when what did we see but a gigantic hairy pig rushing up the road behind us, squealing away like a wounded cheerleader. I guess one had finally managed to escape its old rickety pigpen and come to seek its revenge on the wrongdoers, meaning me. We ran like we'd never run before and the pig ran too. Pigs are not slow. We narrowly escaped the jaws of death that morning by jumping up on a fence. I was very happy that pigs could not fly. My dad told us that once a pig got hold of you, there would be no letting go. They literally have a death grip and they'd rip your arm off before they'd let you go. My idea of pigs has never been the same. *Charlotte's Web* has never held much water with me. You can forget *Babe* as well. Pigs are vicious killers with no regard for a child's young life. I am lucky to be alive. Yes, I am dramatic.

In the fall, Mr. Baldwin, Dale's dad, would always butcher a pig or two so they'd have meat for the winter. This was news to me because I thought meat came from the Woodward's Food Floor at the Chinook Centre. Dale's dad would pick two of the biggest, fattest pigs from the Scots' farm and haul them up the road in his pickup truck. I always thought they looked so funny in the back of that old beat-up truck, like he was taking the pigs to a movie or something. They had no idea where they were headed, and it was just as well. All of the pigs looked fat to me because I knew that every single one of them had eaten at least seventy-six dozen eggs and a million or so onions. The pigs would ride into the Baldwins' yard in the back of that truck, and then be led down a path for a few hundred yards, to a spot just behind a rundown old shed. There they would meet their porcine maker. Their throats were slit and then they were immediately strung up by their back legs on a big tree branch over an old claw-foot bathtub. They'd hang there for an hour or so until all the blood ran out into the tub. I remember looking up at them, hanging there, twisting around in a mad attempt to free themselves, blood spurting out of long, gaping wounds in their throats. It was horrible to see—the life drain out of them into that old white porcelain tub. It was like watching some weird Fellini film. Eventually the squirming and twisting and gurgling stopped. Everything was incredibly quiet. The dead pigs swung from the tree like a grotesque pair of Christmas ornaments. Eyes open and watching you wherever you went.

We kids were lucky enough to have the task of scraping the coarse hair off the pigs after they had succumbed to their injuries. You couldn't butcher the pig until you had scraped all the hair off it. (You learn something new every day in the country.)

We'd use a long, sharp knife that had a handle at both ends, and as you pulled it towards you, you'd scrape off the hair. It was disgusting. That hair was tough to remove. You'd have to go over and over it with the blade. It made a strange sound as it ran across the pale pink skin that stuck with you when you'd lay your head down at night. It was worse than fingernails on a chalkboard. I'll never forget that sound, or the pigs hanging there upside down over a bathtub full of warm, crimson-red blood.

I think about those pigs a lot. I feel guilty that I didn't save them from Dale's dad. Some nights I'll lie in bed and stare at the ceiling with my blankets pulled up underneath my chin, watching the pigs' ghosts flit about the room. I am afraid to even have an arm outside of the covers. I hold my breath and stare at the shadows that seem to swoop down from the rafters to get me. It's scary as hell. And it isn't just pigs that float down from the ceiling, it's the odd cow as well.

One year, Dale's family was heading out on a two-week summer holiday and thought it would be a great idea for me to look after their one and only milk cow. I had never milked a cow in my life, but Dale and his dad were going to teach me and I was going to milk that cow every day so it didn't go dry. I couldn't help but think of the twenty bucks I would make and what I would buy with it.

I was an eager student. I carefully watched how Dale's dad grabbed the teats and pulled on them in such a way that long streams of milk magically squirted out of them into a big steel bucket. He made it look incredibly easy. Dale could do it as well.

"See," he'd say to me. "See what I'm doing?" He'd sit there on the little wooden stool with his head tucked into the cow's side and squeeze those teats evenly and with just enough pressure so the warm milk flowed out of there like it was the easiest thing in the world.

When it was my turn, no matter what I did, no matter how I squeezed and kneaded and pulled on that udder, not a single drop came out. Dale and his dad laughed at me for the first hour and then they were completely frustrated that I couldn't figure it out. Finally, after the third or fourth day of lessons, I got it. Definitely a "ta-dah" moment! On one of my last futile tugs, a stream of milk trickled out of one of the teats and onto the ground. I didn't hit the bucket, but I had at least gotten something to happen. The family would be able to go on their holiday after all and return home to a *not* dry milk cow. I can't tell you how many times they told me that if I didn't milk that cow every day it would go dry. Preventing that from happening was to be my sole purpose for living for those two weeks. Two really long and hot weeks.

Off they drove, out of their dirt driveway, headed for some crystal-clear lake, and there I stood, ready and determined to complete my task. I have to admit that the first day was not great. My mom came with me for moral support and I know she thought that the Baldwins were extremely brave and a little crazy to give me this job. We managed to corral the poor cow (which, I have to say, did not look all that healthy to me), get her into the pen and place the little wooden stool underneath her. As I sat there and looked up at her side I noticed her skin was kind of coming off, but what did I know about healthy cows? Maybe the skin was supposed to do that. I didn't have a clue. All I knew was that I was going to milk that cow, and that was that. My mom stood beside me as I painstakingly milked away until I thought I'd pretty much emptied her out: I got only about a Mason jar's worth. Dale's dad told me that half a bucket was fine if that was all I could get. Three quarters of a bucket would be great, but I should just do the best I could.

Every day I'd walk up the road to the Baldwins' place, call that scruffy-looking cow over to the shed and sit on that little wooden stool and milk to my heart's content. I never did manage to fill that bucket up—in fact, every day I seemed to be getting less and less milk from that cow, and every day that cow seemed to look weirder and weirder. Her hair was coming off in clumps and she seemed bloated. My mom had no idea what was wrong with her, and why would she? We didn't know anything about cows. We both just stood there looking at this ragged thing, wondering what we were doing wrong.

I still had a week to go. I walked up there, rounded up the cow, who was now really reluctant to stand still for me, sat on my stool and began to milk her. She wavered around like she'd had a barrel of vodka for breakfast, making very deep, mournful sounds. I kept trying to steady her and squeeze that milk out. All I could manage was a few drops. I felt the cow's weight suddenly shift from side to side and, before I knew what was happening, she tipped over. She literally kicked the bucket. I screamed and jumped back about ten feet. The Baldwins' cow took one final breath and blew it out of her nose with such a force that the dirt blew up around her head. She made one last throaty moan, and that was it. Her eyes stayed open; they looked like wet pieces of coal.

She looked like she'd been crying.

I could not believe that the Baldwins' one and only cow had just died, right there on the spot. I prayed that she had just fainted, but she was as dead as a doornail. I cried so hard that I could hardly find my way home. I wanted to run but I couldn't catch my breath and my legs seemed to fold underneath me. The half mile seemed more like a marathon. I don't know what I said to my mother when I came crashing through the back door—it was all a snotty blur. I went to sleep that night seeing the sick old cow tipping over again and again.

It's not like we had cellphones back then. There was no way we were going to be able to get hold of the Baldwins on their holiday. They would just have to hear the happy news when they got home. We ended up covering the cow with a tarp and left her where she fell. My dad said that there was no way in hell that we could bury her—it would take a month just to dig a hole big enough, and besides, what if she came to life again? Anything was possible ...

Dale's dad wasn't mad at all. He said that the cow had been sick for awhile; I thought, I wish he had told me that. Dale's little sister Caroline cried a lot over that cow. I guess it was her pet. I didn't know how in the world a person could ever make up for something like killing a cow. Saying I was sorry didn't quite seem to cut it. They never asked me to look after any of their animals again and I guess I don't blame them.

The summers were flying by. The house was more or less finished and we had been living in it for over a year, but dad still worked on it constantly. I had settled into my new school and things seemed easy. Leonard and Dale and I had been roaming the hills and meadows for three years now and we knew every square inch of the land for miles. It's funny how one summer can change everything, though. Suddenly the boys didn't want to shoot or snare things anymore. They didn't want to play with bows and arrows and they didn't want to drive around on the go-cart. They were changing. Me? Not so much. They got so tall over the summer between grades six and seven. Their hormones had started to take over their young bodies. They were much more curious about my body. The funny part of it is that they had seen me without a top from time to time. When we swam in the pond we'd often just go in our underwear. They'd seen me pee more times than you could imagine. But now everything was different.

Apparently there is a big difference between nine and twelve. They wanted to play spin the bottle and Truth or Dare. I didn't know what to make of any of it. I hadn't changed at all; I was still very naive and wanted to stay the way we were. There wasn't very much "truth" involved in Truth or Dare; it was mostly "dare." Their voices were deeper and their muscles were bigger and they were much more aggressive about everything. They were intent on talking me into playing doctor all the time, examining me and wanting me to examine them. Once in awhile I gave in and let them peek into my pants. They would try to bribe me with gum. Gum? What about cash? I couldn't imagine what was so exciting to look at down there. I felt like I hardly knew them anymore.

Leonard was much worse than Dale when it came to the touchy-feely department. In fact, Dale was always a perfect gentleman. He was very gallant for a twelve-year-old. Leonard, on the other hand, was forever trying to persuade me to go into his parents' dark and creepy basement so he could try to kiss me. His bedroom was conveniently down there and I remember it was always cold and uncomfortable. I had no idea what he was trying to do, I just knew it was making me embarrassed and sick to my stomach. I'd lie there and stare up at the faint bit of light coming through the curtained window and yearn to be outside playing. I wanted to be anywhere but there with him. He had one tooth that poked out of the side of his mouth slightly. When he tried to kiss me I could always feel it touching my lips, which were very tightly pursed, I might add. I wondered what had happened to my pal? Where had the old Leonard gone? Hormones had happened, that's what.

I don't know why I didn't just push him off me and run home and tell my mother what he was up to. I didn't know what to do. I didn't really have anybody to confide in. It certainly would not have been either of my brothers. Patrick was five years younger than I was and Duray was hardly ever home. Duray and I certainly never sat down and had long, intimate conversations.

It felt like Duray was disappearing before our very eyes. To say he was becoming estranged from the entire family was an understatement. He was secretive and kept to himself when he was around. He smoked pot and drank my dad's beer and listened to his music and the rest of his life was a mystery to me. (My mom told me later she suspected his pot smoking, but she wasn't exactly sure what to do about it.)

I thought I'd keep the whole Leonard ordeal a secret. I thought that was the best option. I regret that now. I should have said something to someone. I was just very ashamed. Dale probably would have popped him one for me if I had told him. I would walk home from Leonard's house after one of those encounters feeling like I was the worst person in the world, that it was my fault. I think that's a pretty common feeling. We all have similar tales to tell. The shame somehow silences you. Growing up is hard. The person I am now would have taken Leonard by the throat and twisted his little balls off. But when I look back I feel nothing but compassion for both of us, Leonard and me. I often wonder what he recalls of it? Maybe his recollections are different from mine.

It was all so bizarre, and trust me, there was nothing even remotely sexual about any of it for me. I truly thought that Leonard had gone completely bonkers. I thought he had lost every single one of his marbles. I had no clue what was so exciting for Leonard. He wasn't a bad guy at all. He probably thought, what the heck is happening to me and why do I feel like humping fence posts, pumpkins and old cars? He never forced me to do anything. I was just too stupid and shocked to say "stop it!" I suppose that's why they call it learning.

The hardest part was that I knew there would be no going back to who we had been. The wonderful, innocent days of running through the flower-filled meadows, skimming stones in Douglas's Pond and flying kites and riding snowmobiles at midnight were behind us forever. I don't think we fully realized that at the time. Maybe the boys thought we could do both: Leonard could dry hump me from time to time and try and steal a kiss in his parents' basement *and* we could continue to shoot things and have bonfires every weekend and build tree forts. But it wasn't meant to be. That was our last summer. We were headed back to school and I was already starting to spend more time with my other friends, so I didn't speak to them much at school anymore. Leonard and Dale just started to fade like an old Polaroid. I don't even know if they ever graduated. I think they may have gone to another school. All I know is that I'd never had friends like them before in my life and I doubted I would have friends like them again. To say we didn't have a care in the world was the complete truth. Every morning I stepped outside my house and squinted into the Canadian sun, there they'd be, standing with their dogs, their hair blowing sideways, waiting for me to come and play.

chapter five

SECRET HEART

My older brother, Duray, had become pretty much a shadow to me during my Leonard and Dale years. He was three years older than I was, so we didn't play together and I didn't see him much at school. When I was in elementary school, he was in junior high, and when I got to junior high, he had moved on into high school. I was busy running through the pines and riding horses and having fun. I didn't notice him and it was like he didn't want to be noticed. While I had been living like Huckleberry Finn with Leonard and Dale, Duray had been slipping deeper and deeper into incredible sadness. Something terrible had happened to him, and none of us could have imagined what. Later, my mother said that they'd lost him the summer of his ninth year. She said that we'd come back from our yearly summer holiday at Woods Lake in British Columbia, and he was just not the same. Part of him was gone. It wasn't until years later that we pieced together our version of what may have happened. Duray to this day does not discuss that time in his young life, period, no matter how much we prod him. All I know is he became isolated and sullen. The always smiling and happy boy just disappeared. He went from doing incredibly well in school, doing well in sports, being well-liked and achieving straight As, to becoming anti-social and failing at every subject.

It worried my parents no end. They couldn't understand it. I know now that part of the reason they moved us out of the city was so that Duray could attend a smaller school and have the chance to make a new start. I guess they hoped that he might get back on the right path in Springbank. Sadly, nothing was going to get him onto the right path. He was constantly in trouble and my parents were completely helpless to do anything about it. Lord knows they tried everything to get him to understand that his actions would be met with bigger and bigger consequences. My mother always says that some people are determined to ruin their own lives, and he was one of them.

I remember his big brown eyes looking down at his shoes all the time. Duray always seemed to look at the ground. It's hard to see a person's head hang so low, especially a person you love. Even when I was young I knew that something was really wrong with him. He didn't seem to have good friends. He hung around with these guys who thought the world owed them something, and nobody seemed to stick. Kids would just come and go, in and out of his life. You'd see them for a few weeks around the house, hanging out in the basement, and then they'd be gone. He went through people quickly. It's like he didn't want anybody to know him, like he didn't feel worthy of being known. I think he wanted to be invisible.

Maybe that's where the drugs and alcohol came in. They could make him invisible. I was too young to know how to help him or, for that matter, that he even needed help. He always seemed so mad, arguing with our mom and dad. He has said many times over the years that he never felt like he fit in. He was always on the outside looking at all of us, like we were speaking a foreign language. I don't think he knew how to tell us what was bothering him or what had happened to him. Of course, we didn't find out any of this out until it was far too late. He buried all of it away and hoped that it would just stay there, out of sight and out of mind. I don't think that ever works for anybody. It certainly never worked for me.

My brother and I could not have been more different. It's always weird to think that we came from the same two parents. I wanted people to know me. I wanted to nurture new friendships, and I wanted to fit in no matter what I had to do. I enjoyed every minute of my life. Everything was fun. Even when I was alone, which I liked to be as well, I was serene and content. Not Duray. Duray had shadows following him around all the time. He was cloaked in darkness.

Like most siblings, we always fought over some stupid thing or the other, like who ate all the potato chips or where the chocolate bars were hidden or whether I had been in his room and touched his stuff. Touching his stuff was the worst possible thing you could do to an older brother. Stuff was very important and touching somebody else's stuff could and would be severely punished. We'd chase each other through the house and punch each other's arms until faint red marks would appear. It was all pretty harmless and average. I don't know of any kids who didn't fight with their siblings. Duray was much bigger than I was, but I could be mean and wild. I would kick him and scratch him and punch him and throw the odd piece of furniture his way. He never used more force than he needed to. Though I hated it when he sat on my chest and farted on my face. That was never pleasant. He, much like Snoopy, could fart at will. He could also burp the entire alphabet and whistle better than anybody. He stuck his thumb and his middle finger into his mouth and made the highest, loudest whistle you had ever heard in your life. My ears used to ring. Duray taught me how to whistle. It took him about three days, but he managed to teach me how to stick my two fingers in my mouth and blow out a perfect long, shrill note. I am still a great whistler. I can hail a cab from a block away thanks to Duray.

He never knew how much I admired him. He could do anything under the sun; he took after my dad in that way. He could fix absolutely anything that was broken. There was nothing he couldn't take apart and put back together. He was very mechanically minded, but he was an excellent artist as well. He could look at a picture of a truck or a helicopter or a beautiful building and draw it freehand. He was wonderful at woodworking or anything to do with metal or leather or plastics. He could do it all. That always made me jealous. He was also very musical. He loved to play guitar and sing. He made me want to do the same because he made it look effortless. He seemed to be able to listen to a song and then play it back as though he'd always known it.

He was very nonchalant about his talents and abilities, maybe because he didn't think that what he was doing had any worth. My brother was and is incredibly smart but I don't know if he really understood just how intelligent he was. That always seemed sad to me. His self-esteem was so incredibly low. I don't think people even knew what self-esteem was in the seventies, or at least they didn't really give it much attention. A lot of young people slipped between the cracks, and he was one of them. I saw him doing all these incredible things but I didn't really know him. He didn't let you get to know him. I think he thought I was a pest: an annoying little sister who got into his things and got away with everything.

I did tattle on him a lot. He was doing some pretty bad stuff, and I thought that somebody should know. Probably not the best idea in hindsight, because it just made things worse for him at home. I am sorry for telling on him. He needed me to support him, not tell on him every chance I got. Our parents, especially my dad, scrutinized and questioned every little thing he did because he lied about every-thing: where he'd been, who he'd been with, what he'd been doing.

I took no pleasure in seeing him in trouble, I just didn't think about what my actions would do to his life. I didn't look ten minutes ahead of where I was. By the time Duray was a teenager, he'd been stealing from my dad's liquor cabinet and smoking his cigarettes for years. He would stay out as late as he pleased, never telling anyone where he'd been. Sometimes he'd stay out all night without so much as a phone call. He was always in trouble at school, always being suspended. He was vandalizing houses and crashing motorcycles and taking off with my mother's car. I don't know if he was crying out for help or just trying to be the biggest loser in the world on purpose. It's a fine line. He was starting to scare all of us.

One day I remember being out in the yard with Leonard and Dale. By this time, we'd been hanging out less and less but on this day we were riding bikes around the driveway, hanging out, happily wasting the day away. Duray was by the garage, kind of keeping his eye on what we were up to. He had been drinking most of the after-noon and seemed agitated, taunting us and calling us names just for the sake of having something to do. I remember thinking how alone he seemed. Drinking turned him into a completely different person. I tried to steer clear of him if he'd been drinking, but that wasn't always possible. I honestly didn't understand his behaviour. He would usually threaten to break our arms or rip our legs off if we were to tell on him for stealing alcohol. He was a foot taller than any of us so we believed him, even though we knew he'd never actually break our arms. We sort of laughed it off and tried to look like we didn't care when we really did. Leonard and Dale always tried to be brave for me, but this wasn't someone they wanted to tangle with.

Duray could be really intimidating and unpredictable. On this particular day, I watched him down three or four beers and then saunter over to our little beige car and unscrew the gas cap. He put his mouth over the hole and began to huff in and out. He kept breathing in the gas fumes and coughing between huffs. This went on for about five minutes until he flung himself back from the car and started staggering around the yard speaking nonsense. His eyes were big and wild, and he was spitting and hacking and twirling about like, well, a drunk person who'd been huffing gasoline. He laughed like he was possessed and kept yelling things that made no sense at all. After awhile he grabbed his head and moaned in incredible pain. Whatever high he'd climbed up to, he was now rapidly coming down from it.

He repeated the process over and over again until he was exhausted and throwing up. It was hard to watch and even harder to understand. I had never seen anybody huff anything in my life. The only thing I had ever sniffed was a black Jiffy marker. I loved that smell—I still do. But gasoline? Leonard and Dale and I thought Duray was off his ever-loving rocker. For some reason, I didn't tell my mom about those episodes. That was something I should have tattled about, but I was too scared. The huffing episodes became more and more frequent as he disappeared further and further down the rabbit hole.

Duray didn't seem to be all that good at staying out of my dad's way. My dad was especially hard on him. Perhaps because he was the oldest and he was a boy and that's what dads do. They try to groom their sons to be better men than they are. Duray knew how to push his buttons, though. It was a case of my dad saying "black" and my brother saying "white." They were like oil and fire—one spurred on the other. They fed off each other's discontent.

They would argue about everything and nothing. It didn't matter what it was, they just butted heads about it. Their yelling sounded like planes crashing right there in our kitchen and made my stomach fold in on itself. It would very often end in a shoving match or misplaced, angry punches thrown or someone crashing out the back door yelling profanities. Usually when two people yell at each other, not much is accomplished. I didn't want to be around it and, though I'm sure Duray didn't want to be around it either, I doubt very much he knew how to avoid it. It was almost a given that there would be confrontation if drinking was involved: you cannot reason with rum. There was no way in hell I was going to get between my dad and my brother.

My mom spent a lot of time in her ironing room. It was not at all private, since it had two doors and was in the middle of the house, but it was her room. It was going to be a bedroom at one point, but that didn't come to pass. It was small with a pretty decent window that looked right into the side of the garage. Not exactly a million-dollar view. She'd go in there and iron piles of clothes. She never seemed to get through that pile. I am serious when I tell you that it was five feet high at times. I had to iron a few days a week as one of my chores. (I didn't have many.) I'd sit there and watch *Star Trek* and iron T-shirts and slacks and tablecloths and my dad's hankies until I could do it with one foot tied behind my back and blindfolded. I was an excellent ironer. I'd drink Pop Shoppe pop and eat Old Dutch salt and vinegar chips. I could see why my mom liked to be in her ironing room. You could be alone and have a television all to yourself and watch whatever you wanted, and it was quiet. The quiet is what I remember the most about the ironing room. Once in awhile you'd hear the steam pour out of the top of the iron. It was such a pleasant sound, and the warmth of it felt so good. We had three channels we received clearly: channels 2, 4 and, of course, the good old CBC on channel 6. It was a huge deal when we got a fourth channel, even though it didn't have the best programming in the world. Channel 9 was mostly news, and who in their right mind wanted to watch the news?

In the late seventies we got a satellite dish that was the size of the moon. I was afraid to walk by it for fear of developing tumours of some kind. The thing hummed and crackled constantly. I imagined that invisible cancer beams shot out of it, like something from *Star Trek*. We were apparently now receiving all these illegal channels from the States and it was totally exciting. If it was from the States that meant it had to be good. I remember getting the picture a lot of the time, but no sound. That was the satellite company's way of keeping you from stealing their signal, I suppose. We didn't care. We were determined to watch the American movies from the dish without the sound and we all became really good lip readers because of it.

In my dad's book, there wasn't anything worse than a liar. You could burn down a bowling alley, but if you admitted to doing it, you were still a good person and deserved the benefit of the doubt. I don't know when my older brother became a pathological liar. At one time he was the pillar of truth, really. Now Duray lied about everything he did and everywhere he went. My mom would say, "Have you been drinking?" and Duray would lie and say no. She'd always want to smell his breath and check to see if his eyes were red. There wasn't enough Visine in the world to clear up his bloodshot, stoned eyes. Duray called her Sherlock Holmes, which made me laugh. My mom could smell marijuana from five miles away and be able to ascertain whether it had been grown in Colombia or on Vancouver Island. She'd ask him where he'd been, and he would always lie about that too. After awhile I don't think he knew where the truth was. It was gone. There was no truth left in him. He felt that a lie was always the better choice. I didn't start lying until I turned eighteen and, according to my mother, I went bonkers. Maybe I did go bonkers. I liken it to letting the proverbial cat out of the bag. It was a really big bag and I was a late, late, late, late bloomer. (I didn't get my period until I was thirty-seven.)

Every time the phone rang at our house, it seemed like it was somebody calling about something that Duray had done. It was hard to believe that one kid could get up to so many bad things. My mom already had to deal with my dad and his drinking, and now she was also having to deal with Duray lighting haystacks on fire and spray-painting the hell out of the house the neighbours had been building. I don't know how many thousands of dollars my parents spent trying to fix things my brother had ruined. You can only ground a person for so many years, and then it doesn't work anymore. Grounding was a joke to my brother. Duray was an amazing escape artist who could get out of any room and disappear into thin air. He was like Houdini with a drug and alcohol problem.

I don't remember him laughing all that often. He would laugh like the devil when he huffed gasoline, but that was more of a cackle that quickly turned into a scene from *The Exorcist*. It made me feel so hopeless and sad to watch him come undone.

On one of my brother's many escapes he thought it would be a good idea to drive a tiny 75cc Honda motorcycle into Calgary to drink beer. This adventure just about cost him a foot.

My parents had gone somewhere on a short overnight trip, so he simply decided to go on a joyride without a helmet or a licence of any kind in the fading dusk. All hell seemed to break loose with him whenever my parents went anywhere. Duray would find trouble and bring it to the front door. But it was impossible for my parents to be home all the time, and my older brother knew that. He counted on it. I think we were all secretly praying that Duray grow out of his destructive patterns. He didn't. We thought that eventually there would be a light at the end of the tunnel instead of a train coming towards him.

On this particular night, Duray got on the little motorcycle and headed off into town to go to the nearest bar, the Westgate. It was seven or eight miles from where we lived. He actually made it to the hotel without being spotted. He sat there for a few hours drinking, spent all his money and then proceeded to make his way back home. He had gone about a mile when two police officers spotted him buzzing along without a helmet or a licence plate. They turned on their siren, thinking he would immediately pull over, but he had no intention of giving up that easily. The chase was on!

When they got up alongside him they told him to pull over, but he didn't. According to my brother, the two officers in the police cruiser then starting bumping into his motorcycle with their car, trying to get him to stop. He probably got scared and thought he'd outrun them by going down sideroads and trying to head home, but it didn't work out that way. The cruiser bumped him a few more times until it knocked him and the bike over. The police car ran over his leg, leaving him in a crumpled heap on the ground in a pool of his own blood. The way my brother tells it, the blood was spewing out of his boot like a water sprinkler. He doesn't remember much of what happened after that because he passed out. His foot had been punctured by the little metal gear changer on the motorcycle. The pedal went through his boot and into his foot like a steel spike.

I remember picking up the phone when the police called to say that there had been an incident. They asked if my parents were home, and I said they weren't. They asked where they were and when they'd be home. The policeman sounded panic stricken. He wasn't making any sense at all. He was going on and on about what had happened and that it was a "very unfortunate accident."

The police took him to the emergency ward via ambulance to get the mangled mess stitched up. It required hundreds of stitches. To this day my brother can hold water in the divot on the top of his foot where that pedal went in. He's quite proud of that little oddity. If he had not been wearing his heavy leather boots, his foot would have been ripped right off his leg. The police tried to sweep it under the rug by saying they wouldn't press charges. I can't imagine what they were thinking, or what they ended up reporting to their bosses. They more or less got away with running over a kid on a little motorcycle. A few weeks later, he got a ticket in the mail for $30 for driving without a licence. Duray took months to heal. My parents were devastated by the whole thing.

He said he was plastered when he drove home and that he was glad he was because otherwise "it would have hurt a whole lot more than it did."

My dad had begun drinking more himself since we'd moved out of town. He was under a lot more pressure at his job. His hours were longer and he was home less and less. I'm sure building our house was stressful and required a lot of money that he didn't always have. We didn't see him at the dinner table more than a few times a week. I had no idea why he wasn't there; he just wasn't. He was slowly becoming a ghost to me. My mom would caution us not to bring kids home after school because she didn't quite know how dad would be—if he'd be sober or not. His moods were unpredictable, and he could be really cranky and short tempered. Duray bore the brunt of it, unfortunately.

I became a bit afraid of my dad at times, to tell you truth. He was a grouchy guy, always yelling. I don't really remember him ever talking to us. He just yelled. For about five years I thought my name was "Jesus Christ" and I thought my brother's name was "goddammit." We learned a whole hell of a lot of swear words from my dad. They really came in handy at school. I could shock people with my vocabulary. I could spit out words that would leave other kids with their jaws hanging half open. My dad knew some good curses. (And to think he was raised in a Mormon home.) But it honestly didn't bother me all that much. That was my dad—that's the way he was. For some reason I tuned out the naughty, swearing, cursing parts I didn't want to hear. I am pretty sure I wasn't in any kind of denial—I was just always easygoing. I didn't let many things bother me, and his yelling was one of those things. My mom always told me that I knew how to handle him, and I guess I did. For the most part I just retired to the basement to listen to my records.

Making my dad mad was not a good idea, so we all tried not to. I made it a point to be out of the house if I could when he was home. It seemed like everything we did drove him crazy, like not putting his tools back where they came from or not coming home when we were supposed to or fooling around at the dinner table or using his "good wood" to build tree forts and rafts that never floated. How was I supposed to know what good wood looked like? (I must have had good taste in wood because I always used his good stuff.)

My dad didn't like it when you wrecked perfectly good things. He didn't like it if you cut the bread or cheese crooked. I have to say I can't stand that, either. He would get really mad over things like that. Everybody would scatter when he got raving about a ruined block of Velveeta cheese and a lot of goddamns were cast about. A million colourful words came shooting out of his mouth, and we made sure to stay out of their way.

It wasn't the big things but the little things that set him off. That's what made it hard: we never knew exactly what was going to make him angry. I knew that when I was downstairs playing music, he wouldn't come down there for anything. It was my safety net. Nobody went into the basement except Duray and me. Duray's bedroom was down there and it was quite the testosterone-laden den. He had an old waterbed in his room. This was a giant one, with speakers and pot lights in it—it was the mother ship of all waterbeds. He loved that thing. I, on the other hand, have always hated waterbeds. I slept on one once and that was it for me. I dreamed about having to pee all night long, and my back felt like it had been sawed in half. (Also: never let a kitten on a waterbed, as they have very sharp little claws that can make really, really small, slow-leaking holes that you don't notice for days or even weeks.)

He had Nazareth and KISS posters plastered everywhere. He had a black light and black-light posters too, which I thought were amazing. I remember how weird our teeth looked when we had that black light on. (God forbid I should *ever* touch the black light, even if I was absolutely sure Duray was in another country.) My brother was a *very* tidy person. No one had to tell him to clean his room. I, on the other hand, was pretty messy. Making my bed or putting my clothes away cut into my snowmobiling and my tree climbing and my killing of gophers and magpies. Why make a bed when you were just going to get right back into it?

I don't think my dad noticed that I wasn't around much when he was. He was in his own world and I had no idea where that was. I wasn't old enough to understand that he was a person with his own issues and concerns and worries. I somehow managed to be under his radar. I guess it helped that I was short and quick and could get around him pretty well. I would grab a Wagon Wheel out of the cupboard and fly out the back door. (A Wagon Wheel is a godawful chocolate-covered cookie thing filled with marshmallow. We ate them by the millions even though they taste like used sport socks.) I would be outside playing until the sun went down and I literally could not see my hand in front of my face.

By then I had a new dog—Aquarius. My parents had gotten him for us a few years after we'd moved out to Springbank. They'd found him in an ad in the local paper. We drove out to a little town west of us called Priddis and picked him out of a litter of pups. He was the smallest of the bunch. We think he was a German shepherd–husky cross, but the farmer wasn't exactly sure who the father was. I couldn't quite figure out how he couldn't know that. That seemed important to me. My mother tried to explain that you didn't always know who the father was when it came to dogs. I took her word for it. My mother was the one who named him Aquarius. She apparently loved the song as sung by the 5th Dimension: "This is the dawning of the age of Aquarius . . ." Whatever the heck that meant.

My dad had put up an old school-bell from the turn of the century that my mom would ring when playtime was up. I knew that I needed to get home as quickly as my short, bruised legs would take me. No fooling around. You could hear that bell from miles away and, ironically, it was as clear as a bell. Go figure. My dog's ears would perk up and he'd start running for home, and there was no question that he'd be taking me with him. He would always pull at me by my shirt sleeves. Aquarius knew there would be a big bowl of food waiting for him when we got home.

Both my parents worked so hard on the house and in the yard. We had five acres, and they spent months if not years fixing up every square inch of that land: clearing brush and planting trees and mowing and gardening. My dad used to have us haul buckets to water the spruce trees they'd planted. My dad would say, "Go out and water those goddamn trees!" (It wasn't just a tree, it was a goddamn tree.) I would cringe. I would rather have been ironing, because at least then I could watch TV. Picking rocks out of the garden wasn't high on my list.

"Go and pick those goddamn rocks out of that goddamn garden, goddammit!" How did those rocks get there in the first place, I always wondered, and why would a girl need to pick rocks out of a garden anyway? What exactly did the rocks do that was so detrimental to growing things? I never understood the rock-picking at all. It was one of my least favourite chores. I just hated picking rocks. I am quite sure that it served no purpose at all. It was just something my dad made us do when we were in trouble or when he didn't want us in the house. I think he may have been the one who planted the rocks in the garden in the first place, although I will never be able to prove that. He will undoubtedly take that secret to his grave. His last words will be like that final scene in *Citizen Kane*. He will utter the word "rocks," and slip into the vapour of the unknown. Yes, I am dramatic.

My dad liked to pick a fight and win it. It's like that old saying: Do you want to have peace, or do you want to be right? My dad wanted to be right. He always thought he was right and the hard part was that, more often than not, he *was*. He seemed to know everything about everything, and that made it hard to win an argument. My dad was very, very stubborn, and I know that drove my mother crazy. My mom wanted peace. We all wanted peace. Who doesn't want peace, for crying out Christmas?

Usually their fights ended with my parents not talking to each other. The silent treatment was a much-used weapon in our house. Silence is creepy and eerie when done on purpose and executed properly. You cannot talk to the other person, ever. You must hold out as long as you can. To win at the silent treatment game you may have to stop speaking for at least a year, sometimes longer. That's what it seemed like, anyway.

I could walk around our house and be able to hear hearts beating, clocks ticking, floors creaking, wind throwing leaves around outside, mice walking on the snow . . . Everything was amplified. Silence is never all that silent, when you really think about it.

Mom did her best to protect us from all the mood swings that the drinking was causing in my dad and from all his irrational behaviour, but the rug wasn't big enough to sweep everything under. You can't just go out and buy a bigger rug, although we all would have liked to have done that for my mother's sake. Maybe a bigger rug would have made things easier for her. It would have bought her some precious time.

I don't know how it happened, because it was so gradual, but eventually my dad just kind of disappeared. He was working around the clock and by the time he got home, I was in bed, and by the time I was getting up, he was already gone again. That's just the way it was. Ever since he'd gotten his new job at a concrete and construction company, he wasn't home very much. It seemed perfectly normal to me. It's probably because my mom picked up so much of the slack. She drove us kids everywhere: to swimming lessons and hockey practice and volleyball games and track and field and badminton and you name it. I don't know where she got the time to magically show up to pick me up and drop me off, but she did. She drove my friends everywhere too. She never said no to any of them.

Because school was so far from home, we didn't get to go home at lunchtime; we were there pretty much all day and had to bring our lunches with us on the bus. Eventually they converted a classroom into a kind of cafeteria, but until that happened, Patrick, Duray and I brought our lunches from home. My mom tried to switch it up to keep things fresh and exciting. It couldn't have been easy to please our complicated palates. We were, after all, used to complex gourmet food made in a Crock-Pot, so she had a very high bar to leap over.

She made all kinds of different sandwiches—bologna or tomato or Cheez Whiz. (We went through nine gallons of Cheez Whiz every week, I'm sure. I can't wait to see what the long-term health effects of that will be.) There were certain items we'd always have in our lunch boxes. Rock-hard Dad's oatmeal and chocolate-chip cookies that took the skin off the roof of your mouth and, yes, those dreaded Wagon Wheels. We'd also take a Thermos of something to drink, either juice or milk. Pop was not a good idea because of the explosion factor. I had a baby-blue plastic lunch box with a matching Thermos that my mom bought me at the Co-op. It lasted me all through elementary and junior high school, but I went through about four hundred glass Thermos inserts. I was forever breaking them. If you dropped those old Thermoses from four inches off the floor, they'd shatter into a million pieces. If you bumped them on the side of a chair, or into the back of someone's head, they'd break. I am just saying that it didn't take much to break a Thermos insert. But my mom was always mad when she had to buy me yet another one.

My mom tried to get more creative with our lunches as the years went by. Sandwiches had become a thing of the past; it was high time to move on to bigger and better things. One morning she boiled the kettle, filled my Thermos with hot water and sank a hot dog wiener into it. She wrapped the bun in plastic wrap, already loaded with ketchup and mustard and onions. She even had a dill pickle sliced up and wrapped in tinfoil. She figured the wiener would be perfectly heated and ready to put into my bun by lunchtime. When I sat down and opened my blue lunch box, I knew something was different. Where was my sandwich? What was this bun for? I unscrewed the top of my Thermos and couldn't figure out what I was looking at. I could see a beige bubble looking out at me. I poked at it with my finger and it hardly moved. What was it? I got out my pencil and stabbed at the thing, still not knowing what to make of what was in there. It turned out the wiener had absorbed all the water and had expanded into every possible bit of space in the Thermos. I had to pull out the wiener piece by piece with my pencil and put the pieces into my bun. My mom swears to this day she never put a wiener into my Thermos. Well, she did, and, although it didn't look like a hot dog when I finally got it out, it did taste like one. I have to give her credit for trying.

There was also the case of the exploding chili, but I guess I don't have to expand on that. It speaks for itself. I became more and more cautious about unscrewing my Thermos lid all through elementary school. I would have been happy to have soup or hot chocolate in there, like the rest of the kids, but I was always getting sloppy joes or spaghetti or beef stew. I remember eating my spaghetti with a spoon. It kind of disintegrated after a few hours in my baby-blue Thermos, but it was still good.

I guess I should have been grateful that I was getting lunch at all. I knew kids who came to school with a few oatmeal cookies in a brown paper bag and a bologna sandwich on white generic bread every single day. The contents of their lunches never changed. And a few kids sat there with nothing at all. I remember this one girl who just sat and read her Nancy Drew books all through the lunch hour because she didn't have anything to eat. I sometimes wonder what happened to her. I don't even remember her name, which makes it even more sad. I could kick myself for not just marching over to her and offering up some of what I had. Surely she would have appreciated chunks of my beige hot dog wiener? Surely she would have enjoyed a spoonful of my atomic chili? I can't go back and change that but I would in a heartbeat if the universe would let me. I had years of school lunches ahead of me, and I will say this, they were always interesting. Thank God we finally got a cafeteria in junior high, though it was total crap for the most part. Everything they had came from a frozen box. There wasn't a vegetable within a hundred miles of our school. For a buck I could buy a mini cardboard-like pizza with mystery meat on top of it, a generic root beer and a greasy paper bag full of french fries. My nutritional needs were not even close to being met, but I didn't have to risk having my own head blown off by my baby-blue Thermos anymore.

chapter six

MY FATHER'S DAUGHTER

think my fourth grade teacher had the most lasting influence on my somewhat crazy career choice. (I didn't really choose it—it chose me—but we'll get to that.) Music was the last thing on the planet my parents could ever have fathomed my being involved with, I am sure. They thought I would just end up lighting things on fire and watching them burn, or that I would somehow become involved in the circus. They may well have prayed that I might consider entering a convent at some point, but a circus was pretty much the only place that would welcome a fire-wielding girl like me anyway. Nuns, of course, don't really like anything burning—too much like hell. (There was a singing nun I really loved growing up. She sang a version of the Lord's Prayer that became kind of a pop hit back in the day.)

My mother will often say to me that she had no idea I liked singing or, for that matter, that I *could* sing. My grade four teacher discovered that I, Jann Richards from Alberta, had a singing voice inside of me that was just screaming to get out. (It actually *was* rather like a scream and a bit like rubber boots walking on wet Styrofoam, but it was a singing voice nonetheless!)

My teacher's name was Judith Humphreys and she was probably just barely into her twenties. I couldn't have taught a single soul how to spit when I was in my twenties. I was an idiot, but at least I knew I was an idiot. When you're an idiot and you don't realize it, well, that's where the danger lies. When you know you're an idiot, you're halfway to salvation. (I used to think salvation was when your mouth got all watery. Boy, was I wrong.)

She had long red hair that was always swept to the side with a barrette of some kind. (Ms. Humphreys had the good kind of red hair, not the wiry kind that Mrs. May had.) She had a permanent smile on her face, complete with dimples! For some reason I always think about her nice, straight teeth and her big, rosy cheeks. Some things just stick in your memory like flies on apple pie. I think she must have showered right before she came to school every morning, because she was always shiny. She made me want to start brushing my hair on a far more regular basis. Leonard and Dale had somehow changed me into a tomboy with no sense of personal grooming whatsoever. I had to try and correct that.

Ms. Humphreys got married about halfway through the year and shortly thereafter became Mrs. Snyder, but that never really seemed to stick. I don't think she minded what you called her, Ms. Humphreys or Mrs. Snyder, she was just happy to be called "teacher." It's so nice when teachers actually like their jobs—it makes a kid's life a lot easier for about twelve years. Ms. Humphreys loved her job, and we all felt it when she swept into the classroom every morning. She seemed to glide past our desks in slow motion, brandishing a fairy wand. I always felt like I was being covered in glitter.

She was unbelievably friendly and straightforward. She didn't have any airs about her. I heard one of the other teachers call her "Judith" one day, kind of by mistake, I guess. I don't think I had ever known a teacher's first name before. I didn't know teachers even had first names. I thought they just had last names, and that they lived in the school after we all went home on the bus. I figured they had little cots in the teachers' lounge where they slept at night. I wanted so badly to call her Judith, too, but I never did. I thought about it in my head, though. I imagined saying things like "Um, Judith, what time do you think we'll be breaking for lunch today?" or "Judith, did you happen to see the news last night? It was very interesting."

I had many imaginary conversations with Judith, in which I was very smart and grown-up. We'd go for coffee together in my head. It was always fun. We'd shop for skirts and watches and new cars. And then Judith would ask me a real question and I'd just sit there at my desk with a blank look on my face.

"Where were you just now, Jann Richards?" she'd say. I couldn't very well tell her that I had been with her the whole time, shopping for new skirts and Chevrolets.

"Um . . ." was all I could ever reply. She never got mad at me, though; she always had a slight smile that meant, "Well, just pay more attention from now on, time for daydreaming later." I did try to pay attention. I tried with all my might. I beat back my imagination with threats of never talking to it again. But you can't reason with imagination, it's just too powerful. You give in to it eventually and end up riding a silver unicorn to Saturn during math class. Reality is big, but imagination is even bigger.

I was an extremely imaginative kid, and it didn't help that Elbow Valley Elementary was a lot different than my old school in Calgary, and not just because it was out in the sticks. My new school was considered very progressive in its day: its design was called "open area," so you could always see every class and what all the other kids were doing. It was a sprawling free space with a lot going on at any given time, which made it hard for me to concentrate on anything, especially with Ms. Humphreys just floating around like she did. I was forever looking about and eavesdropping on conversations other kids were having or lessons from other teachers in entirely different grades. Maybe I was just being nosy; that's probably a good description, now that I think about it. I had, after all, become a pretty decent lip reader from trying to figure out the movies we'd been stealing from American satellite.

All the activity was like a drug for me. I felt like I was a bee in a hive and all the words were one big, crazy buzz. Leonard's mom used to tell me that I was like a bear with a bee up its ass. Not quite the same thing as a bee in a hive. To think that I was one of the few people that she even liked says a lot about her. Leonard's mom also told me that if I wasn't careful my face would stay like that. *Stay like what?* Leonard's mom drank a lot of beer so she said some funny things.

The school was kind of shaped like a wheel and all the classes were spokes coming off the library, which was at the centre. It was completely open and airy. No matter what classroom area you were in, you could look right into all the rows of books. I would gaze over at all the bookshelves lined up with book after beautiful book, filled with who knew what adventures. I would spend every spare moment wandering around those books, opening them up and looking at the illustrations, smelling the paper and reading countless random paragraphs, not knowing which book to devour first. It was literary overload. Reading was a real experience for me. I could be absorbed into a book within moments. I loved that my mind could shut everything off, and just be there in a book looking around at everything. Reading became an important aid in times of disaster and discomfort and heartbreak. It still is. My favourite author in grade four was an English writer named Enid Blyton, who wrote amazing stories about children solving mysteries and getting themselves into all kinds of trouble. I would read her books over and over again under the covers at night with my dad's flashlight. He might have been mad about my wearing down his flashlight batteries all the time, but he never said anything. I loved the library and I loved reading, but it turned out I loved music even more. Ironically, music made me feel still. I needed to feel stillness—being static was extremely difficult for me. Maybe I did have a bee up my ass.

When I was seven or eight years old, I used to take my dad's precious transistor radio off a shelf in his office and put it under my pillow at night. It was a big radio, probably the size of a shoebox, so my head would be eight inches off the bed. I'd feel his hand come sliding under my pillow a few hours later to gently pull it out. I used to look forward to him coming into my room to take it back. I don't know why, I just did. I can remember vividly how he smelled. His scent would linger in my bedroom long after he'd gone.

I found out later it was Old Spice aftershave lotion. I can't smell it without thinking about my dad. There were commercials on TV back in the seventies for Old Spice in which all the men were on sailboats with the sea breeze blowing through their hair. They had giant moustaches and navy peacoats and they looked rugged and confident. My dad did not look like any of those men. My dad looked like a dad. He looked worried, for the most part. Maybe wearing Old Spice made him feel like a sailor. I hope it did. The guy deserved a damn break, that's for sure.

Still, I was always in trouble for running the batteries down in that radio of his because they were expensive, after all, or rather "goddamn expensive." I would often hear my mother in the background somewhere saying, "Do you have to say 'goddamn' all the time?" My dad would mumble something back to her and so it would go. Were there any other kind of batteries other than goddamned ones? I didn't think so. Everything was goddamned in my dad's world. If he couldn't open a jar, it became "this goddamn jar!" If the TV didn't work right, it became "this goddamn TV." He was pretty good about my absconding with the radio, for some reason. He was probably relieved that it wasn't a box of Eddylite Easy Strike matches I had under there. (I wasn't stupid. I kept those under the mattress.)

He still has that radio. He listens to it all the time. Sometimes I go into his woodworking shop when he's not there, walk over to it and turn it on. I'll run my hands over the black-and-silver casing, remembering all the songs that seeped into my pillow and then into my brain at night. All of those songs stayed right there in my head and never came out. I summon them up and steal from them from time to time when I am writing. (I don't tell anybody, though, as I don't want to involve lawyers. Nobody is the wiser.)

Music class with Judith was so exciting I felt sick to my stomach every morning before we went in through that big steel door. I had butterflies diving around in my chest and running up and down my legs. The music room had three huge tiers of carpeted stairs and looked like a mini-amphitheatre. There were no desks or chairs or tables, which I found to be unbelievable. It was a carpeted heaven in a space behind the school stage, which was attached to the gym. We could always hear balls bouncing around and kids yelling and laughing from the gym class. We'd all lie on the giant stairs, practically drooling, as we peered down at Judith and waited for her to play us songs from the albums she brought in from her very own collection.

The record player looked like it was covered in canvas, a rectangular box about the size of an apple crate with a sticker on it that said, "Property of Elbow Valley Elementary School." I always wondered why they needed to put a sticker on it. Like we all didn't know where it was from? Did they actually think we'd try and steal a record player? We were three and a half feet tall, for God's sake. How would you even begin to figure out how to get something that big out of the classroom, never mind onto the school bus? (Now that I think about it, maybe they were more worried about the teachers stealing it than the students.)

Judith would flip though the big cardboard box full of her well-worn vinyl records, scanning the covers, looking for just the right song. She had so many wonderful artists in her collection. She had Anne Murray and Carly Simon and Simon and Garfunkel and Janis Ian and Judy Collins and James Taylor and the Beatles and the Rolling Stones and Joan Baez and the Carpenters. I loved the Carpenters even more than I loved driving Leonard and Dale's go-cart. It was like Judith had poured chocolate into my ears. She played a song called "Ticket to Ride" and it flooded out over the classroom and made me feel like I had been struck by lightning. Every hair on my body shot upwards, electrified by the sound of Karen Carpenter's voice. I had heard plenty of songs in my life, but this song, this girl's voice, made the world stop.

We always sang at the top of our lungs to every song Judith played. She'd bring in photocopied pages of song lyrics and hand them out to each of us delicately, like they were little baby chicks. I would read them, careful not to bend any of the corners, and I would marvel at how the verses looked like long poems and made my tongue feel like it had salt and lemon on it as I read them to myself. Reading song lyrics was like solving a mystery. You had to figure out what they meant, and it seemed like each kid had a different idea of what that was.

Beneath its snowy mantle cold and clean,
The unborn grass lies waiting for its coat to turn to green.

That was the first line from Anne Murray's song "Snowbird." I had no idea what it meant. I read it over and over again. I didn't know what a snowy mantle was and I wasn't sure that unborn grass could have a coat, but who cared anyway? Judith dropped the needle on the record player, and we'd all start singing like we didn't need the money. I remember her taking me to the front of the class and having me sing all by myself. I had no idea why she'd do that, but I didn't mind. I remember thinking how good it felt to have all that sound rumbling around in my chest. I felt weightless. (I remember my mom talking about Anne Murray. She'd say, "I don't know why that girl won't put shoes on her feet." Then she'd shake her head and figure out what to make for supper. I hated being barefoot. To this day I wear shoes and socks whenever possible.)

Judith also had us dance in music class. We waltzed and tangoed and discoed ourselves into a delightful frenzy. We had an odd number of students in our music class, so someone inevitably ended up dancing with Judith. You'd think that dancing with your teacher would have been the worst thing in the world, but it was actually the opposite. We fought over who would be the last man standing without a partner. I got to dance a polka once with Judith, and I've never forgotten it. She'd put on a record with some crazy guy yelling instructions at us: "Allemande left and allemande right! Do-si-do!" Whatever in God's name that meant. For me it meant spinning around like one of those dervish people until I couldn't keep standing. I'd fall exhausted on the carpeted floor and watch the ceiling whirl around my head.

Judith taught us practical things as well as the fun stuff. She taught us the basics about notes and scales and keys and chords, but it was just her plain old passion for music that lit our spirits. Her music class was my favourite class in the world. That was followed closely by gym class and, of course, art class. I can't remember those teachers' names so they obviously didn't leave a huge impression on me. I do remember my art teacher wearing a purple bra under a white sweater. It's so funny that that image has stuck with me all these years.

Math was impossible. I figured that math was for kids who had no hope of ever making friends. What in the world would anyone ever need math for in their entire lives? What was useful about a fraction or a square root? Math was nothing more than twelve years of blur for me. I never retained a single usable thing. I can't even count the days between my periods. I am always in a public place when I get my period, and I always say "goddammit" under my breath when I do because I am my father's daughter.

When I reached junior high I did end up with one math teacher whose class I actually kind of liked. His name was Mr. Milton and he was at least 130 years old. He wore the same suit every day and he smelled like mothballs. He had white hair and glasses with thick, black frames that had a Cary Grant vibe to them. That was about the only thing remotely cool about the man. He didn't really teach—he stood at the front of the room with his golf putter, and would continuously putt a golf ball into a paper cup. He'd tell us to open our math books to page such-and-such and then he'd start putting. He rarely looked up to see what we were doing, he would just shuffle back and forth, collecting the ball from the cup again and again. The bell would ring and we'd all look at each other in disbelief. The first week or so, I couldn't quite believe that this was going to be a common occurrence, but it was. Everybody in the entire school talked about Mr. Milton and his putting. I don't know how the principal couldn't have known what he was doing in that classroom. Maybe we were being taught subliminally?

It wasn't just the golfing thing that was strange with him— there were also skits. I have no idea why we did it, or what he was thinking, but off he'd send us into little groups in the far corners of the room to spend the class making up something stupid to perform. The only requirement would be that the skit needed to have something to do with numbers. After all, it was math class. I remember one we made up that was supposed to be about a long and bloody brain operation. We dressed up like doctors and nurses and doused our class-mate, who was the patient, with ketchup. One of us called out made-up equations, which apparently had something to do with the brain pro-cedure, while the rest of us laughed our heads off squirting ketchup around the room. Mr. Milton sat behind his desk with his arms folded and laughed too.

What a nutty old bugger he was. Likeable, but a dead-on nutter. I don't remember him ever saying anybody's name. I am positive he had no idea what our names were. He'd say "You there" or "Look where my finger is pointing, I mean *you!*" It was scary if his finger was pointing at you but I guess I survived it all right. Nowadays there would be some kind of parent or school board intervention and Mr. Milton would most certainly end up pushing mops and brooms somewhere. He certainly wouldn't be able to continue being a math teacher. I'm glad I went to school in the seventies.

My friend Theresa lived up the road from us, in the opposite direc-tion from Leonard and Dale's place. She was one of seven kids, and had Dutch immigrant parents. We met in a lineup outside of Elbow Valley Elementary School. I don't know what we were lined up for, but there we stood with our lunch boxes in hand. She was about a foot taller than I was, and as shy as a person could possibly be. We somehow became fast friends. I was very grateful for Theresa, who became my link to civility. I actually had a fighting chance of remain-ing a girl around Theresa. She had a bunch of sisters, too, so that was an extra-special bonus.

I would pedal my bike the few miles up the road to her house whenever I had the chance. I was always dodging swarms of mosqui-toes that hung in the air like buzzing black clouds. Getting a few bugs in your mouth was completely unavoidable. I crashed a dozen

times trying to swerve around them so sometimes swallowing them
just seemed like the better, safer option. Mosquitoes, I have found,
can live in your hair for a few days if you don't take the time to pick
them out. I was not good when it came to brushing my hair. For
whatever reason, I hated doing it. If I could have a braid down the
back of my head that lasted a week, I was happy.

Theresa's house was like a weird fantasy playground. Her dad
had a garage full of the craziest things, which he and his wife had
bought at auctions. Most people would have thought that the garage
was full of piles of junk, but I thought it was like a mountain of free
candy. I didn't know which lovely heap to climb first. Their yard
looked as though Alice from *Alice in Wonderland* and Dorothy from
The Wizard of Oz had hosted an after-grad party that involved a lot
of cheap liquor and drag queens.

Mr. and Mrs. deCrom loved a good auction. If Theresa's dad
thought it was a bargain, it ended up in the back of his truck. I remember him having six or eight of those professional hair dryer chairs
lined up next to his pickup truck in the garage. I guess he figured that
with all the kids he had he could save a bundle on hairdressing. I don't
think they ever used those chairs, although we'd sit in them from time
to time and pretend to get our hair done. They came in very handy
when we were playing "pageant."

"Pageant" was a way better game than "put Dicky in the dryer."
I had never heard of a single soul going to hell for playing "pageant."
I was always, always the host of the pageant and Theresa, her sister
Audrey and their next-door neighbour Sherry were the contestants.
Theresa's dad had bought a whole whack of assorted bridesmaids'
gowns at one of his auctions. They certainly did come in handy when
we had the evening gown segment of the game. I was always a bit
jealous that I couldn't be the one dressing up in the gowns and the
shoes. Instead, I was the one who had to make up the theme songs

and ask all the skill-testing questions. It was hard work. World peace was a very popular thing to want, even back then. World peace and, of course, feeding all the starving children in Africa, which Theresa would always include in her speeches. I think that's what clinched her many wins. (It's tragic that we are still struggling to feed the starving children of the planet. Mothers everywhere still say to their kids, just like my mother did to us, "Finish your dinner because there are children starving in Africa who would love to eat those Brussels sprouts." I have this sinking feeling that it could be another four hundred years before we feed the children of the world.) The talent part of our pageants was a bit sketchy but always entertaining. Baton twirling and interpretive dance seemed to top the list of things the girls wanted to do. I think there were even a few cooking demonstrations.

There were times that I wished Theresa and I had a go-cart to drive back and forth in between costume changes, and there were certainly times when I missed dangling from the trees and shooting at things. But Leonard and Dale and the killing fields were starting to fade behind me and the deCroms were engulfing me with their giant family. I didn't mind one single bit. I decided that I was going to like Dutch people. They were outdoorsy but they didn't kill everything within rifle sight.

Theresa's dad swore a lot like my dad, too, so I felt like we had an understanding, only Mr. deCrom swore in Dutch. I learned how to say "goddammit" in an entirely different language. I also learned how to say "thick socks" and "pinch it off," which were apparently things you'd yell at a family member if they'd been in the bathroom too long. I liked those expressions.

Theresa's mom always had a big pot of soup on the stove, with noodles, carrots, onions and mini-meatballs in it. It seemed like a bottomless pot, and it made the house smell like Sunday afternoons in a church basement. The only thing missing was the bake sale, though

Mrs. deCrom made her own bread. You had to slice it yourself. My dad would have killed me on the spot if he'd ever seen how thick and crooked I cut that bread. I got in trouble with Theresa a few times over how I sliced into their hunks of ham and blocks of Dutch Gouda cheese. It was hard cutting free-form. Maybe it was because I was too short to see where the giant knife was headed. It wasn't like I was trying to cut it crooked.

They had a huge, black cast-iron frying pan always sitting on the stove with an inch of grease in the bottom of it. Mrs. deCrom fried up everything imaginable in that big, black iron skillet. She used to scorch large pieces of thick, homemade bread in the hot grease, and then sprinkle sugar on them. It didn't look very tasty, but it really was. Theresa told me that it was because of the war. What war? I thought to myself. I knew that a big war had taken place, but I thought that it had ended at least a hundred years ago. I was alarmed to be reminded that it was only 1945 when that war ended for the Dutch people and that it was still a touchy subject. I guess in Europe during the war grease of any kind was like liquid gold. Forty years later, the whole family was still deeply programmed by World War II rationing. I didn't know you could use grease more than one time—boy, was I wrong.

In our house, the frying pan was nearly sandblasted clean after every use. My mother would stand over the sink while all the windows fogged up with steam, scrubbing the living hell out of our pots and pans. Her hands would be bright red from the combination of hot water and S.O.S pads. To this day I can't touch an S.O.S pad. They make me feel like grinding all my teeth off to the root.

My dad used to put four or five strips of bacon into a pan and fry them up, but Mrs. deCrom would put an entire pound in and move it around like a brick until it was done. Miraculously, it all came out perfectly cooked. Then she'd drop the eggs into two inches of pure pig fat and boil them in oil. After the feeding frenzy came to an end and the breakfast plates were cleared away, the pan would be put right back on the stove filled with all that grease, awaiting the big fry-up that would undoubtedly happen the very next morning. The deCroms were a very frugal family. Nothing was wasted, nothing was thrown away—and I mean nothing.

Theresa told me that the family was driving back from church one Sunday when suddenly the car swerved and there was a subtle but audible thumpity thump. They came to a rolling stop and everybody waited to see what they had hit, if anything, and what damage had been done. Mr. deCrom stepped out of the vehicle, and to his delight discovered that he had hit a rabbit. He grabbed it by the ears and tossed it into the back of the car with his terrified children. Theresa told me that the bunny was not quite dead, which only added to the chaos. Theresa swears they took that poor little bunny home and had it for dinner. I remember my dad hitting the odd gopher or squirrel as we drove around those back country roads, but I am pretty sure we never ate anything he ran over. Mind you, who knows what went into my mom's brown-and-gold Crock-Pot.

I can't say that I loved junior high school. I felt awkward, to say the least. My body felt like it belonged to someone else entirely. It was changing on a daily basis—they were subtle changes, but changes nonetheless, and they scared me. I had always been stick-thin and wiry, but I was starting to put weight on my hips and my legs and my stomach. I was still tiny, but I could see the differences from month to month. My clothes were becoming a bit harder to squeeze into, and I hated it, because I would have to go out and buy new ones. Shopping wasn't all that high on the list of things I liked to do. Mom would take us once a year for new school clothes, and that was about the extent of my shopping. I'd pick things out in about two minutes and be done with it. A lot of my clothes were hand-me-downs from Duray. I liked his worn-out jeans and his plaid shirts. People pay big bucks for clothes that look like they've been worn for years—apparently they call it "distressed" and charge a bloody fortune for it. I was ahead of my time.

In junior high school I kind of became popular. Well, I don't know that for sure. I just decided that I would try to be. My goal was to not be one of the kids that got picked on. I wanted to become like Switzerland: so neutral that my classmates would have no idea what clique I belonged to. I would have to belong to all the cliques and be convincing. First I had to figure out if we even had any cliques, and then what the cliques were.

Thankfully none of the forty or so kids in my grade exerted any pressure to be dressed well, so there was no fashion clique. Half the kids who got on the bus in the morning smelled like chicken poop, so the bar wasn't exactly set all that high. In fact, if you came to school and didn't smell like some kind of farm animal, you were considered weird. Being "in fashion" was foreign to everybody apart from a few silly souls who had just moved to Springbank from the city. For some reason, they still clung to the idea that they were supposed to look coordinated. If anything I was wearing matched, it was simply by chance. The new kids hadn't been conditioned yet. Soon they would be in generic running shoes and used Levi's from the Salvation Army, skipping Mr. Milton's math class/putting lesson to drink Lonesome Charlie by the river. (Lonesome Charlie was a very cheap, incredibly crappy pink wine that was basically a headache in a bottle but was also sweet and bubbly and therefore very popular.)

There were a couple of sisters who had moved to the area from California, of all places. Their names were Kim and Debbie Dunning. Our whole school turned upside down when they arrived one fall day in September. They were both so pretty! When they laid eyes on all of us farm-looking people, they looked as though they would cry.

We probably all looked like extras from the movie *Children of the Corn*. I don't blame them for feeling upset. They were stared at for at least a year. I am sure it was their worst nightmare to be sitting in their graffiti-covered desks, having poorly dressed pubescent boys that smelled like chicken poop staring at them. These two lovely girls had gone from sand-covered beaches and sunshine to cow patties and haystacks. Theresa and I felt sorry for them, although we were jealous. They were the most beautiful girls any of us had ever laid eyes on. They looked like the girls on TV—all tanned and glowing with long, straight, shiny hair. They always seemed to be moving in slow motion. You didn't know whether to kiss them or punch them. (As it turned out, they were both very nice, and it didn't take long for them to learn how to smoke cigarettes and drink Lonesome Charlie and date very, very far beneath them. Sometimes you can't fight fate.)

Some of my friends had started developing breasts, and I'd seen them before gym class trying to cover themselves up by changing in the bathroom stalls. All the girls seemed mortified about having to wear a training bra, and I was too. Well, there were one or two girls who started wearing bras two years before they had to. God knows why. They even went so far as to stuff them with tissue to fill them out. We all knew. Some girls were completely out of their minds when it came to things like that. Who would want breasts any sooner than they had to get them? I wanted to keep mine at bay for as long as I could and I kept wearing looser shirts so no one could see what was going on. Eventually, my mom took me into Woodward's and bought me a training bra. I did not want to have to wear one, but I wasn't given much of a choice. For whatever reason, even trying it on was humiliating to me. I felt like I was losing control over my own body, and it felt terrible. My mother said that I would get used to it and that there would be no discussion. It was already completely embarrassing, so why would I want to discuss it anyway?

Things got even worse when my mom wanted to discuss my impending period. I couldn't quite believe what I was hearing. My period? Please, dear God, Lord Jesus above, do *not* make me discuss my period with my mother. I didn't plan on ever getting my period, for one thing, and for another thing, I already knew about my period because there was a girl who blabbed all about hers in biology class. Fitting really, biology class.

Out of the blue one day, my mother marched me up to her bedroom and opened the drawer second from the top of her dresser and pointed to the biggest menstrual pad I had ever seen in my life, and I'd seen a few in my day. These things were like mattresses and they had to be attached to giant belts that looked like they should be holding up hockey socks. My mother gave me a tutorial on how to use the pads and how to connect the belts and, quite frankly, after that, it all started to feel and sound like I'd been huffing helium at a clown's birthday party. I never again ventured into the "period drawer." What I ended up doing, when I did finally start my period, was roll up wads of toilet paper and then stuff them into my underpants. I kind of clamped my legs together to keep everything in place. It was an art form for sure. I felt weird about the whole period thing and kept it to myself until I was about eighteen. My mom must have thought that I was really late to come to the menstrual party, but she didn't say anything to me, thank God. Most of the girls I knew from school got their periods when they were fourteen or fifteen. I was sixteen when I started, and really didn't want to tell my mom.

But the problem with the homemade toilet paper maxi-pads was that they crawled up your bum crack and right out of your jeans whenever you walked or moved, which was fairly often. I was always trying to figure out how to cram the pad down past my waistband and back into position. I would only have to take a few jaunty steps before all of a sudden my toilet paper wad was making its way towards my training bra. I really wanted to learn how to use tampons—anything seemed better than going into my mother's period drawer—but my friend Elise's mom told us that they were for married people. We never quite figured that one out. (If you're ever considering making your own pads, know that you can get serious chafing down there from wads of toilet paper.)

I went through hundreds of rolls of toilet paper during that time, and eventually my dad started to notice. I heard him upstairs one morning yelling, "Where is all the goddamn toilet paper disappearing to in this goddamn house?" He went on to spew out about twenty-seven Jesus Christs and at least one F-bomb. We very seldom heard the F- bomb, but on the occasion it did slip out of his head we all ran for cover. I wondered how you said the F-bomb in Dutch. I would have to remind myself to ask Theresa's dad about that.

chapter seven

GROWING PAINS AND FISHING RODS

I didn't like growing up at all. It felt, well, quite simply, odd. It's not easy becoming a person. Even my thinking had begun to change. I started thinking about God again. God was always poking around somewhere in the back of my mind, but I was beginning to seriously consider who and what he was. Was he even a *he*? Where did he live? Did he wear clothes? Did he have a penis? That one really bothered me to think about. I knew even picturing that was a terrible sin punishable by a trip to hell.

I had so many questions about the universe. I didn't know where to start. I began to pray a lot. I didn't really know what I was doing, but I would lie in my bed at night and talk endlessly to whatever it was that was out there. I would whisper all my secrets into the ears of the abyss and fall asleep right in the middle of some important wish. I couldn't quite get my head around the concept of death. To think that I would die seemed laughable. Where does someone go when they die? Would I get another body? Do you get to eat up there? Surely they give you clothes to wear. Would I know anybody in the afterlife? I hadn't even begun figuring out the "before" life yet. I had certainly killed enough things in my youth to understand that death was a very serious thing. You're here and then you're not, that's what my dad always said. One day I woke up startled because the thought of perishing had never crossed my mind, and then there it was. *I am going to die!* Just like that, jumping up and down right in front of me, taunting me before I even had time to eat my morning Pop-Tart.

It's an innocent time in your life when you can actually say you don't know of a single person that has passed away. My dad's father had died before I was born, so that didn't really count. So technically I didn't know personally anybody who had died. I do feel, however, that I came very close to being killed several times in my young life, thanks to my dear friend Sue McLennen. Sue was the female version of Leonard and Dale. We were always on some sort of outdoors adventure, but Sue didn't have the desire to kill anything. She didn't even own a gun, which was good. Sue lived in a little town called Bragg Creek that was much closer to the wilderness than we were in Springbank. We loved playing down by the river, throwing rocks and wading in the water looking for treasures that people may have lost hundreds of years ago. Once I found a hubcap and pretended it was part of a spaceship that had crashed. We used that hubcap to pan for gold all summer long. (We must not have been panning correctly, because we never managed to unearth a single nugget of the glimmering stuff. We would have been happy finding cold, hard cash if it were underneath that water somewhere as well.)

Sue and I were chased by a bear one day when we were panning for gold down at the river. I remember being taught survival skills in Brownies. You were to lie down and play dead when encountering a bear, but lying down in the bushes seemed beyond crazy to me at that moment and Sue and I made a run for it. I decided then and there that Brownies was as dumb as a bear turd and I vowed never to

Me and my brother
Duray in 1962.

Me and my little pal Shelly in 1964.
Notice how my shins are covered in
bruises while Shelly doesn't have a mark
on her. We look like a before-and-after
poster for hemophiliacs.

Me and my mom in 1965.

Duray looking happy in 1964. That's me on the left.

Me and Duray, pleased with our new little brother, Patrick, 1966.

Me and my dad riding a moped in 1967. Obviously I am beyond thrilled.

Gary and me at my house in town on Louise Road, 1966. One thing is for sure: Leonard and Dale would have eaten him alive.

Leonard and Dale: playmates, wilderness guides, cousins.

My grade one class in 1968. I am third from the left in the front row.

A family photo op in my gram's garden, 1971.

My magical fourth-grade teacher, Judith Humphreys. This photograph was taken on a school trip to overnight camp.

Me (on the left) and Sue McLennen at about the age when we were attacked by a bear. We didn't have photo booths in Bragg Creek—we took this in the city, so it was kind of a big deal!

Me, Dad, Pat and Duray in the mid-seventies doing yard work (apparently). I look thrilled.

My gram, 1998. She loved a good joke and had the most wonderful laugh to go along with every punch line.

Me and my half-blind, half-deaf grandmother Richards.

Entertaining in the inaccurately named "coke machine room" of my high school.

Duray in Dad's chair, having a cigarette during one of the rare times when he was at home in the late seventies.

With my grad date Stuart in 1980. I still had my awful perm but my mom took me to the hairdresser to blow it out for one night only.

It was a truly awful perm.

Me and Theresa on our first big trip abroad, 1980. Hawaii felt very far away from Springbank, Alberta.

I played my guitar on the beach in Hawaii, got sunburned and was sick for two days.

Patrick, me and Duray at Christmas in 1981. I was becoming fashionable by the looks of my hair—I cut the perm off!

A rare performance in our living room in 1981, after my grad debut.

Making myself useful around our property in 1982. I would have been just about to get my pacemaker.

Norman Earl, on his mystical, magical salmon trawler.
I think I probably gutted five or six hundred fish a day.
(Used with kind permission of Norman Earl's family.)

My family in 1983. We all look homeless because we'd spent the whole day outside working in the yard.

Mom in our infamous video store, Fairview Video, in 1987.

I captured my family at the dinner table and that "look" on my dad's face, 1986.
From left: Duray, mom, dad, gram and Pat

My dad and me, 2002. I don't know where we are but the plastic cups sure say "formal."

go again unless it was Cupcake Day, in which case I would make a one-time exception.

I have never run so fast in my life. We could hear the bear crashing behind us as we tore through the brush to get back to the road. Now that I think about it, that bear could have been running away from us, but that makes the story less interesting. It was a little brown bear that was probably three hundred pounds at best. It certainly wasn't a grizzly or anything like that. All I know is that the brown bear was after us and if we were to be eaten by him it would be the most sensational story ever told at my junior high school. For a split second I thought of letting it catch up to us, but then my common sense took over, thank God.

Another time, Sue and I were playing with a very long fly-fishing rod, casting a lead weight into the trees, when *by accident* I whacked her across the thigh, leaving a really long, red welt. She, of course, had to retaliate, and started running after me, intending to whack me back. It's hard to run when you're laughing as hard as we were. I remember trying to hide behind a telephone pole. Sue was flicking the fishing rod at my legs trying to hit me when all of a sudden a car veered off the road and smashed into the pole. We must have been really carrying on and not heard it coming, because it seemed to roar out of nowhere. The crash itself was deafening. The ground beneath my feet shook so hard it knocked me over.

Sue and I stood there looking at each other in disbelief. I was inches away from being squashed between a wooden pole and a large four-door vehicle moving at fifty miles an hour. People came running from the house next door trying to figure out what had happened. The poor guy had had a heart attack behind the wheel and lost control of his car. He was clutching his chest and muttering, "I'm so sorry, I'm so sorry . . ." While everyone waited for the ambulance, I wondered if he was going to die. His wife, who had been in the passenger seat, had a bloody nose that looked a lot worse than it probably was. She was staggering around with her purse dangling off her arm. God forbid she should lose that purse! After the ambulance drove them to the hospital, Sue and I wandered home with our fishing rod, still in shock. It was one of the most exciting and frightening things that had ever happened in Bragg Creek. We never did find out if that guy died. He was still moaning when they hauled him off, and we assumed that was a good sign.

In bed later that night, I cried for an hour, replaying everything in my mind. I don't think I realized how close I had come to dying. It was nothing more than a split second that could have changed everything about my existence. Sue never did whack me back with that fishing pole. I guess she figured being almost hit by a car was payback enough.

Sue was so much fun to be around. Her parents lived in a real log cabin that her dad had built, and I thought that that was completely fantastic. It looked like a quaint little pioneer home that Hutterites would have lived in, only edgier. The people in this log house smoked and drank.

Sue's folks sold antiques and ran the local postal outlet, among other things. Sue's mom was a landscape painter. She'd sit in the post office part of their house and paint these amazing mountain scenes. The oil paint looked edible and, believe me, I was tempted. I had never seen anybody paint a real honest-to-God painting before, and I was completely entranced. Someday I wanted to do that too.

Sue's dad always had a pipe hanging out of his mouth, and he liked to drink whisky. (I think he may have been drunk all the time, but I never knew what he looked like sober so I never actually figured that out.) He hardly ever spoke a word to any of us. He grunted and waved his hands a lot. I was kind of afraid of him. Sue told me that her dad was Scottish and that's why he was the way he was, whatever that meant. His hands were as big as baseball mitts, and they were riddled with scars and cuts and gouges. Not only had he built their log house, but he built log houses for a living, and his hands reflected every single hour he put into building them. Sue's parents seemed like hippies but I knew they weren't. They marched to their own band, that's for sure.

Sue was one of six girls. Her mother had two sets of twins. I often thought that her dad must have shaken his Scottish head back and forth every time another girl popped out of his wife. You'd think a Scottish man would have pined for a son. If he did, we never heard him say anything about it. He'd just sit at his wooden kitchen table (which he'd made himself) with billows of smoke gathering over his head. He'd flick the newspaper, peer over its pages, and ask us if we had anything better to do. I guess that meant, get your asses out of my house and go play. He did it with a glint in his eye; even though he was kind of scary, he smiled with his eyes all the time. He tugged on the braid down the back of my head once, and I took that as a sign that he actually liked me.

One day Sue and I puffed away on his old pipe until we both turned green. It was like eating a half-burned log dipped in kerosene. I tried to throw up but nothing would come out. My eyes just watered madly and I stood hunched over in the trees, feeling foolish for having tried smoking at all. Sue was so afraid that we'd get caught that we made sure to put everything back just so. We wiped the pipe down for prints, and we fluffed up the tobacco in the pouch so it looked full. Her dad had a temper that we didn't want to trigger under any circumstances. We both hoped our cover-up job was professional. I vowed to not smoke again until college.

Bragg Creek was like the Canadian version of the Ozark Mountains, complete with the distant strains of banjos. I think there were a few folks out there whose parents may have been cousins. I won't name any names, but there were some interesting sets of teeth for sure. Bragg Creek had one decrepit little gas station that had a single, old, rusted gas pump and an ancient pop machine that froze solid in the winter. There was one kind of gas—*very* leaded—and two kinds of pop, if you were lucky. The machines had glass bottles that pulled up through metal sleeves. I remember drinking Orange Crush or Dad's Root Beer. A bottle of Crush cost twenty-five cents and made my entire mouth orange for several hours. The store also sold a small selection of penny candy so it was the place to hang out for sure.

Gene Fullerton and his wife, Eva, owned and operated the gas station and also bootlegged beer and an odd assortment of hard liquor out the back door. Everybody knew what was going on. It didn't matter if you were fourteen or ninety-seven, you could buy alcohol from Gene and Eva.

Gene was a big man with a red face and his wife was like a barrel with legs. They both looked like you could roll them down a hill and they'd be none the worse for wear. Gene combed his hair from one side of his head right over to the other, like those thirty-five strands of hair would disguise what was actually going on up there. He had beady little eyes, the whites suffused with red veins screaming out for oxygen. He also had what they called a gin blossom growing off the end of his nose. It looked like a mangled lump of purple cauliflower. My mom told me people got them from drinking too much. I would find myself staring at his nose whenever I saw him. He always smelled like whisky and his wife, well, she did too. Eva wore the same muumuu-type dress for years. She swayed from side to side when she walked, but never spilled a drop of whatever she was drinking. I remember her having one big tooth in her head that stuck out under her top lip, and I mean one tooth. I don't know why she decided to keep just that one. I'd see her out in her yard with that dress on, holding her red plastic cup. Sue said she drank rye and Seven. I had never heard of rye and Seven. It sounded weird.

There was something so melancholy about that pair. They certainly weren't unkind people—in fact, they were endlessly jovial; just drunk, that's all. They had all these wild kids who drank like crazy too. All you had to do was mention the name Fullerton and people knew it meant trouble. All their boys dropped out of school very early on and just drank themselves half to death. They were so young and good-hearted, but alcohol ruined their lives. They were simply born with an addiction. Sometimes people come through the veil already saddled with problems. It's just a theory, mind you, but that's the way it seems. My mom would often say that the Fullerton kids didn't have a chance from the word go.

Gene and Eva sat there and watched their entire family just drown in booze. First the man he takes the drink, and then the drink he takes the man—my dad always said that. My dad was a drinker, but he didn't look like Gene Fullerton. My mom told me that people didn't always look like drunks even when they were. Some can blend in and seem normal for the most part. I think my dad was one of those people. He blended in, he seemed normal, his drinking seemed invisible—except that my mom could see him and Duray could see him and I could see him. I hoped my dad would never end up with a gnarled purple chunk of cauliflower on the end of his nose.

Sue and I got beer from Gene once in awhile. He charged twenty bucks for a case of beer, which was outrageous back then. It was more than double what a case of beer went for in town, but he knew he had you over a barrel. By the time you were buying liquor from Gene Fullerton, you were probably half in the bag and desperate to keep the party going. Sue and I would buy a case, go down to the river and laugh our fool heads off. We certainly didn't drink an entire case, but we'd each have a bottle and maybe split a third. The rest we hid in the bushes for the next time we were down there. Somebody always found those bottles of beer and drank them and we were pretty sure we knew who it was: the Fullerton boys.

We occasionally played spin the bottle with one or two of the Fullerton boys. They were always up for anything so we figured, why not? They were kind of cute when they were young. They had pretty good teeth, too. Why kissing anybody on the lips for a one-one thousand count was such a big deal, I will never understand. There certainly wasn't a tongue in sight, so it was all pretty tame. We'd watch the river gurgle past us and sit around a bonfire kissing each other or daring each other to do silly things. We'd become bored of it all fairly quickly and just move on to skipping stones or melting the bottom of our shoes on the fire. I still enjoyed a good fire.

Sometimes Sue and I would take some of our bootlegged beer and go to dances at the Bragg Creek community hall, where we'd see Theresa and our other friends. (I may have stolen change from the bottom of my mom's purse from time to time to do this.) My parents didn't know if I was out late because I was staying the weekend in Bragg Creek with Sue's family and they knew that Sue and I were harmless—which we were—and that we didn't go out of our way to find trouble. Sue's parents didn't have a curfew of any kind and maybe didn't worry about us because the community hall was a thousand yards from their front door. Sue was very much like me, and I think that's why we got along so well. We were mischievous, not stupid.

There was always a live band playing bad country songs at the community dances. Everybody knew everybody so we were pretty much assured a fun night. All the dancing enticed everybody to drink their body weight in beer. It was fun watching people whirl around the worn-out hardwood floors, drunker than skunks and dancing with such reckless abandon. Dancing makes people thirsty. It never failed that they would run out of booze before the dance came to an end, and that caused problems. The organizers always seemed amazed that people could drink that much and still be standing. There would most certainly be a fist fight or two and then handshakes afterwards implying that there were no hard feelings. It was usually the Fullertons punching it out with each other anyway.

I wasn't much of a dancer, not that anybody ever asked me to dance. I pretty much stood by the wall watching everybody else stumble about. Theresa would usually be the one to rescue me from my "wallfloweryness." She was wallflowery herself. In a pinch we would dance together. Sue was always asked to dance. The boys were crazy about her and I could see why. She had a face like a cherub and her freckles were like stars on her face and she was confident. She had the fellas lined up all night long. She was like cute little flame holding court with a bunch of homely, hairy moths.

At the end of the night there were always four or five busted-up chairs and a couple of broken tables. There were broken windows, broken bottles and puddles of vomit scattered about. Someone always seemed to back into the hall with a pickup truck and take off a good chunk of the wood siding. We didn't miss very many dances, or "dos," as my mom would call them. The community hall threw them every three or four months. It took them that long to make the various repairs on the building.

Of course everybody got into their trucks and drove off with one eye shut to make sure they were on the right side of the road. I think drinking and driving was what pretty much everybody did back then. I don't think I'd heard of a DUI until the eighties. It wasn't a big deal, although it should have been. Nobody I knew was ever pulled over for drinking and driving. I am amazed that my dad was never pulled over. I am amazed that I was never pulled over. Well, sort of . . .

One night when I was tipsy and driving home too slowly, probably swerving back and forth (ever so slightly), I did in fact get pulled over. I saw the red and blue lights crawl up beside me and I thought my heart was going to explode. I had been drinking but I didn't think I was too drunk to be driving. (Everybody thinks they're fine to drive.) The officer asked me how much I had had to drink and I told him the truth—that I didn't exactly know. It was probably a couple of glasses of draft beer. I don't remember him asking me for my driver's licence or anything like insurance or registration. He told me that I probably shouldn't be driving around this late at night by myself, that it was dangerous. So believe it or not the police officer drove me home! There I was, in the back of an RCMP police cruiser, heading towards the open arms of my understanding, loving parents. God help me.

We left my locked car sitting on the side of a gravel road. The cop told me to make sure I picked it up the next morning, because he did not want to drive down that road the next day and find it still parked there. I told him that, yessir, the car would *not* be there! I prayed that he wasn't going to talk to my mom and dad. So far I had gotten away with near murder. I knew they would be asleep but my mother could be awoken by a bird on the windowsill so I knew I needed a miracle—another miracle.

I made small talk all the way home about the dance and who was there and how much fun it was. I don't think I ever shut up. The poor guy just kept saying "Uh-huh" and "Oh yeah?" I was probably driving him crazy. He brought me right to our front door and said, "There you go." *There you go?* I just hopped out. He told me to have a good night. It was twenty after two in the morning. Good grief, I thought to myself, as I crept in through the unlocked back door as quietly as humanly possible. Inside everything was dark and still. Would I be ambushed by my mother shining a large flashlight in my face, and questioned until sunrise? I couldn't believe my luck— my parents were actually sound asleep.

The washer and dryer were right at the door when you came in, so I took off all my smelly beer clothes and washed away any evidence of a good time. I felt so relieved and so guilty all at once. My parents never found out about that little incident, thanks be to God, the giver of all miracles. I might well have been killed if I'd ended up in the slammer. In fact, the slammer would have been my preference over facing the wrath of my father. My experience with the police was obviously a lot different from my older brother's. They drove me home but they ran him over.

Sue's folks used to let us sleep outside in a tent near the side of their house. Even in the summer the temperatures would drop enough to leave you shivering half the night. It was always so exciting to be out there in a tent, but frightening too. I was always scared of that bear showing up or, God forbid, one of the Fullerton boys coming to harass us. We'd lie there with flashlights and bags of chips and just chatter the hours away until the sun started coming up, and then we'd finally nod off for an hour. When I could hear the birds chirping and we finally did get up, I could hardly think, I was so exhausted. We'd go rushing into Sue's log house, where her dad would be sitting and smoking his pipe, and brush our teeth, make our lunches, change our clothes and head for the yellow school bus, our own private taxi.

I loved going out to Bragg Creek—and it was probably nice for my mom not to have to drive me around those weekends—but I was always so glad to come through our back door and be home. I was happy to be the only daughter again after a weekend with Sue and all those sisters!

One year Sue didn't return to school in Springbank. She just seemed to disappear into thin air. I don't know where she went. So many things could change in a single summer. She was a dear part of my childhood, and I missed her a lot as the years went by. People come and go, I was learning that more and more. Maybe Sue thought I was the one that went somewhere.

I was by now a seasoned country girl. I had earned my stripes, as it were. I had the world's best dog, Aquarius. I had peed outside, slept outside, shot and killed small animals, built tree forts and rafts and ridden the school bus long enough to be considered a "Springbanker." I could hardly remember ever having lived in the city. My parents had slowly but surely finished our house, and we had all settled in to our new lives. Well, we thought we were settled. It's easy to mistake a sandbar for solid land if you're not paying close attention.

Complex undercurrents kept trying to pull us apart. Mom and dad were the ones mainly feeling the strain. It wasn't anything you could put your finger on, but the atmosphere was getting thicker as the days were getting longer. I felt the undercurrents at night under the bed, reaching up to grab an arm or a leg. I hated having my arms or my feet hanging out of the covers at night. I felt I was inviting big, creepy trouble by having them stark naked right out there in the open. I often tried convincing myself that I was not afraid of the dark and that there was no such thing as demons. It rarely worked. (As I got older I always kept a night light on for protection. Demons are deathly afraid of night lights.) Then I'd fall asleep due to a lack of oxygen, since I'd be underneath my blankets hyperventilating most nights.

My dad came and went and came and went, and my mom kept shuttling us around to all our activities, trying to keep us as busy as possible. We seemed to keep just busy enough to ignore what was actually going on. My parents were definitely not getting along. I would often hear raised voices after I had gone to bed at night. I'd lie there and try to make out what was being said, but I never could. It was muffled and fragmented. The one thing I could make out was my mother saying "Keep your voice down!" which seemed somewhat ironic. It must have been hard for her to deal with him coming home late after he'd been drinking.

Looking back, I wish I could have carried some of that weight. I knew there were things going on that weren't good, but I kept so busy that I didn't give myself a chance to worry. I talked myself out of a lot of what I witnessed going on between my mom and dad. I suppose part of me was scared to death of the possible outcome of their discontent. I could tell that his behaviour was wearing her out. She'd pack us up and take us to gram's house once in awhile for sleepovers. Mom probably needed a break from the constant arguing.

My gram was one of seventeen children. She was born on a small farm that one of her nephews runs in southern Alberta. It's hard to fathom that my gram's mother had *so* many kids, especially knowing that they were all born into such hard times. You'd think it would have been in everybody's best interest to stop at two, but my mom told me that people back then had to give birth to their own labourers. Every kid worked on the farm; that's the way it was.

Apparently my great-grandfather was nothing short of a bastard who never let up on my great-grandmother, and that in and of itself was the main reason they brought seventeen beings into the world. My great-grandmother was never not pregnant. My mom tells me her grandfather was a drunken, dirty old man. He exposed himself in front of his own children and grandchildren many times. My gram's sister, Ern, told him on one of those occasions that if she ever saw him pull out his penis again she'd cut it off. I guess that scared him enough to stop whipping it out all the time. It's hard to think that man is part of me and I am part of him. Genetics are bizarre.

Gram's mom died during childbirth at forty-six from a massive hemorrhage. I think about that all the time. I have seen one picture of my great-grandmother, from when she was about thirty-six years old. She looked so much older than that. Her lips were pursed and her eyes looked like the light had left them. They were sunken into her head. People didn't smile for pictures much in those days but even still, she looked worn out and defeated.

Even though my gram had a terrible childhood, she was a delight to be around. She was altruistic, kind and funny, helpful and full of goodness. She was little when her mom died, maybe seven or eight. She could have turned out to be a bitter, cranky woman, as a few of her sisters did, but she was an angelic human being. We all adored her. She loved to have a cold beer and a laugh. I wouldn't say she was a smoker by any stretch of the imagination, but she enjoyed a few puffs here and there on a weekend. I remember her letting me roll her cigarettes in one of those weird little tobacco machines. It was so much fun. I made a huge mess and ruined hundreds of the filter tubes, but she never got mad at me. She was so patient and tender. I never heard her say a discouraging word about anyone or anything. She liked everybody and everybody liked her.

When mom drove us to gram's house to stay for a few nights, I was relieved somehow. I knew it would be a welcome break for my mother—a chance to think and breathe and regroup. I didn't know exactly why we had to stay there, but it didn't matter, I was happy just the same. It felt like a holiday. My gram always had ice-cold milk in the fridge and a jar full of peppermints by her couch. She was so good to us. She and my mom were so close, they were like the same person. They talked effortlessly. They were bound by some wonderful bit of heavenly, golden thread. I think my gram saved us many times.

Most days my dad would be gone before I got up in the morning. He was working long hours, and mom was so frustrated with him. There were countless ultimatums that were never acted upon. She couldn't seem to follow through on any of her threats and I don't blame her for that. Nobody wanted to break up our family, least of all her. I didn't know how close she was coming to running out of options. You can only take your kids to sleep over at your mother's house so many times and then something has to give.

I don't think we were unlike most families. Most families are complicated and hard to understand. My mom would always tell me that we weren't the only weird family out there, as if she was trying to convince herself. I was happy to hear it coming from her mouth, anyway. I knew families who ran over bunnies and had them for their dinner. I knew families who hung pigs in trees. By all accounts, we were as normal as normal could be.

I was glad to have my weird little family. I wouldn't have changed a single thing about them even if God had given me the option to. (There were worse things out there than brothers—those things were called sisters.) But I felt that because I had a brother who was always in trouble, it put extra pressure on me to be good. And it wasn't always easy. I felt like I couldn't do anything to rock the boat because my parents wouldn't be able to stand another thing going sideways. Not that I wanted to do anything bad and not that I was bad, it just made me very aware of what I was doing at all times. My dad's temper helped keep me on a fairly straight and narrow road too. When he yelled my heart just about stopped. It was that loud and that ferocious. Half the time I wondered if he knew what he was so bloody mad about. My mom would tell us that he was just like his mother. That made him yell too.

Patrick seemed to get along with everybody. He had such an easygoing nature. He was so smart and empathic—a sensitive boy with a really great head of hair! He would feather it to near perfection every morning using a blow-dryer that could have started a forest fire. It had one setting: atomic. If you weren't careful with that crazy thing, you'd burn an ear off. He spent more time in the bathroom than any of us. He was the only one who seemed to really care about how he looked for school every morning. It took him hours to decide on an outfit. He worried about having everything perfect. He put a lot of pressure on himself, which I didn't realize until many years later. He'd be so nervous about getting on the bus every morning he'd almost make himself physically sick. All his worries and troubles paid off academically. Thank heavens my parents had one child who would bring home a really great report card twice a year without fail.

Patrick had not yet outgrown his asthma and was riddled with symptoms every spring, but he was game to play all the sports right along with the other kids. It was hard on his lungs to keep up with all the cardio required for football and track and field. He spent most of his time just trying to breathe. I remember seeing him in his over-sized football uniform. His legs were so skinny and his shoulders were so hiked up around his jaw line he looked like a grasshopper. It didn't help that the school uniforms were green. He looked so proud to be in that uniform. He never stopped trying to be just one of the gang. Everybody deals with shadows in their own particular way. Patrick's way was to be as close to perfect as he could be.

Duray was smart, but he didn't care about being perfect. He didn't care about how he looked. He was one of those guys who could get up in the morning and splash water on his face and be ready for the day. He didn't agonize over little things like his clothes or his hair. He made everything look so easy and so hard all at the same time. He could have slept through math class and still received a good grade if he'd shown up to take the tests. He was strong and athletic despite his pot smoking and his gas huffing. He would outrun everybody at school track meets, with no training or practising or anything. He was always good at running away from life.

My dad showed up to watch him run one year. Out of the blue he came and sat with the rest of the crowd and watched Duray compete at the track meet. Duray always talked about that. He was so proud that dad had taken time from work to sit in the bleachers and watch him race. Dad talked about it too. He'd often tell the story of Duray being half a mile ahead of everybody else in the race, that he couldn't believe his eyes. Dad told us that nobody else stood a chance, running against Duray. Knowing he had made dad proud of him, Duray's face would beam with pure happiness.

chapter eight

PARKING LOTS AND
GIRL POWER

When I was twelve or thirteen, my mom began taking guitar lessons. The only reason she took up guitar was because she wanted to have something to do while she waited outside the school arena for me while I was at hockey practice. It would have been pointless for her to drive home and come back to pick me up and she said she was going to get hemorrhoids sitting on those cold bleachers. "It's like sitting on a block of ice," she'd say.

As the story goes, the preacher of the local church was offering beginner guitar lessons to all ages, which meant, please dear Jesus, let somebody show up and take lessons from me. The church was close to the arena and he was offering the lessons around the same time we practised on Saturday mornings. My mom had always wanted to learn an instrument and this seemed like just the right opportunity.

I liked sports of any kind, so when they put the sign-up sheet for the Springbank Sweethearts girls' hockey team, I was first in line. I hadn't really skated much at that point, but I thought, what the heck, it looks easy on TV. My favourite team was the Montreal Canadiens. I thought Frank and Pete Mahovlich were quite handsome. If they could play hockey, so could I. I couldn't have been more wrong—I was a terrible hockey player—but what I lacked in talent I made up for with enthusiasm.

My parents bought all my hockey equipment from a second-hand store called Sport Swap. Some people were weird about second-hand stuff, but I couldn't have cared less. I had a friend who didn't want to admit that her skis were used. I knew they were used because they had somebody else's initials on them, but I never said a word. I knew it would've hurt her feelings. You could hardly see me when I put on my helmet. It must have belonged to a giant Russian defenceman at some point, because it swallowed my whole head. I had to tip my neck back to keep the darn thing on. It's pretty hard to score a goal when you can't even see your feet.

I think mom would have preferred to learn to play the piano, but we didn't have one of those. I did, however, own a plastic air-powered organ with an impressive one-octave range, but I doubt that would have been useful for lessons of any kind. It only had twelve notes in total and the sound of the air whistling through was louder than any note you played. I likened it to a bagpipe with keys.

For eighty bucks my mom got not only a gorgeous binder filled with the popular sheet music of the day, but a guitar tuner, a professional finger chart, a faux leather strap and, lo and behold, a brand-new guitar! It was bigger than my mother. It came in its own case, made of fabric that looked like worn-out blue jeans. It was the most beautiful thing I had ever laid eyes on.

It was the first time I thought my mother was really cool. I was jealous of her new-found interest and, deep down inside, I would much rather have been taking lessons with her than pushing a puck around a freezing cold patch of ice while a bunch of crazy parents screamed insults at the referees from the stands. I was enamoured of my mother's guitar—I wanted to hold it and touch it and strum it. I could hear her practising at night in the living room. The sound of her patiently strumming away would drift up and around my head like smoke. I'd sit at the top of the stairs and listen to her trying to make the chords and sing along. It really hurt her fingers, to the point where they became so sore from pushing the various strings down that they almost bled, but she kept on trying to get it right. If you've ever learned how to play guitar, you know how difficult it is. The ends of your fingertips become blistered and crack open. My mom had such delicate hands to begin with, so I am not sure how she did it. The preacher told his class that if it hurt, chances were they were doing it right! My mom kept right on learning, despite the pain it caused her. I guess it was kind of like being married . . .

My mother had a beautiful voice, but I already knew that. She sang to me a lot when I was little. I was a terrible sleeper, so she'd rub my back and sing songs until I drifted off. She said her arm would just about fall off stroking my back—up and down and up and down—trying to get me to go to sleep. If she stopped for a second I'd wake up again. It's like if you fall asleep with the television on and someone comes along and shuts it off, you immediately wake up. Her song selection was kind of crazy, or at least different. She used to sing songs from a movie called *Paint Your Wagon* with Clint Eastwood and Lee Marvin. I loved those songs, "Wand'rin' Star" and "I'm on My Way" in particular—I knew them by heart because she sang them so often to me. I thought my mom sang them at least as well as, if not better than, Clint Eastwood. And my mom was *way* better than Lee Marvin (that was a no-brainer, as I didn't think he could sing at all). Songs from *Fiddler on the Roof* were popular around our house too, but they weren't my favourites. "Sunrise, Sunset" is the only song that ever made any sense to me; the rest seemed to be about farm animals or unrequited love, neither of which appealed to my ears at the time. My mom also attempted to sing Harry Belafonte tunes, which I loved, but she lacked the accent needed to really pull off "Come, mister tally man, tally me banana." What the heck was that all about? Tally your own bananas.

Before too long, my mom was playing songs like "Country Roads" by John Denver, "Goodnight Irene," originally recorded by Huddie "Lead Belly" Ledbetter, and "Edelweiss" by . . . whoever the hell first sang that song. She was sounding so great, so professional! I was amazed, to say the least. I couldn't believe that this was the mother that belonged to me.

I went to a lesson with her once. I sat in the corner of the church on a metal chair and listened to eight or ten people who were concentrating so intensely that they looked like they were trying to go to the bathroom. They all strummed away madly and sang songs for an hour at the top of their puffed-up, gleeful lungs; I was in heaven. I loved the tones that poured out of their big guitars. I loved that together they could make a sound that seemed to seep underneath my skin and crawl ever so slowly towards my heart and then just sit there, humming like a long laugh. Everybody looked so darn happy, and it was contagious! Any one of those people who had a trouble in the world when they walked into that lesson walked out an hour later not knowing what those troubles could possibly have been. My mom looked happy in that guitar class, and she didn't look happy very often.

Her brow was usually furrowed, and for good reason. Because building the house had put such a strain on my parents financially, my mom felt she had no other choice but to go back to work. She didn't want to, but she knew she had to. She was thirty-nine years old, and had to figure out some way to support us all in case something went—well, just in case . . . She honestly didn't know if my dad would be able to keep his job at the concrete company or not. There was a lot of infighting where he worked and sometimes there was real fighting. My dad worked with two crazy brothers who could both drink like the devil in a desert and who beat the hell out of each other on a weekly basis. Things were unsteady and unpredictable. The company was one truckload of concrete away from crashing onto the tarmac.

I know that at that point my dad was drinking so much he'd stopped eating, and managed to get himself down to about 130 pounds. I don't remember him being thin. I didn't see him around enough to even notice if he was thin. My mom told me that often when alcoholics drink they don't want to eat. That was news to me. Drinking was nothing like smoking pot, then, because when Duray smoked pot he'd microwave a package of wieners and eat the entire thing with a loaf of white bread followed by four or five Wagon Wheels and a gallon of homo milk. Duray would eat car parts if he had the munchies and there was nothing else around. Sometimes I think my mom got a part-time job not just for the money but so she could get out of the house. Who could blame her?

She worked a crazy assortment of odd jobs to earn a bit of extra money for us. One of them was sorting eggs at a chicken farm about a mile down the road from where we lived. Mom said it was a horrible job because of the smell. She had to peel her clothes off at the back door and bleach them in hot water to get the stench out. Everybody who lived within a few miles of the egg farm knew what it could do to a perfectly good summer day. When the wind blew in the right direction, the smell of chicken shit was so bad it could almost peel the red paint off a barn. I can't really describe it but I'll try: if you put a loaded diaper in a pot of boiling sock juice with goat balls you'd be about halfway there.

My poor mother stood in front of a conveyor belt, holding up egg after egg to a 40-watt light bulb. Her job was to see if the eggs were fertilized, which I thought was disgusting. She worked there just long enough to afford a third-hand clunker of a car called an Epic. It had a top speed of forty miles per hour and could fit two people comfortably and four people really uncomfortably. She quit her job at the egg farm the day she got the last cheque she needed to buy that car. She drove us everywhere after that. It was nice for her to be able to get around without having to depend on my dad.

I don't know how she did it. My mom worked a full-time job for several years as well. She somehow managed to get a job as a dental assistant, of all things, though she had no experience. She saw an ad in the paper and went and filled out an application, did the interview and Dr. dePledge hired her right there on the spot. She went out and bought dental technician outfits and everything. I was very proud of her and I think she was proud herself too. My mom sold Avon for awhile in the seventies, but she didn't really like the door-to-door part of it so she gave it up. I don't blame her. The dental technician job was a lot more serious than the Avon gig, although I did miss the flavoured lip glosses that came in the giant flower rings. I would have to settle for the plastic diamond rings I got from the dentist.

There she was, with the suction thingy and the teeth-picking tools and the cotton swabs and the paper-spitting cup—just like she knew what she was doing. Of course she made us all go to Dr. dePledge because he gave her a good deal. I don't know what the good deal was, but she may have had our fillings and our cleanings done in trade for ironing all his shirts. My mom said she had a hard time getting Dr. dePledge to even give us a bill for our dental work. He was a very nice man, and I know my mom was very grateful for his generosity. He also gave a good needle. I never felt a darn thing. I would anticipate pain, and it never arrived. Before I knew what hit me, my nostrils were frozen and one of my eyelids was hanging down over my lip. Sometimes it felt like he froze one of my ears. Better safe than sorry, I guess. It took days to be able to drink anything without pouring it down the front of my shirt. His hands always smelled like Jergens lotion—very almondy. It's funny the things you remember. He would ask you a question and then cram his fingers down your throat. Why do dentists do that? They ask you something that you can't answer without sounding like you've had a stroke.

It was a bit embarrassing having my own mother as my dental hygienist. It was really weird to have her sitting there beside me, staring down my throat, picking away at my teeth and telling me that I needed to be flossing more. She was big on flossing.

"Just floss between the ones you want to keep," she'd say. Someone once told me that flossing your teeth on a regular basis can add seven years to your life, but that the flossing itself will literally take up the seven years, so it's kind of a moot point. (And by the way, don't floss and drive; I've tried it and it makes it really hard to text and drink.)

My mom came home one day and told us that that afternoon a patient had died in the dental chair. Yes, died. A patient had *died* in the chair? I wondered what she had done to him. My mom told us that the patient was a very old man and had to have one of his teeth extracted. Apparently he didn't make it. I wondered how badly you'd have to screw up a tooth extraction to actually kill somebody. She went on and on about how much blood there was spewing out of his elderly mouth. She said they just couldn't stop it and so he basically bled to death. I felt queasy just listening to her go on about that old man and all the blood pumping out of the empty socket in his head. Of all the ways you can leave this planet, death by tooth extraction is not all that bad, I guess. It's pretty weird, but not bad as far as deaths go.

My mom never minded blood. She told us that, growing up, her dream was to be an operating-room nurse. What kind of a dream is that? What happened to flight attendant or actress or, God forbid, a famous singer? I can't even stand the sight of a needle going into my arm, never mind the gore I would encounter in an operating room. I realized there was a lot I didn't know about my mother. She wasn't even that upset that the old guy had bought the farm. I guess an ambulance came and hauled him away to a morgue somewhere. I do not want to die in a dental chair unless I have the laughing gas on full blast and my Latin lover Philippe straddling my body with the suction thing going. (That could mean anything, couldn't it?) Then, and only then, would I be prepared to die in a dental chair. Oh yeah, and I would like to be a 107 years old with a glass of champagne in one hand and a cheese and onion sandwich in the other.

We ate a lot of meals out of a Crock-Pot when my mom was working at the dental office, and I know that doesn't have anything to do with the guy dying in the dental chair. Before she headed off to work, my mother would stick a chicken or a roast or a ham in that yellow-and-brown Crock-Pot with a few carrots and onions, and, nine hours later, voilà! It would turn into dinner. It was always good, though. No matter what kind of meat you put in that thing, it would turn it into a stew that was always dark brown in colour and would taste exactly the same. Even the carrots gave up their orange eventually. No vegetable could withstand the colour-sucking power of my mother's Crock-Pot.

As I got older, I cooked dinner a few times a week just to help out while she was at work. We needed a break from the unmerciful stews on occasion. My so-called cooking consisted of opening a lot of cans and putting them all together into a casserole dish with tuna and Cheez Whiz and baking it. *Surprise! It's dinner! I don't know what it's going to taste like and that's why it's a surprise!* No one was thrilled when I was in charge of feeding the family, least of all me. There was generally a lot of mumbling going on around the table. I swear there were times when my dad tried to bury his uneaten casserole under his mashed potatoes. I'm no dummy. I have to say, I am pretty sure that I came by my cooking skills honestly—I say that with a lot of love in my heart.

Mom really enjoyed going to her guitar lessons, and I enjoyed her going to those lessons too. It was something that she was doing for herself and nobody else, and I paid close attention to that. I know she was relieved to be working at the dental office too. It was a fairly big office, as there were three full-time dentists and they all had assistants and receptionists, so it was a very social place and she was making new friends for the first time in a long time. It was important for her to have other women to talk to and now she had a whole gaggle of co-workers. I'm sure it was nice for them to get together in the lunchroom and discuss how rotten their boyfriends and husbands were. I don't think my mom found herself quite so alone after she started working for Dr. dePledge. She had found herself some girl power!

My dad was still very seldom at home and when he was it was tense. Whenever my dad took the time to speak to me I was always shocked. I'd look around and think to myself, are you talking to me? I mean, I was thrilled that he was talking to me and not yelling, but I felt awkward. He would say things to me like "What are you doing with yourself?" or "Where do you think you're going?" It was always kind of random. I was very intrigued by my dad. I wondered what was going on in his head most days. He was a puzzle to me.

One summer day I got to go into town with my dad to run some errands. Most of the time I felt I was a nuisance to him so this was indeed a rare occasion. It wasn't very often that I got the chance to do things with just him. My mother looked at my dad out of the corner of her eye, somewhat suspicious. Maybe she knew something that we didn't. Whatever it was, she seemed uneasy.

Sue was staying over at our place for the weekend, so of course she came along and then Patrick wanted to come too. Dad told us he'd take us to an arcade to play a few games once he was done his running around, so we were all beside ourselves with excitement. I was thrilled to have Sue for a sleepover as I didn't get to have them very often. My mom always cautioned me not to bring kids home after school as she never knew what kind of mood my dad would be in and whether he would embarrass us. But Sue's dad was a drinker too and she knew all too well what it was like to have to cover up a situation. She was a kindred spirit and one of the few friends I knew I could have stay over without feeling at all weird. My dad liked Sue a lot: he even went so far as to remember her name.

We piled into my dad's company car, rolled down the windows and headed into town with giant grins on our faces. I remember it being a particularly hot day so we were dressed in T-shirts and jeans. We didn't have jackets with us, just the clothes on our backs. Dad drove around to a few stores, stopping here and there for whatever it was he needed. We went in with him when he picked up things for the house at the hardware store. We went in with him when he returned the bottles to the Pop Shoppe. We went in with him everywhere until we rolled into the parking lot at the Tradewinds Hotel and Bar. When we got there he told us to wait in the car and that he'd be back in a few minutes. Something told me it wasn't going to be a few minutes but I just shoved that thought to the back of my mind.

A few minutes went by and then a few more minutes went by and then at least an hour went by and there was still no sign of my dad. The sun was pelting down on us and we sat there in the car engulfed in its giant orange glare and waited. Cars were coming and going and people were walking by looking into the car with eyebrows raised.

We were all getting thirsty. It was hot that day. We kept the windows rolled down to keep the air moving, and we were keeping ourselves busy playing games like I spy and "name that car." Then Patrick said he was hungry and that he wanted to go home. Dad had the keys with him so we couldn't even listen to the radio to find out what time it was. It was hard to tell how long he had been gone. I felt anxious. I hated that feeling.

My mom was at home, pacing.

Looking at the clock.

Worried.

I was relieved when I finally saw him coming towards the car with a big smile on his shiny, red face.

"I'm gonna be a little bit longer, but here's twenty bucks for you three to go to the arcade," he said. That seemed reasonable. It was twenty bucks, after all. The arcade was across the other side of a very busy road called Macleod Trail. It had three lanes going in each direction and it was always bustling with heavy traffic. There was a decent stoplight and a crosswalk, though, and I figured we'd make it in one piece if we hurried. Maybe this wasn't going to be that bad after all. I watched him walk back through the glass doors of the hotel and, without another glance at us, disappear inside.

We took our windfall and raced across the road, weaving through the traffic to the mall, where we headed straight for the Orange Julius stand to buy drinks and hot dogs. We had enough money left over to play the pinball machines and the electronic Ping-Pong thing that was all the rage. We were all so happy to be in the arcade and not sitting in the parking lot at the Tradewinds. We stayed as long as the money lasted and then we figured we'd better go back to the car.

We thought we'd be in trouble for sure, as we'd been gone at least an hour and a half. We walked as fast as we could back across Macleod Trail to where the car had been sitting all afternoon in the sun, convinced my dad would be standing there beside it with his hands on his hips, tapping his wristwatch. He wasn't. He wasn't anywhere in sight. It was starting to get dark, and I was feeling more and more unsure of what to do. Sue and Patrick and I got back in the car and waited. We didn't know what else to do. The sun seemed to be giving up too.

My mom was frantic.

She stared out the window at the road.

Every car that went by she thought, *maybe it's them.*

We had been gone five hours.

Patrick was beginning to come apart at the seams. He didn't do well with any kind of stress, and this was stressful to all of us. He wanted to go home. He'd been crying quietly to himself for the last half-hour. I don't blame him—I wanted to go home too. His tears were heartbreaking to both Sue and me. We didn't know what words we should be saying to him. We'd eaten all our candy and drunk all our pop. Time was scraping its nails on the roof of the car. My mother was going to kill us all. My dad had never left us like this before—ever. I decided one of us had to go into the Tradewinds and fetch my dad out, and it was going to be me. I knew they didn't allow kids in a place like that, but they were going to have to make an exception.

I went in through the glass doors and was instantly engulfed by grey clouds of cigarette smoke. It was dingy and dark in there—filled with men drinking glasses of lukewarm draft beer and engaging in clumsy, droning conversations. I went on a hunt for my dad. No one seemed to notice me at all. A girl wandering around in a bar filled with drunk people was invisible, apparently, which I found hard to believe. I walked around tables covered in empty glasses, looking for my dad's corduroy pants. I walked down the long bar, gazing up at all the talking heads bobbing back and forth like those plastic dogs stuck in the back windows of cars. I finally spotted him sitting at a table with men I'd never seen before; he was laughing and carrying on like he didn't have a care in the world. When he finally spotted me, he looked shocked. He excused himself from the table and asked me what the hell I was doing in there.

I told him we were tired and cold and that we wanted to go home. I told him he'd been in the Tradewinds long enough and that mom would be really worried by now. I told him we'd spent all our money and that it was time to go. I was scared of him and I didn't want him to be mad, but I was willing to take that chance. I needed to get Patrick home. Sue and I could have managed, but Patrick was little. Enough was enough. I don't know if he heard one word I was saying, he just muttered something and threw some money on the table where the strange men were sitting.

He looked madder than I'd ever seen him, but then he caught himself. It was like he had a moment of clarity. I was relieved. He came out with me to the parking lot and got into the car, started it up and drove us home.

My mother didn't say a thing when we drove up.

She just looked at us with a thousand pounds of relief.

She looked at my dad with complete and utter disappointment.

He looked at the ground.

Mom and I drove Sue home to Bragg Creek. I was sad that my sleepover had ended the way it had. I am pretty sure we stayed at my gram's house the rest of the weekend.

My mom was so busy trying to shield us from dad all the time that it was taking a toll on her well-being. I knew she was anxious even though she pretended not to be. She worried constantly about what she should do about his drinking, because he didn't seem too worried about what he should do about his drinking. I don't think he saw it as any sort of a problem, and that was the problem. My dad wasn't used to anyone telling him what to do so it was hard trying to convince him he needed to make some changes in his life. And he needed to make quite a few.

The options for my mom were becoming fewer and further between. We were in a holding pattern, like a plane trying to land in a storm. We were circling the runway, hoping somebody would tell us we could land. Eventually you run out of fuel and crash.

chapter nine

I SWEAR ON THE ORANGE BIBLE

wanted to learn how to play the guitar just like my mom, but I didn't want anybody else to know—not my mother, not anybody. For some reason I felt embarrassed about it. It seemed like such a serious thing to do, and I wasn't a serious girl. I was a funny girl who wasn't really passionate about anything in particular. I liked doing everything, but I didn't know what being passionate was. Sue was passionate about skiing and Sue's mom was passionate about painting, so I knew what passion was but I didn't know what mine was. I guess I was waiting to see what I'd be good at but it just hadn't happened . . . yet. My mom was always telling me that I was good at everything I tried, but moms are supposed to say that. Being good at something doesn't mean you're passionate about it. I loved watching *Star Trek*, but I was pretty sure that didn't count as a passion.

I didn't think anybody would understand the sudden interest I had in learning an instrument; I certainly didn't. How could I possibly tell anybody that singing pulled at me like a giant red magnet? It seemed so detached from my goofy personality. I didn't dare hope that I was even the slightest bit musical but I must have decided at some point in my heart that I was willing to give it a whirl. It was going to be my secret, and a tricky one to keep.

What if I picked the damn thing up and couldn't make it play one simple chord? I'd seen enough people playing guitar on TV to sort of know how to hold one, but not really. If it was too big for my mom, it was going to be even bigger for me. When I finally strapped it on to my shoulder and placed my arms over it, I felt like I was trying to strum a canoe. It seemed impossible. Maybe I was crazy to think I had a hope in Havana.

For the first time in my life, it felt like I was experiencing a grown-up desire. I felt like I was falling in love, whatever that meant. I would even go as far to say that it was an awakening of sorts. I was waking up (and I wasn't really a morning person at all—my mother would have to bribe me with cartoons and cereal to get me to come downstairs and get ready for school). This desire was a new feeling for me. It stood on my shoulders and yelled "amen!" at anything that moved. Desire took up a lot of space in my head. It was like God saw me standing there in the middle of my bedroom and he handed me a silver bolt of lightning and said, "Here, put this inside your heart." I don't know how else to explain it.

After my mom finished her own practice sessions and put the guitar away in its case, I would find a way to fish it out and drag it down to the basement. I'd listen carefully to make sure nobody was going to come down the stairs to surprise me. I knew every single creak in the floor, so that came in very handy in establishing each separate individual's whereabouts upstairs. When everybody was accounted for, I had some time to be alone and begin to figure this thing out.

I opened up her big orange song bible with all the songs in it and flipped through every page, looking for a song I knew. The first one I recognized was Janis Ian's "At Seventeen." I started with that one. I had that record so I knew how it was supposed to sound. (I couldn't have chosen a more difficult song to learn if I tried. To this day, I cannot play it properly.) I became convinced, after having tried to form the first chord on the chart, that Ms. Ian had seven fingers on each hand.

There was an illustration on the very first page of the binder that basically showed you where to put your fingers on the strings to make the various chords. The fingers were labelled one, two, three, four and five. That made sense so far . . . The C chord had three numbers, which meant that there would be three fingers on three strings, and so that's where I began. That first attempt was nothing more than a buzzing mess of noise that didn't sound like anything at all. It was so disappointing. I expected something to ring out into the air that sounded like angels singing. I kept trying and kept trying and kept trying until finally the buzzing stopped and something that sounded like a note droned past me towards the rust-coloured brick wall in front of my face. I was giving myself a headache and I had to remind myself to breathe. It was only music, after all.

I must have spent at least three hours trying to make one chord sound decent before I was forced to quit. My fingertips had divots in them and were close to splitting apart. I had never had anything hurt quite as much as this. Theresa used to sneak up on me and crack my knuckles when I wasn't watching, but not even that hurt as much as learning to play guitar.

For the next few months that was all I did. I didn't care how much it hurt. I ran off the bus right after school, snatched my mother's guitar from her bedroom closet and practised for hours in the basement. I was usually alone in the house after school. It was just me, Janis Ian and a big orange binder full of songs to tackle. The first few weeks were hard, but after three or four months I had mastered five or six chords and was able to play almost every song in the binder. I was amazed with myself. I couldn't read music, I just knew the finger charts and had memorized their corresponding positions to make the chords, but that was almost like reading music, wasn't it?

The only chords I was having trouble with were the bar chords, which involved having one of your fingers lying flat against all the strings to cover them up entirely while using your remaining digits to form a chord higher up the neck of the guitar. I still had hands the size of golf balls, so it was next to impossible for me to make bar chords. But it didn't take long for me to learn that I could make up my own techniques and it would still sound like something. If it sounded like music, chances were that it was. That was my motto. I loved every second I spent in the basement all by myself. The rest of the world disappeared and my soul soared around my head like a meteorite.

I had managed to teach myself the guitar and learn how to sing along without anybody in my house knowing. I don't know how I kept it a secret but I did. Nobody would have a clue about my hidden talents until I performed at my high school graduation ceremony, six years after first strapping the thing on.

Upstairs, my parents were struggling to get Duray back on the right path but trouble followed him wherever he went. They put him into counselling and enrolled him into a new school with tutors that they couldn't afford. They enrolled him in Cadets, which he actually attended for awhile. They tried tough love. They tried to get him involved in sports. They tried bribery. Nothing worked. My dad tried yelling a lot, but that only seemed to make things worse. Duray's troubles were getting bigger and bigger and they took up all his time and stole his happiness. You could see his troubles perched on his shoulders, chuckling to themselves, and now they invariably involved the police in some way, shape or form. The long arm of the law reached into our house in Springbank and wrapped itself around Duray's throat.

He was now headed towards jail time—no more slaps on the wrist. There were court appearances and probation things and sentencing things. There were people he had to report to now, and there wasn't a thing any of us could do about it. Duray was in his very own version of hell, complete with demons and wicked temptations. (At least he had a constant flame burning so he could fire up a joint whenever necessary.)

My brother was this guy who came to our house once in awhile to change his clothes and rummage around for change in the bottom of my mom's purse. (We all did that, though; it wasn't just Duray. I think my mother would have been a millionaire had she been able to keep all the coins we stole.) I never really saw him anymore; not around the house, not at school, not anywhere. Maybe he was around somewhere, but I don't remember him. He wasn't even in his room downstairs anymore. I know that because I was in the basement all the time.

After I tore through my mother's orange binder of songs, it dawned on me that perhaps I could make up my own songs. If John Denver could make up a song, well, by hell, so could I! "By hell" was one of my dad's favourite curses.

"By hell, I'm gonna ring your neck!" he'd holler. (He never really rang anybody's neck.) Sometimes "by hell" was a good thing. Like if the Stampeders, Calgary's beloved football team, happened to win the Grey Cup, my dad would yell, "By hell! They did it!" It was a very versatile curse.

I remember gazing at the back cover of Janis Ian's album *Between the Lines* and reading with much amazement that *all* the songs—words and music—had been written by Ms. Ian herself. I was in shock sitting there thinking about what that meant. It had never occurred to me that somebody had to write the music that was on the radio every day. It had never crossed my mind. I also couldn't believe that Janis's real name was Janis Eddy Fink. I had read that in a *Tiger Beat* magazine. I assumed that all singers must have to change their names to make themselves sound more professional, but I wondered why Janis's parents thought it would be a good idea to call their daughter Janis Eddy Fink. It might have had something to do with Woodstock.

My friend Michelle, who had all the *Tiger Beat* magazines, was also the only person I knew lucky enough to have her own record player. It had detachable speakers that she had spread out on her dresser. Michelle loved music too, and she took great pride in playing all her favourite songs for me. She had a lot of records I had never heard of. She played me songs by a band called the Runaways that was made up of all girls. There wasn't one all-girl band in my entire record collection, so this was truly an incredible discovery. As I pored over the liner notes on the back of the Runaways album, I found more proof of people—girls—writing their own music and playing their own instruments!

It took me an hour to make up my first song. I called it "Paradise" and it was about my parents dying. I set the bar very high early in my career to write the most depressing songs possible. Soon I was writing a new song every day. I had books filled with lyrics and chords secretly stashed away in my bedroom. I was mortified that somebody might stumble across them, so I made sure they were some place no one would think to look. There was a crawl-space you could access through a little door in my bedroom, which was more or less a junk space. The angle was too sharp for it to be part of the actual room, so it was just left unfinished. I stuffed my writing books up underneath the pink insulation. My hands and arms were always itchy from shoving them so far inside it. Eventually I had to find a new hiding place because there were just too many books to stash there.

Writing songs was all I did. I never intended a soul to ever hear any of them, they were solely for my personal enjoyment. I don't think I realized how badly I needed to express myself. I couldn't wait to get out of school. I sat at my desk and stared at the clock on the wall and willed the arms to spin themselves around to 3:30. The bus ride home seemed to take nine hours. I can't recall learning anything in school between 1974 and 1980. It's truly a miracle that I can write my own name.

I was surprised by what came out of me, to tell you the truth. All the songs were drenched in blues and greys. I was such a funny kid. I loved laughing, I loved humour and I loved being a jackass. To make somebody laugh was very empowering. Being funny helped me out at school a lot. Kids were afraid to pick on somebody they knew was quick on her feet. I can't remember a single kid in my class who ever engaged me in a battle of wits. I was grateful for that. I never used my humour to make fun of anybody else either. I didn't have the stomach or the heart for bullying. In fact, I hated seeing any kid get picked on, and I wish I had done more to stop it when I saw it happening around me. Being silent about bullying is just as bad as being the bully. You're either the good guy or the bad guy. You can't sit on the fence. I wish I had known that then, but wisdom is not for the young. Time doles it out. That's the only way to get your hands on it.

I was very seldom, if ever, serious around my house. I felt that somebody had to provide a bit of levity there and that somebody was me! It made me feel good to see my mom laugh.

There was nothing like standing in front of a group of people and making them burst into guffaws over something I'd said or done. It was like a drug. Perhaps that's why I had a hard time understanding the polarity in my songwriting. My music was profoundly serious and morose and reverent, while my personality was just plain zany and offbeat. There was never a morsel of humour to be found in any of my songs. Music was off limits to humour and even to irony. I don't know why, but I protected my songs from that part of my personality. I guess there was a part of me that knew she'd have to be taken seriously someday.

I spent hundreds of hours in the basement listening to records. My parents had a whole bunch of old albums that had been sitting in boxes for far too many years. I fished them out to discover what in the heck they'd been rocking out to before they had kids. I came to the conclusion that they never rocked out, certainly not to any of the albums I found in that cardboard box. They had Sammy Davis Jr. and Nana Mouskouri and Roger Whittaker and Neil Diamond. Duray's collection included Frank Zappa, KISS, Jethro Tull and the Guess Who. My influences were far flung, to say the least. You wouldn't think that Frank Zappa would be high on my list of influences, but he did teach me one very important thing and that was that you could say anything you wanted in a song. I thought that was awesome. One of the lines he wrote in a song was "Billy was a mountain, Ethel was a tree growing off of his shoulder." I never forgot that line or that song. Frank taught me that I could say anything, so I did.

My sensible dad, for some strange reason, had a moment of utter weakness and let us join the Columbia Record Club. I could not believe that he said yes. I don't think he had a clue about what we were getting ourselves into. For *one cent* you could buy *ten* albums that would be rushed right to your door. *Yes, right to your door!*

It seemed too good to be true, and of course it was. My dad said a few goddammits about the Columbia Record Club before it was all over, let me tell you. Yes, we did receive our ten albums for one cent and then every month after that they'd send us one that we didn't order and definitely didn't want, and they'd charge us full price for it. If we didn't like the album that they'd sent we'd have thirty days to send it back and not be charged but otherwise we were. (Insert small print here. I am already confused.) Who had the time to ship unwanted albums back? They didn't exactly make it easy—there were many serial numbers to fill in on long, complicated forms and the return address was some place in Buffalo, New York, and that required postage to the States. Holy Moses, my dad was so mad that I thought his heart would explode. I learned even more swear words than I thought existed in the English language.

For years we received wacky unknown albums from the Columbia Record Club and we never sent one of them back. Sometimes I'd know who the artist was, but not very often. We filed them all away in the basement with KISS and Frank Zappa and Olivia Newton-John. Our Columbia Record Club pile just kept getting higher, and our pile of ridiculous bills kept getting higher and higher too. My dad said he wasn't going to pay the bastards ten red cents. (We did actually pay them the initial ten red cents, just so you know.) Sometimes it was good to have a dad like mine. Nobody messed with my dad, myself included.

I was always excited to get the newest record in the mail from the Columbia Record Club, even if I hadn't heard of the band. Nobody else seemed as interested as I was. I'd stare at the covers for hours. One month we received Herb Alpert and the Tijuana Brass. I played a song called "The Lonely Bull" about forty-five million times. My dad used to stomp on the kitchen floor and demand that I turn it down. That's when headphones really would have come in handy, but sadly we didn't own a pair. Headphones hadn't even been invented yet. (I hope I'm kidding.)

The one album I did get that changed my entire young life was the new Carpenters record. When it showed up in our mailbox I nearly fell over. They were so popular—you heard one of their songs on the radio at least every hour. I'd loved them since I first heard them in

Judith's music class. They were fascinating to me because they were so young.

Michelle's *Tiger Beat* magazines showed the Carpenters performing in Japan, of all places! They were becoming famous all over the world. I wondered what that must feel like. I bet it felt weird. Karen Carpenter looked to be the same age as me. All of the other singers that my parents owned on vinyl seemed to me to have one foot in the grave. Roger Whittaker whistled, for crying out loud, and Nana Mouskouri had big, thick, black glasses. Only old people wore glasses. Only old people whistled. My shop teacher whistled and wore bifocals, that's how I knew the singers on my parents' records were ancient. I was grateful to finally be exposed to artists with whom I had something in common—first and foremost among which was being alive.

I couldn't get down to the basement fast enough. I carefully but quickly ripped the Carpenters record out of its package and steadied my hand to put in onto the turntable. (I had to tape four pennies onto the needle to get it to play the records. Otherwise, the needle popped off and the record would skip. I discovered the penny trick all on my own. It beat holding my finger on the needle, as eventually my arm would freeze up.) There is nothing like hearing a song for the first time and letting it wash over you. You become addicted to it. I became addicted to the Carpenters. The sound I heard when the needle hit the spinning record was magic. That white static crackling noise that suddenly filled an entire room with possibility. (How the heck did they get the music to fit onto those plastic grooves? It didn't make sense to me. Modern science was a marvel. What would they think of next? Pretty soon we'd be calling people from anywhere in the world using a little phone that could fit in your ear and TV would play on a screen on your wristwatch. That would be the day.)

Albums were so much easier to play than 45s. We never seemed to have that middle plastic thingy that kept the 45 from doing a loop-the-loop while you were trying to centre it. Duray used to put masking tape over the inch-wide hole and then punch the steel rod in the middle of the turntable through that to keep it steady. I always thought that was so clever. Duray was clever.

I played the Carpenters record over and over, and then I played it some more. It was on repeat for six months. I learned to strum along to the songs by ear and eventually had them all memorized. I moved from the Carpenters to Olivia Newton-John's *Come On Over* LP and then onto Carly Simon and Bette Midler and James Taylor and Jim Croce. I tackled so many records I lost track. School definitely took a back seat, if not a place in the trunk.

The Columbia Record Club was turning me into kind of a recluse. I had a big secret, and it felt fantastic. I had something that was mine. I don't know what my parents thought I was doing down there in the basement, but I am sure they were glad that I was home and not getting myself into any trouble. They already had one kid who was doing plenty of that.

When I was thirteen or fourteen years old, my mother finally came to the end of her very frayed rope. She said it took her a long time to find the courage to tell my dad he was going to have to move out. She didn't know what to expect. She had no idea how he'd react to the news that she wanted a separation. She assumed that he'd fly off the handle like he usually did and start hollering at the top of his lungs, but he did no such thing. He was actually very sullen and quiet. He was probably shocked that such words had come out of my mother's mouth.

She said the hardest part of telling him was finding a moment when he was sober enough to understand what she was asking him to do. She told him that she could not live with someone who thought drinking was more important than his family and that he'd have to find somewhere else to live. My dad didn't say anything; what was there to say? He went upstairs to their bedroom and started throwing clothes into a suitcase. He grabbed four or five suit jackets, his shaving kit, socks, underwear, T-shirts—all the usual suspects—and he walked out the back door to his company car. My mom said she bawled her head off as he drove out of the yard and then she went into her ironing room.

The plane had finally come down for an emergency landing.

My mom didn't have a clue about where he was going or what he was going to do. She didn't ask and I don't think she cared. She was relieved to have it over and done with. That was that. Things were going to change around our house.

I remember her having the talk with us about what was going on with her and dad and what was probably going to happen. She wasn't sure how long we'd be able to stay in the house. She told us that she didn't know if he was going to come back or not. She told us that he had to do something about his drinking, because she couldn't live with him anymore. It was too hard. She told us it was up to him now.

That didn't sound very promising.

It was very quiet around our house those first few days. It was like it had been raining hard for months and months, and then suddenly it stopped. You don't know how noisy it is sometimes until the noise goes away. Patrick and I sat silently at the dinner table and ate our sloppy joes and drank our milk and wondered what our futures would be. My mom pushed her food around on her white CorningWare plate and stared out the window. I am sure she felt completely and utterly alone. (CorningWare plates were supposed to be unbreakable, so we decided we'd throw them onto the kitchen floor to test that theory out. They do break into a million tiny shards of white glass, just so you know.)

—

I didn't want to have to move. I didn't want to lose my dog, Aquarius, and I didn't want to have to change schools and start over again. I wanted everything to be normal—whatever that meant. I didn't think about how my mother felt. I feel terrible about that now. Looking back is sometimes harder than looking forward. At least you don't know what the future is and there's always hope, whereas what's behind you never changes; in fact sometimes it seems to just get worse. The mind is a funny thing that way. It can take a memory and twist it a thousand times over.

A week or so after my dad left, he came by the house because he hadn't taken any pants with him. He'd been in such a hurry that he'd packed up his jackets but not the matching pants to go with them. It was awkward for everybody. Maybe he did it on purpose. Maybe he wanted my mom to say, "Just kidding! Come home!" She didn't. He gathered up a few more things, put them into a plastic bag and drove off again. He looked incredibly sad to me.

For the first time I felt like crying. I hadn't done that yet. I was going to miss his Saturday morning fry-up breakfasts. I was going to miss going to the drive-in on Friday nights. I was going to miss . . . I couldn't think of anything else I was going to miss, but I really tried to. I felt like my world was falling apart. It was, however, very good songwriting material.

My dad moved into a little apartment with his friend Mel, who had also been booted out of his house by his wife, for reasons unknown to me. My mom was relieved because Mel was apparently very clean and for some reason she felt better about my dad living with someone who knew how to keep a house tidy. Mel could also cook. I knew who Mel was because he and his wife had been good friends with my parents for years. I remember visiting them at their half-built house out in Millarville, a little country town an hour or so outside of Calgary. I remember playing with Mel's three wild kids. They were very likeable children—slightly weird and a bit rough around the edges, but I loved that.

I don't know why they didn't finish building their house, but they never did. Its lonesome frame stood in the middle of a big field with plastic sheeting over the windows instead of glass. The sheets would flap back and forth like an old, tired flag. The prairie wind blew through the tar paper–covered walls, causing a constant faint whistle. It was a singing house, complete with dancing arms and legs. The floor was covered with planks of wood that you could look down through to the basement. The appliances just stood in the middle of the kitchen, waiting to be put into place. None of the cupboards had doors. There were plain wooden shelves filled with unmatched plates and glasses. It all looked sad to me. It felt sad, too. There wasn't a tree in sight. No matter which way you looked, there was mile after mile of nothing—just a whole lot of dirt and endless open range. I guess that's why they call it the prairies. Maybe that unfinished house was why Isabel kicked Mel out.

In happier times, mom and dad used to sit around the kitchen table with Mel and Isabel and drink pot after pot of coffee and laugh. (There may have been something in the coffee, one never knows.) We kids would throw back a pop and a handful of potato chips and head outside to play. It didn't matter what the weather was like, we'd be out there running around like a pack of wolves. We always had fun because Mel and Isabel had a barn full of horses and cats and giant piles of hay. Patrick nearly died after playing in that haystack; he could barely suck in a single merciful breath after ten minutes of climbing around on the bales. It was a risk he was willing to take, though— that's how much fun it was.

Mel and Isabel's wild kids, Billy Ruth, Bobby June and Tyler (Tyler was the only boy), were skilled yet creepy horse whisperers.

They could make a horse do things that defied rational explanation. Their horses could sit and stay, shake a hoof and practically roll over. I swear they could almost talk! I heard it with my own ears. Those kids had been on the back of a horse before they could walk or talk, and they made sure they told us that every few minutes.

"We been ridin' since we wasn't walkin' or crawlin' . . ." (Yeah, you just told us that). Patrick once asked me if they were "normal" kids. I told him that they weren't. I told him that I didn't quite know what they were. I think Patrick was really asking if they were dangerous. Fearless is what they were. They were completely themselves, which I thought was spectacular. I envied them. I assumed that they were real country kids, complete with running noses and red necks, unlike us. Patrick also asked me if they went to school. I honest-to-God didn't know. I never thought about it. Let's assume they did.

I don't think Mel was a big drinker; I think he and his wife split up because she just didn't love him anymore. That was a fate worse than what my dad had suffered. Yes, he got kicked out, but my mom still loved him; he just had a drinking problem. Mel, on the other hand, had quite simply been set adrift.

I guess my dad started going to AA shortly after he moved in with Mel, because he called up my mom and told her that he was sober. Even though Mel was a good housekeeper, and a somewhat decent cook, my dad wanted to come home. My mom had laid down the law, though, and she had a list of things that he had to do in order for him to qualify for re-entry into our house. I'm not sure what was on that list, but *no drinking* was at the top of it. I was proud of my mom for sticking to her guns.

My mom was constantly worried about money so she balanced her chequebook a lot. I would see her hunched over my dad's desk, shuffling through piles of papers and bills. "It never ends," she'd lament. It couldn't have been easy being there alone with us, paying bills and fixing things and driving us all over hell's half-acre and all that other stuff you have to do when you're running a household. It must have been scary at night, thinking about people breaking in and murdering us all. (Maybe she didn't think about that but I did.) We didn't have an alarm system. We did have Aquarius, but he wasn't much of a guard dog. He licked complete strangers like they were cheeseburgers.

We didn't talk about my dad for weeks. We all tried to keep busy. The first time my dad came home for a visit sober, he came bearing a brand-new iron for my mother. It was a very weird gift to bring to a woman you wanted to woo back into your life. She said to him, "What's this?" and he replied, "Well, I knew you needed a new iron." My dad knew the way to my mother's heart. You'd think he would have brought flowers or chocolates but no, he brought a new Sunbeam steam iron. I think my mom was happy to get it, though; it's the thought that counts, and she did iron more than an entire legion of Chinese dry cleaners.

It was a Sunday when he came out to see us so he stayed for supper. My dad seemed relieved to be sitting there around our white kitchen table eating a meal with us. He was a new version of himself; he didn't holler or lose his temper once. I waited for him to throw around a few goddammits, but he never did. He just ate his supper quietly and then he left. I could hear my parents talking at the door before he got into his car, but I couldn't make out what they were saying. Believe me, I tried.

He came back every weekend and worked on repairing his marriage and his reputation. My mom was cautious but hopeful, I think. She didn't have any grand expectations of how things would turn out. Patience is indeed a virgin. Or something like that . . .

My mom needed to be sure that the soberness was going to stick. Who could blame her? Alcohol is like air: it's everywhere you turn. Hard to avoid putting it into your mouth. We just hoped that the twelve steps of never were going to work for my dad. My mom would always say, "It's up to him." I am pretty sure she didn't mean God. My mother was never terribly religious and I was happy about that. Her views on religion were always very practical, thank God.

The AA people had a poem that my dad had put onto a plaque. He would recite it at all his AA meetings.

> *God grant me the serenity to accept the things I cannot change,*
> *Courage to change the things I can,*
> *And the wisdom to know the difference.*

I always thought that it was a great poem. It made sense to me, unlike some poems that left me scratching my head and wondering what was wrong with artistic people.

I went to an AA meeting with my dad every now and again. I loved going because, as I found out, alcoholics love sugar, and so they had enough donuts and coffee and cola and candy at their gatherings to make a kid feel like she had died and gone to tooth-rotting heaven. All the recovering drunk people would eat a dozen donuts each as they guzzled pot after pot of thick black coffee with, you guessed it, five heaping tablespoons of white sugar. AA meetings were A-okay in my books. I was glad my dad was going to them and meeting other people who had trouble with rum from time to time.

When my dad eventually moved home a few months later, he stuck the AA poem plaque in their upstairs bathroom. I read that verse every day for the next ten years. It was like I couldn't even begin to think about having a poo without reading that damn thing. It was very Pavlovian. I guess it was a better option than having to read the Lord's Prayer every time you went to pay your respects to the septic tank. That would have been a surefire way to have eternal constipation, as it was an extremely long poem.

The only other thing we had in the bathroom to read was, of course, a copy of *Reader's Digest* magazine. It was at least ten years old. It looked like the dog had eaten it and thrown it up again. I had each and every page committed to memory and I am not kidding.

There was one story I read at least a thousand times about a woman who had survived a bear attack only to crash-land in the plane that had flown in to rescue her. Now that's bad luck, or good luck, it's hard to know . . . The woman somehow survived the plane crash as well as the bear attack, and went on to become a life coach and professional speaker. I would have liked to attend one of her speeches. Perhaps they began with: "Don't ever go into the woods or get into a plane, and then your life will work out just fine." I'll never forget that story. I will also never forget the word "reciprocity," as it was in the "Expanding Your Word Power" section of that very same issue. I never managed to use it in a song, although I tried rhyming it once with "velocity" but it didn't work out. It did, however, work quite well with "atrocity," which was much more up my songwriting alley.

After he moved home, my dad went to AA meetings whenever he could. He drank a *lot* of coffee and said it gave him the runs. It's no wonder the *Reader's Digest* magazine looked so beaten up.

My mother forgave him in tiny little bits. Trust is a hard thing to get back.

chapter ten

BEING REBECCA

High school was a really wonderful time in my life. It was smooth sailing, except for the home perm my mother gave me in grade twelve. The story goes as follows:

I had stick-straight hair that I couldn't do anything with except braid or put into ponytails. I wanted to change up my look slightly, more like the wavy look that a lot of movie stars seemed to be sporting. A few girls in my class had perms and I thought that they looked really great. My mom brought home a do-it-yourself box of "perm" from the Co-op, as per my request, and said that we'd put it in that weekend. I was so excited I couldn't wait to show off my new do at school on Monday.

That Saturday my mom opened the box and spread its contents on the kitchen table. There were rubber gloves, perm solution, dozens of tiny plastic rollers, "taming" solution (whatever the hell that was) and, finally, the all-important instructions. I was in charge of reading out the instructions to her. It was painstaking work getting all the little rollers in, and it took at least ninety minutes. There seemed to be an awful lot of them. I only wanted a little wave but we were following the instructions, after all, so we carried on. Step two was the perm solution. My mom drizzled it onto my head, careful to keep it from dripping down the back of my neck. The smell was horrible. It was like someone had thrown a cat onto a fire. I could hardly keep my eyes open.

After fifteen minutes or so, it really started to burn. I told my mother that my head felt like it had Tabasco sauce on it, but she insisted that we follow the instructions to a T. I figured she knew what she was doing. She kept checking my scalp and saying that everything looked good and so I sat there watching the minutes on the oven timer tick painfully by. After ten more minutes I couldn't stand it. I told my mom that something was definitely wrong and that she had to get it off of my scalp. She told me she would test a roller and unwound it to check the hairs to see if they had any curl. She thought the roller needed a little more time. I felt like I was going to have to submerge myself into an ice bath after it was all said and done. I couldn't believe that my hair wasn't melting right off my head. The instructions called for forty-five minutes with the perm solution on. I was then to give my hair a thorough rinse and, as the final step, apply the taming solution, followed by a double rinse. I couldn't wait to get the damn plastic rollers out of my hair. It started to smell like someone had thrown up onto the cat that was on fire. Mom pulled the rollers off and stuck my head under the tap at the kitchen sink. The taming solution smelled not bad at all compared to the perm chemicals. Mom thought it looked great. I wanted to see it!

When my hair was wet it looked pretty good. I could see curly waves, even little ringlets. My mom said that we needed to blow it dry to see the full effect. I sat on the white swivelling kitchen chair and waited as my mom brushed and dried my newly permed hair. My mom was brushing and blowing for a really long time. She seemed somewhat perplexed about the whole thing.

"That's odd," she mumbled under her breath. "Hmph . . ."

I was getting nervous at this point. "What's the matter, mom?"

"Well, it seems to have really worked," she said anxiously. "It's got really good curl, that's for sure."

I wanted to see it immediately.

"I hope that's what you wanted," she called out as I raced to the bathroom mirror to see for myself.

What I saw was nothing short of a major disaster. I would never be able to show my face at school ever again. My mom had given me an Afro! I had the smallest, tightest curls on my head that I'd ever laid eyes on. It took force to pull them straight and when you let them go again they'd spring back into a compact coil. I was so shocked I didn't know what to say. My mom came into the bathroom behind me and said that it didn't look that bad. I strongly disagreed.

"We followed the instructions on the box," she insisted.

I know there are a lot of people who have nightmare stories of how hard high school was for them, but that wasn't the case for me. I had been with the same kids since grade four, so we all knew each other and we pretty much got along. School was like a big party as far as I was concerned. I loved all the team sports, and I played everything: basketball, volleyball, flag football, badminton, track and field and, of course, hockey. It was easy making it onto the teams because there were so few kids who tried out. All I had to do was show up for practice and I was a shoo-in! I guess that's what happens when you have forty-two kids in your entire grade.

We'd be lucky to find nine people to play baseball. God forbid we should have one extra kid who could sit on the bench. If one player got hit in the head with a bat and was bleeding to death he'd have to keep playing because there wasn't anybody who could take his place. Our gym teacher, Mrs. Neilson, quite often had to be the back-catcher as well as the umpire. In addition to being the gym teacher, she was our English teacher, our social studies teacher, our math teacher *and* the coach of all my sports teams.

She was always in her gym clothes and wore her whistle and her stopwatch to English and math class and actually used the whistle on occasion. It's weird having a whistle blown when you are in the middle of writing a math test. For whatever reason, I don't think Mrs. Neilson liked me. I certainly didn't care for her much, so that was probably half our problem. For some reason she gave me the creeps. Maybe it was because she blinked way too much—I'd heard that people who blink a lot seem nervous. She certainly made me nervous roaming the halls with that whistle around her neck.

I had some very interesting teachers while at Springbank High School, some of whom seemed like they'd been fired from Hogwarts and some of whom seemed no older than we were. My art teacher looked like she was sixteen. All the boys thought they had died and gone to heaven because she had a body like a Russian gymnast. (All the girls were secretly jealous, I'm sure, that she had stolen the boys' attention.) But however young, Mrs. Denyse was an amazing art teacher. She was fresh out of university and ready to take on the world, only she ended up with us instead of the world. Must have been slightly disappointing.

I had no idea what I was going to do when I got out of high school. Everyone seemed to be talking about which universities they had enrolled at and what they were going to be.

I had no idea what I was going to be. I was still trying to figure out who I was, never mind who I *would* be. I felt like I had lots of time to sort that out. I still had a whole year before I had to start thinking about any of that career crap. I had things to go *do* before I had to go *be*. Didn't that stuff just sort itself out? I hoped it did. It did in the movies anyway. There was always the scene with some sappy music and the heroine running in slow motion through a field of golden daffodils towards her dazzling future. That's the way I pictured my life unfolding. Alas, I had a ways to go.

Most of the parties I went to as a teenager were harmless. A bunch of us—anywhere between six and ninety-seven, depending on the weather—would drive our crummy old cars to an empty field somewhere, and we'd start a giant, blazing bonfire and drink warm beer somebody had stolen from their parents' secret stash in the basement. If we were lucky, somebody remembered to bring a few bags of potato chips. We'd stand around like a bunch of bowling pins, staring at the sparks flying through the black sky. Every so often somebody would say something funny and we'd all laugh. We were happy to be there, with the flames kissing our faces, pretending we were grown-up. One of us would usually have a car or truck door pried open so we could hear the radio blaring from the crappy little built-in speakers. We were all glad when Frank, who drove a T-roof Chevy Camaro, showed up at a party, because he had an eight-track stereo tape player and we'd have decent, loud music to listen to. Frank would always have a huge bottle of whisky with him as well. The guy could drink like a sailor and still drive as straight as a ruler. Between the giant fire and the booming music, it was easy to find the party on even the blackest of nights.

I thought Frank was like James Dean because he smoked cigarettes and wore his hair long and brushed back. He was one of the few guys who looked like he knew how to drink a beer. The rest of us just appeared awkward holding those brown stubby bottles in our hands. Not Frank—he was very manly. He would tip the beer bottle back towards his head and barely brush it with his lips, letting the malt beverage drain down the back of his throat. He didn't seem to even have to swallow. After each drink he'd take a long puff off his du Maurier cigarette and blow the smoke up over his head. I thought it was marvellous, I really did. I don't remember him ever talking. He was such a quiet kid, kind of mysterious, if that's possible at sixteen years old. He came to school about once a week, whether he needed to learn anything or not. I always wondered if he even had parents. I wondered where Frank lived and who bought his clothes. I am pretty sure he didn't know I existed, which is funny considering how much I thought about him and his mysterious life.

We'd listen to his eight-track player until his car battery died. (In hindsight, it would have been a good idea to just leave the Camaro engine running, even if the exhaust did make us all sick.) Somebody would end up giving his car a boost, so it all worked out. If there was one thing everybody had in the trunk of their car, it was jumper cables. Nobody in Canada would be caught dead without a set of those. (One year I got jumper cables in my stocking for Christmas. It doesn't get any more Canadian than that. They were red, and my mom said that that was the only colour she could find and if I didn't like them she could take them back. I would have preferred plaid, but red would have to do.)

I remember listening to so much great music at those bonfire parties underneath the brightest, shiniest stars. Boston, Rod Stewart, Queen, Cat Stevens, Fleetwood Mac, Journey, Martha and the Muffins, the Beatles, Jethro Tull, Ozzy Osbourne, Black Sabbath, Nazareth, Simon and Garfunkel, Hank Williams, Lynyrd Skynyrd, Johnny Cash, the Eagles, even Barry Manilow. There's something about being a bit drunk and singing "Mandy" at the top of your lungs that makes you feel like you'll never die. We put on a great show for all the horses and cows that would surround us. None of us thought it was the least bit odd to have livestock five or six feet from us. It was like they were part of the gang. I am sure we were very interesting to observe.

As the parties wore on into the night, inevitably someone would drink too much and wind up throwing up in the bushes. We'd all laugh, secretly grateful it wasn't us getting sick. The "thrower upper" would often rejoin the party after a quick trip into the trees and, unbelievably, drink some more, which I found astounding. And there would always be a few unsuitable couples who drifted off into the privacy of the trees to make out. (It was best to avoid the puddles of vomit). Of course the unsuitable couples wouldn't speak at school that Monday because that wasn't cool. You had to act like you'd never seen that person in your life. You had to act like you didn't care one little bit if that person lived or died. You had to be aloof, tossing your head back (in slow motion if possible) and laughing madly if you thought they were looking at you. Even if it was true love, you had to sacrifice yourself for the greater good. Those were the rules.

I kissed a boy named Mark for half the night at an indoor party that took place at the Hungarian Cultural Society, of all places, and, yes, I too was ignored the next day at school. I tried to be the "ignorer," but I wasn't quite quick enough. I made eye contact with Mark purely by mistake, right next to my locker, and when he quickly looked away, I became the "ignoree." High school was complicated.

Mark was such a nice guy—tall and slim with curly, light-brown hair. He was very athletic and smart and popular to boot. I guess you could say he was a triple threat. I always thought I was lucky to have kissed him at all and kept wondering how it was that he had picked me. There were so many other girls at that party. I certainly wasn't tall and willowy or the least bit pretty. I thought I was cute given just the right lighting, but how often do you get just the right lighting? I didn't even have boobs at this point. I felt like I had swallowed a canary all the rest of the week. Being the "ignoree" only bothered me for about fifteen minutes and then I was over it. I may have blushed ever so slightly as we passed each other in the hall later that day, but that was the extent of my shame. I was relieved in a way that we didn't have to rehash our very short romance. I didn't think we were all that good a match anyway, because our teeth kept clinking together when we kissed. If my head went left, his head went right. We never had that good seal that was of paramount importance for a successful lip-lock. Neither of us knew what we were doing in the kissing department (and I was pretty sure we didn't look anything like Kristy McNichol and Leif Garrett when they kissed on the TV series *Family*).

I remember the Hungarian Cultural Society had a jukebox. It looked more like a spaceship than something that played records. For twenty-five cents you could play four songs, which I thought was highway robbery, because my friend Patti had her very own jukebox in her parents' basement and it was free. To this day I can't hear a Juice Newton song without thinking about kissing Mark and how our teeth made sparks in the dark. (There is some kind of poem begging to be born right now . . .) I remember Leo Sayer singing "The Show Must Go On," and thinking it was the worst song I had ever heard but I liked it anyway.

The funny thing about going to a small school is that you were either the type of girl who got pregnant between English and math class in the school parking lot, or you were like Rebecca of Sunnybrook Farm, virtuous and more or less completely inexperienced. There didn't seem to be anything in between. I was in the Rebecca of Sunnybrook Farm category.

I was a late bloomer in many ways, well, in every way. I hadn't really had many romantic encounters. Yes, I had kissed Mark and had let Leonard dry hump me in his mother's basement, but that was pretty much it. Oh yeah, and in the fourth grade a little boy named Greg said he'd give me a big piece of bubble gum if I kissed him on the lips. It was only a one-one thousand, so it was totally manageable. I kept my mouth shut as tightly as a pickle jar.

Every year it seemed like we lost a couple of girls to "the sinful deed you should never do." It was always the girls you'd never dream would be engaging in sex of any kind, certainly not the kind of sex that involved a real honest-to-God penis. I'd hear whispered rumours by the lockers at lunchtime about this girl and that boy and the next thing I knew the knocked-up girl in question would be whisked off to some school for pregnant teens in Edmonton. That very same girl, pregnant no more, would reappear in the classroom the next spring, and not a single word about the illegitimate baby would be breathed by anybody. Not even the bullies dared go there. Eventually the whole sordid affair was swept under the boards of the football bleachers, never to be spoken of again. Well, at least not in front of the sinners themselves . . .

I always wondered why the boys who impregnated these young girls got off so easy. They stayed in school and graduated with their classes and were more or less held up as heroes by their male friends, with a lot of wink, wink, nudge, nudge going on. I am not saying that the boys didn't suffer some pain and anxiety, but they didn't have to be pregnant. The boys seemingly glided through all the embarrassment and the shame while the girls ate and slept in it.

The girls always looked so changed, so defeated, when they came back to school. I don't know how anyone could not be changed after giving birth to a real, live person. It must have been horribly hard giving the babies up. These girls were probably going to be spending the rest of their lives wondering how their babies were and who they were and where they were.

I knew one girl who gave up her baby her very first year of university. Just when she was starting her life, she got pregnant and had a very sudden change of plans. She was only seventeen or eighteen. She was in my grade but she'd skipped a year because she was so darn smart. I saw her a few times after her baby had been adopted and she was different somehow. The whole baby thing made her cynical and mean. I guess if she was going to feel miserable, she was going to make damn sure everybody else was miserable too. I felt sorry for her. She was too young to be broken.

I had a hard time giving an old pair of jeans away, so I couldn't imagine giving away a person. I think it was very brave of those girls to do what they did. They gave their babies a real chance to have wonderful lives. We had adopted Patrick when he was ten days old, so I knew full well what a gift it was to have a new soul come into your family. I knew that some young girl had given him up in order for him to be with us. We were all very grateful to his biological mother for putting him on the planet. Apparently she was only sixteen years old when she gave birth to him. It was hard for me to get my head around that. Pat was such an amazing addition to our family. We were all thrilled when he arrived with his little, blue blanket and his tiny hairbrush. He had the cutest face and the biggest ears. He was completely adorable, and we loved him the minute he came through the door.

I read an unbelievably crazy statistic once that said that four out of four girls have had sexual contact they did not want. I read it about six times to make sure I was reading it correctly. It's a tongue-in-cheek comment, but I can sort of guess where the author was coming from. It's more of a comment about our society than a statistic. It means that every girl has a bit of shame following her to bed at night. I knew I did.

When I was about ten years old one of my relatives at a family event got me alone in a basement and lay on top of me. He was older than I was so he certainly knew better, but he did it anyway. "Don't tell anybody, 'k?" he quietly insisted. "We didn't do anything, right?" *Who's we? I didn't do anything but you, on the other hand . . .*

He somehow lured me downstairs and got me onto the crappy couch with the springs sticking out of it, and eventually managed to get his fat, sweaty body on top of me. He writhed around, making these low moaning noises, his sweat dripping onto my face. I had no idea what he was doing but somehow I also did. Does that make any sense? I knew it was bad. I knew it was dirty, and I knew beyond anything else that it made me feel terrible.

He had all his clothes on but that didn't make it any easier to stomach. He went back and forth on top of me, rubbing over my body for what seemed like three weeks, and then he came to an exhausted sudden halt, huffing and puffing away like his big, fat body had been running after an ice cream truck. His breath was hot against my neck, and I struggled to avoid it blowing into my face. He lay there, still, not really knowing how to let me up. Maybe he thought I was going to do something like run and tell somebody? I felt like a rabbit in the jaws of a wolf.

I am sure I was only about eighty pounds when I was ten. He must have been at least twice my size. I certainly couldn't move out from underneath him. I was pinned there like a rag doll. I should have screamed, but I didn't. I should've hit him or kicked him, but I didn't. I didn't do anything at all. I cried a lot afterwards and locked myself into the bathroom down there in the basement, hoping he'd be gone when I finally had the courage to come out. Like so many girls, I thought I had done something wrong. I thought that I had done something to make him do that to me.

My ten-year-old self couldn't process any of it. I tried not to think about him and "it," but as I got older I'd occasionally see him at a family get-together and I'd do my best to act normal, whatever that was. I felt like everybody around me could see my memory floating through the air like a black balloon. It still creeps into my head on a sunny Sunday afternoon.

I want other girls to know, yeah, it happened to me too. You're not alone. I wasn't raped, but I was violated. The brutality against so many women on this planet defies goodness on every level. Sexual assaults have lasting, lifelong effects on the human soul.

I should have told my mom sooner than I did, but eventually it all came out. She was very understanding and empathetic. I realized, years later, that my cousin was going to be the one who had to live with the shame, not me. That was a good realization. I don't let the memory hurt me anymore.

Becoming a person can be difficult, to say the least. You are inundated with so many experiences and so much information. There are trillions of tiny bits and pieces of universal information that sift through your head at any given moment, like how does my brain make my fingers move, what kind of sandwich should I make, should I pull off this hangnail really quickly or clip most of it off to avoid the pain I know it's going to cause if I just yank it off? I found myself lying in bed, wondering how I was going to make sense of it all. If getting my period was the only thing I had to worry about I would have been laughing, but, oh no, there were myriad things far worse than a menstrual cycle.

For two or three years I felt completely overwhelmed by everything. My hormones were running around my body like hungry truckers at a buffet. Hairs popped up in places I never even knew I had. I was plucking them out as fast as my tweezers could tweeze. I finally had to give up on the hair removal because I was starting to look like a rotisserie chicken. And the mental and emotional part of growing up wasn't any easier than the physical part. When I dragged religion into the whole equation, I started feeling like I was certifiably nuts.

I wondered more and more about who in heaven's name God was.

Was God:

A)   A really big person?

B)   A UFO?

C)   A lost astronaut from another galaxy?

D)   A friend of my Mormon grandmother's?

E)   None of the above?

I had a Buddhist friend who told me that I was God. That God was *in* me. No wonder I was feeling like I was putting on weight.

I prayed every night that I would wake up with all my spiritual queries answered. I was prepared for whatever answer God wanted to give me. I just wanted to know one way or the other what the hell was going on. I prayed constantly and read the Bible religiously (how else can you read a Bible?). I enjoyed parts of it, where there was an actual story, but for the most part I was completely and utterly lost. The "begats" made my brain hurt. Did we really need to know who begat whom and for that many pages? To tell you the truth I skipped through most of the begats and ahead to the parts where everybody was killing each other. (Nothing has changed, it seems, we're still doing that today . . .)

The Bible had a lot of rules that I knew full well I was not going to be able to abide by. Two thousand years ago, my menstrual cycle would have really caused me some problems. For instance, I would have had to either live in a tent with some other broads for the entire week or leave town altogether. If Biblical men were the ones having the periods, it would have been a time to drink and feast and have full body massages. Eating pork would have also posed a big problem for me back then since that's what my mother had bubbling away in her Crock-Pot at least once a week. I would have been stoned on the spot. They revise a dictionary every year, for crying out loud! High time to revise the Good Book, I would think.

I didn't like the fact that according to my dad's very Mormon mother—my grandmother Richards—God knew what I was thinking and could see everything I did, including when I was having my period. It was hard going to the bathroom after that without wanting to completely cover myself with a towel, and sometimes I did cover myself with a towel and I am not kidding.

I wondered how God could see every single person on the planet and know what they were doing, never mind what they were thinking. It seemed impossible that God could keep track of us all. My head felt like it was going to cave in on itself. My mom told me I was too young to be worrying so much about God, and that it was actually God's job to be worrying about me. She was probably right. My mother always knew what to say to make me feel better.

My grandmother Richards told me that all people were sinners, and that I was a sinner too and that I needed to repent and work harder in school. She told me that I needed to remain steadfast, whatever that meant. I always thought she smelled a little bit like a Kleenex box, if that's possible. Maybe because she had so many Kleenexes stuffed into one of her bra cups. (She'd had a breast removed due to a cancer scare in the fifties.) Whenever she wiped my face, I knew exactly where she got the tissue from. It was a bit creepy, but handy just the same. I think she kept a deck of cards in there, too, and a Yahtzee game. My grandma loved to play Yahtzee. Growing up, I must have played two million games of Yahtzee with her. I would be in her good graces, and God's, if I let her win. I threw the games on purpose almost every time.

I think my grandmother Richards would have been a lot nicer and happier had her husband, my dad's dad, not passed away so young. She was left with a young family to raise, and it must have been hard being alone. She didn't have a lot of friends, according to my mother. She had church friends and that was it. She wasn't the type of person to invite the neighbours over for coffee because A) she didn't like the neighbours and B) she didn't drink coffee. My grandmother had Jesus and she made sure we knew that practically every time she spoke. I wanted God to be anything but what she believed him to be. Her version of him seemed really scary.

Her God was mad at everybody, handing out punishment and fear, stomping his feet on the ground when he didn't get his way. Her God had more rules for getting into heaven than I knew what to do with. I wasn't going to be able to abide by them all. She told me that families were forever and that she hoped I was going to be able to come with her into eternal life. Not at the rate I was going, I thought. If drinking coffee or beer or wine was going to keep me locked out of Eden, well, I guess I was a lost cause. (Maybe decaf would have been okay, but I'm not sure. I'll have to go back and check *Mormonism for Dummies*.)

Grandma Richards and I didn't quite see eye to eye about God, that's for certain. I guess she would be travelling to wherever it was in the ether of the afterlife without me. I didn't have any plans on dying, anyway, so I could wipe that off of my worry plate for the time being. I was planning on living a long, long time.

chapter eleven

THE LAST SUMMER

managed to graduate from high school, but just barely. I never studied for a single test, I never listened to instructions and I didn't care about anything even remotely academic. Other than that I was a great student.

I was short only three measly credits going into my last semester of high school, but I had to somehow make them up in order to pass. I was sent to my school guidance counsellor to figure out what I could do. He informed me that my choice was to take an extra class or take an extra class—so, well, I took the extra class. It involved me staying after school to work with and learn from a local farmer. I was the only student who was going to be taking that extra class, which had something to do with fertilizer. I didn't think that that sounded all that bad, but I ended up standing on the back of a manure spreader pulling a lever that shot cow poo a hundred feet into the air. Nobody told me that fertilizer was *poo*. I thought fertilizer was fertilizer. For that simple act, which perhaps took me three or four hours at a time, I earned the three lousy credits that enabled me to graduate with my class. The lowest possible number of credits needed to graduate from an Alberta high school is one hundred. I graduated with 101. I had never been so proud. My parents were beyond relieved, as you can imagine.

I wasn't even on the ballot but my classmates elected me grad chairman. I was in charge of organizing our party, hiring the band, finding a venue, selling the tickets, planning the meal: the whole nine yards. I had never done anything of the sort but I was excited. Thank God the rest of the grad committee were smart and talented and organized because I was useless. I couldn't organize my own sock drawer.

Because there were only forty-two of us, our grad wouldn't require as much planning as grads for Calgary High School, which usually had about fifteen hundred students. Going to a small school had its advantages. We could have had our grad at a KFC but we didn't, thank God.

The hardest part of planning the entire thing would be finding someone to go with me. I hadn't thought about that a lot; I was too busy worrying about God watching me when I was in the bathroom. The scramble to find a date started in March for most people and most of my friends were all set. I was one of the only girls who didn't have a date.

There wasn't really anybody that I liked all that much. Mark was out of the question, and the boy I sort of liked was already spoken for as well as most of the boys my age and older. I had known most of these boys since the fourth grade so they were all kind of like my brothers and not grad-date material. But I don't think that was the point—the point was I needed to not be going alone. It would have been really easy to go with Theresa but I don't think her boyfriend would have been too keen on that. I was going to have to do the unthinkable and ask someone a grade below me, *oh the horror!* I would almost certainly be ridiculed but it was a chance I'd have to take. Asking someone a year older would have been no problem whatsoever—I would have been considered incredibly cool—but asking someone a year younger meant I was a desperate loser.

I don't know where I found the courage but I finally managed to go up to an eleventh grader named Stuart Richardson and ask him if he wanted to go to grad with me. He actually accepted, which I was totally unprepared for. In my mind I had already heard him say, "No, thank you, I have to bathe my ailing South African grandmother that night." Stuart probably had no idea how important it was for me to have him accept. I am pretty sure that he didn't want to hurt my feelings and that's why he agreed to go with me. It was not a perfect scenario: my parents drove Stuart and me in their car and my mother made the dress I wore and there were still a few pins left in the hem, but the night turned out to be a great success. As grad chairman I could be proud. All I had to survive now was making it through my debut performance.

As I sat through the dinner, I worried about singing my song. It took up all the space in my brain. I hadn't ever sung in front of anybody before, so I wasn't sure if I would faint or not. I couldn't imagine what it was going to feel like. In fact, I didn't know if I could go through with it, period. My thousands of hours of secret singing in my parents' basement had in no way prepared me to play in front of a live audience. I had spent a number of months trying to figure out how I was going to sing a song I had written for my classmates. No one in my family—never mind my school—knew that I played the guitar and wrote songs, so it was going to be a bit complicated. I didn't want to be made fun of. I was known as the class clown, not the girl who sings a serious ballad about having to say goodbye to life as we knew it.

I had practised the song a thousand times in the basement and had tried to visualize my classmates sitting there at the grad ceremony in their underpants. (I had read somewhere that that's how

Karen Carpenter got over her stage fright.) I told myself I didn't really care what the kids thought since I was going to be getting out of Dodge anyway, but I was worried about what my mom and dad would think. More than anything else, I did not want my parents to think I was crazy. I was sure they'd be shocked, considering they didn't know I was the least bit musical. Trust me, I was shocked myself.

I finally walked up to the band leader and explained that I had written a song for my classmates and wanted to sing it to them. I am not sure he trusted me entirely, but he lent me his guitar and set me up behind a microphone. (I had forgotten I would need a guitar!) I don't think I have ever been so afraid in my entire life. My lips went completely numb, and I felt like I was going to fold in on myself. One of my eyelids kept twitching—I would have glued it shut if I could have. My mouth was as dry as dirt, and I found it incredibly hard to swallow. I don't remember singing at all, only the fear and the panic and anxiety. I stood there in the dress my mother had made me, with this huge electric guitar flung over my shoulder, and looked out at a sea of dropped jaws. My classmates were looking up at me on that stage in total disbelief and I watched their faces change from surprise to confusion. I felt like flying around the ballroom and like throwing up. I wondered if a person could throw up and fly around at the same time.

My mom and dad looked like they were going to bawl, and maybe they did cry a little bit—I couldn't see that far away and besides, my eyes were watering profusely. I finished the song and to my great relief I was not booed off the stage. I don't remember anybody clapping, although I think they must have, even if it was just because they felt sorry for me. The rest of the night was a blur. Everybody danced and drank and laughed and made promises to keep in touch. We all felt like we'd completed the most important chapter of our lives. None of us had the slightest inkling of what lay ahead. The band played until about one in the morning and then, as quickly as it had all begun, our big night wound itself into a tight little ball and rolled itself to bed. (There was a fairly wild after-party, which of course entailed a bonfire, beer, potato chips and someone throwing up in the trees.)

My mom and dad didn't say much about my song. My mom said, "I didn't know you liked music." I shrugged and said, "Yeah, I guess I do." A decade later my mom told me that she and dad thought that I was as good as Anne Murray. I thought that was adorable.

The day after the grad party, I went to Hawaii with Theresa and two other girls for a week. For some reason still unknown to me, my parents actually let me go. I guess Theresa told her folks that my parents said it was okay and I told my parents that her parents said it was okay. I was eighteen years old and on a small island twelve hundred miles from home. I felt like I had won the lottery! For $400 each we flew to Oahu and stayed in a two-bedroom hotel suite twenty-seven floors above the beach. We were all thrilled to be there. I had $200 of spending money with me, which I blew through in a few days by tipping every person that looked at me and smiled. Theresa, God love her, paid for me for the rest of the holiday. We still laugh about that trip and about how young we were. We were so incredibly naive. None of us had ever been anywhere before.

Theresa saw her first penis on that trip. She went on a joyride with a local boy she'd met at the bar, who thought it would be incredibly romantic if he "pulled his goalie," so to speak, right there in front of her. Theresa didn't even touch him but she thought that some of "it" might have gotten onto her pant leg. She was so upset she cried. Believe it or not, not a single one of us knew for sure how sperm worked. We had an idea but we didn't trust our biology class completely. You can never be too careful when it comes to sperm, so we bought a pregnancy test at the pharmacy just to be on the safe side.

I had no idea what I was going to do with my life when I got home from Oahu. I didn't like thinking about it too hard or too long. I felt like I had to grow up overnight. My mother used to tell me that one day I would have to be the one buying my own toilet paper and toothpaste. One day I would have to be responsible for my own well-being. One day I wouldn't be able to live at home and just pull things out of the fridge and scarf them down. One day I would have to be my own person and look after my own life. What an outrage.

There was nothing carefree about the rest of the summer in Springbank. The days all felt fragmented and chaotic. I wasn't going back to high school in September to daydream the hours away, hanging out with my friends and playing basketball and badminton. I wasn't going to be standing around my locker in the hallway gabbing about who was going to be having a party on the weekend. I was going to have to grow up and find a job.

My parents prodded me about what I wanted to do. I kept telling them that I wanted to go into drama. (*Drama?* I didn't even *like* drama.) Why the hell that came out of my mouth I will never know. What I really wanted to be was a teacher of some kind, but my grades weren't good enough to get me into any of the college-level courses I'd need to take. To upgrade my high school diploma would take time and effort. Teaching would have to be put on the back burner—in fact, teaching wouldn't even be making it onto the stove.

I decided to enroll in the drama program at Mount Royal College in Calgary, even though it wasn't even remotely what I wanted to do. Drama wouldn't require me to do anything but breathe in and out, and I wouldn't need to upgrade my academic status. I never once thought that I could go into music for a living. Someone like me didn't do something like that. I let any grandiose ideas about that just pour out onto the basement floor.

Thank God my parents helped me to buy an old Ford Pinto that summer, simply because they were sick and tired of driving me around. Now I had a way of getting myself into Calgary. The Pinto was white with a red racing stripe, and I thought it was gorgeous. My dad's friend had painted it in his garage, but it still looked really good. It only had 270,000 kilometres on it, which made it practically brand new! The radio worked and it had a functioning cassette deck so I felt like I had hit the vehicular jackpot. You could get it up to a whopping fifty miles an hour in twenty seconds *if* you were headed straight down a mountain with the gas pedal matted to the floor.

Note to self: Check the oil if the little red oil light is on.

P.S. If the oil light is on, it's probably too late.

It dawned on me one day in my parents' basement that I had never actually heard myself sing before. I mean, I had recorded my songs into my little cassette recorder but they sounded pretty terrible. I started going through the Yellow Pages to see if there were any professional studios in the city where I could go and record a couple of my songs for real. I found two, one of which was called Circa Sound and the other of which was too far across town to even consider getting to it in my Ford Pinto. I didn't know how to go about booking anything, or what I was actually looking to do, so I figured I should simply call the number in the book and take it from there. A guy named Bruce picked up the phone. I probably gave him too much information about myself and what I wanted to do because he kept saying "I see" and "I understand." He told me that he had time available that Thursday and that all I needed to do was come in with my guitar and he would do a demo of my songs. It sounded simple enough. It would cost thirty-five dollars an hour to record them onto a two-track, whatever that was.

I was excited to hear what I sounded like on a real recording. Surely I could come up with thirty-five dollars. All I had to do was get there! I practised like mad trying to decide which two songs to record. The songs I chose to record were two of my very best: "Never Love a Sailor," penned on my Oahu graduation trip, and "Disillusioned."

When Thursday finally rolled around, I realized that I didn't have any gas in my tank. I ended up siphoning gas out of my mom's car and, trust me, it's a really horrible thing to do if you don't know exactly what you're doing. But Duray was a good teacher when it came to things like that, and I soon had a quarter of a tank, which would get me to town and back if I didn't get lost or go too fast. I grabbed my mother's giant Yamaha guitar and I was off!

I was surprised to arrive at an old house—nothing like what I had pictured—but I parked outside and went up to the front door to ring the bell. Bruce was about forty-five years old. He had little round glasses like John Lennon and was very soft spoken. I thought that he looked a bit nerdy. He wasted little time getting me set up to sing. He got me a stool, propped me in front of the microphone and said that we could begin anytime. He told me to relax and be as natural as possible. So that's what I did. I started strumming and singing, and about forty-five minutes later I had my two songs on tape.

Bruce told me he was amazed at what came out of my mouth. I told him I had written the songs myself; that seemed to amaze him even more. We sat behind the console in the studio and listened back to what I'd just done. I was so surprised to hear my voice clearly for the first time. I thought it sounded pretty good. Bruce asked me a million questions about my writing and where I had been performing and how long I'd been singing. He went on and on. I told him that I had never performed anywhere but at my grad. I don't think he believed me.

As I turned to the door with my cassette tape in hand, he said that for $1,500 he could hire a band and really do a professional demo for me of the two songs I had just recorded. Fifteen hundred dollars was a far cry from $35. I had no idea how I was going to swing that but I really wanted to.

I told him I'd get back to him and I started off again towards the door. Then he said, "Well, I could probably do a good job for $1,000." A thousand dollars seemed a little more doable to me but it was still a stretch. I only knew two people who might have that kind of money: my mom and dad.

I told Bruce I'd have to call him in a few days, that I'd talk to my parents and see what they thought of the whole idea. I told him it was a lot of money and he told me that he thought he could get me played on the radio. I couldn't believe it. I was completely twisted up inside just thinking about it. Me, being played on the radio. How in the world could that be?

I was nervous about bringing it up with my parents. I didn't have a job and I wasn't going to school. I kind of already knew what the answer was going to be from my dad. It was going to be no. In fact, it was probably actually going to be a "No, goddammit," and "Do you think I'm made of goddamn money?" Believe it or not, instead he said, "When do you need it?" He wanted to meet this Bruce to see if he was on the up-and-up. He told me that I would have to pay him back in full or that would be the last goddamn dime I ever got from him. I thought that was a fair enough deal.

Bruce hired a band and I went in a few weeks later and recorded my very first professional 45 rpm. It seemed too good to be true and, of course, if something seems too good to be true, it usually is. Bruce somehow talked us into ordering two thousand copies of the 45 and it ended up costing my dad a heck of a lot more money than a thousand dollars.

I drove myself right to the radio station downtown and handed my 45 to the lady at the front desk of the Canadian Broadcasting Corporation; I told her to give it to the DJ if she didn't mind. I told her that I hoped he would play it on his show that day. She looked at me like I had just been let out of the loony bin. Obviously I had no idea how these things worked. I was just naive enough to be a tiny bit confident. A few days later I was in the car with my mom and we heard "Never Love a Sailor" come on the radio. We both looked at each other in utter disbelief. After the song played, the CBC announcer said my name and called me a local singer/songwriter. I just about died and so did my mother. It was exciting beyond anything I had ever experienced. I never heard it again, although a few of my friends did.

I had made it onto the radio and that was something. A few short weeks later, I was feeling so very low. I wasn't really enjoying adulthood. It was far too serious, as far as I was concerned. I still had 1,999 bloody copies of my 45 and I had no idea what I was going to do with them. I guess I would be storing all those boxes in my parents' basement, right next to my dashed hopes. My parents could have said "I told you so," but they didn't.

One day in late August, I got a call at my parents' house; the voice on the line asked to speak to Jann Richards. (I thought that was really odd because I seldom got phone calls—when the phone rang it was either work for my dad or the police looking for my brother.) I told him that he was speaking to Jann Richards. My heart skipped for a moment because I hoped it was going to be something about me being on the radio. Maybe it was a big record producer from Los Angeles who was going to ask me to sign a recording contract.

The voice identified himself as a teacher from my former high school and said that he had some very tragic news. The worst possible things started racing through my mind—one of them being that I hadn't graduated after all, that it was all a huge mistake and I was going to have to go back and work some more on the shit-spreader. I wish that had been what he was calling me about, but it wasn't. One of my good friends, Marilyn, had passed away from complications following a colostomy. I remember hanging on to the phone like it was a life preserver. My ears buzzed with the emptiness of silence. I felt my heart begin to beat madly in my chest, and I broke down sobbing. I didn't know anybody my own age who had died and certainly not anybody I'd loved so dearly. It was so beyond my comprehension.

I loved Marilyn; everybody did. She was athletic, smart, funny; she glowed. She was one of those people who honestly never said a bad word about anybody. She floated around like she wasn't human. I know people always talk about the dearly departed like they were saints, but she really *was* a saint. To think she was somehow just gone broke my heart and everybody else's too.

I had known Marilyn since the fourth grade. I sat beside her in many of our classes and we'd laugh our heads off at silly things and write goofy love notes to boys. We didn't hang out much after the bell rang, but we were still very close "school friends." Marilyn was there when I had to pick my wiener out of my Thermos with my pencil. Marilyn was there when my Thermos exploded from having atomic chili in it. Marilyn was there with all of us, standing around at the bonfire parties with a beer in her hand, singing along to Fleetwood Mac. Marilyn was on all the teams with me, basketball and volleyball and baseball. When I did silly things she'd throw her brown hair back and just giggle like mad—nothing was off limits when it came to making her smile. She had the whitest teeth and the most beautiful skin. I remember her putting Jergens lotion on all the time. Every day after gym class, she'd slather half a bottle of the almond-smelling liquid all over her body. She always looked tanned to me, like she lived in Miami half the year. She seemed far more mature than her years let on.

She missed a lot of high school and none of us really knew why. There would be months when she just wasn't there. Her friends finally found out when she gathered up a few of us to tell us about her illness. She had struggled with colitis for many years and had finally, after a long battle with the disease, opted to get the "bag" installed. She was only eighteen, and I am sure it was a monumental, life-altering decision to have to make. She had so much going for her. She was engaged to a great guy named Gary, and we all thought she was destined to be the most successful of all of us.

I had just seen Marilyn at a little cocktail lounge in Calgary a few months before. She was heading out to British Columbia to go to college. We all got together for a bite to eat and a beer to see her off. She looked so happy and healthy.

The voice on the line told me that there was going to be a memorial service for Marilyn in Kamloops, British Columbia, later that week, and asked me if I could go to represent our class. I was trying to absorb all the information coming at me. I didn't know what I should do. Kamloops was nine hours away and there was no one to get a ride with. I was going to have to figure out how to get there myself.

My Ford Pinto had blown its engine a few weeks earlier, so it wasn't going to be an option to drive the 442 kilometres—through the Rocky Mountains, I might add—without it catching on fire. By the time I hung up the phone I decided I was going to have to borrow a bit of money out of the grad fund to take the train. I wasn't going to borrow any more money from my parents at the risk of my own life.

I was the grad chairman, after all, and I still had access to the leftover funds in the bank. Our graduating class had yet to decide what we were going to do with the $1,500 we had left over in the bank. We had talked about having some kind of stupid big rock engraved and plunked in front of the school that said "Grad '80," or repainting the gym floor with the school emblem, neither of which I thought were interesting options. I knew that attending Marilyn's funeral was the best possible thing to do with that leftover money. I was going to represent the entire class and go to her memorial. I took out $600, bought train tickets for myself and a few of her closest friends and a large bottle of Alberta vodka, and off we went to pay our respects to a really wonderful girl.

We stayed for a couple of nights at a hotel in Kamloops; we ate out at some crummy little restaurants; we visited with Marilyn's family and cried buckets of tears in between. I was so glad to have gone.

A few days after I had come home from the funeral, I got another call from a teacher who wanted me to come out to the high school to see him about some missing money as soon as I possibly could. Feeling defiant, to say the least, I took my mother's car and drove out there the next day.

He acted like he was a Supreme Court judge and I was in the witness stand begging for my life. But I wasn't one of his students anymore. I was a real person now. I simply said to Mister Whatever-his-name-was that he needed either to drop the whole thing or call the police because I wasn't the least bit sorry about what I'd done, and furthermore I didn't appreciate the way he was talking to me. He looked at me like I had three heads and one nostril in each of them. He kept tapping his pencil on the top of his desk lamp and telling me how serious it all was, that what I had done was illegal. When he wasn't tapping his pencil, he was shuffling papers like he was looking for some kind of new and damning information. I sat there, staring at him as hard and as long as I possibly could. I tried my very best not to blink more than twice. Blinking just makes people look nervous. I didn't want to look the least bit nervous, because I wasn't.

"I'm going to let it go this time," he said. "You could have been in a lot of trouble, young lady." He went on and on about ethics and honour and trust. My eyes were dried out and on the brink of falling out of my head from not blinking once while he droned on. When he was done, I took a deep breath and let him have it. I told him that it wasn't his money, nor was it the school's money. I told him it belonged to the graduating students of the class of 1980 and that they would be the only ones who could press charges of any kind. (I hoped they wouldn't press charges.) He told me to watch my mouth and I mumbled "fuck off" under my breath and it just about sent him through the ceiling tiles.

I left his office feeling puffed up and victorious. The class of 1980 never pressed charges. A few of the kids even expressed happiness that I'd gone to the funeral. I knew the whole school would have been there for her had she passed away in Springbank. Marilyn would have been smiling from tip to toe knowing what I'd done, I knew that for sure.

Dying didn't seem so far away from me now. Losing Marilyn to that giant, unknown void was a huge awakening for me. I lay in bed for weeks afterwards, worrying about dying. It was parked at my front door, right beside my blown-up Ford Pinto. Marilyn's death was a wee glimpse into what it was going to be like to be a grown-up person. Grown-up people had their hands full of hurt most days, or at least that's what it looked like to me. Perhaps the universe was going to test my ability to fail with grace. Whatever it was that was coming, it felt ominous.

I still hadn't started college. I had to wait and enrol in the second semester because I had missed the fall deadlines, so I had some more time to kill (or waste, more like it). I was pretty much wandering around, watching the world go by on the back of a truck. I watched TV and thought too much. I wondered why God would choose to call someone like Marilyn, of all people, home? Why in the world wasn't it one of those bastard bullies at school? Why wasn't it me? I thought about the ever-expanding universe my dad had told me about. What was my universe expanding into? Never mind.

All my friends were off and running, attending classes at university, becoming something, and I was still in my parents' basement, strumming the guitar and writing songs that no one would ever hear (except one or two people who listened to the CBC, which was better than nothing).

My parents weren't sure what to do with me. They kept hoping I'd make up my mind about my future and at least start down a path to somewhere. They didn't discourage me from pursuing music as a career, but they also didn't want to see me have my heart busted into a million pieces. My parents were very practical: they knew as well as I did that people like me didn't dare imagine a life in show business. I knew they were right. It didn't bother me all that much, to tell you the truth. I wasn't a dreamer by any stretch of the imagination. But I wasn't realistic, either.

Duray had dropped out before he finished high school, so they were more or less counting on me to make something of myself. I felt a constant pressure to get it right for them. Duray had moved into a whole new league of bad behaviour: getting charged with impaired driving and assault and vandalism. He was in and out of court and it was costing my folks a small fortune in lawyers and fines. Drugs and alcohol had moved into his body and taken over his life. It was like watching a house on fire and having no way to put it out. I was pretty sure that there wasn't enough water in the world to put my brother's burning house out. He was far too busy drinking gasoline.

My mom told me that if I wasn't going to be going to school that fall, I would absolutely have to get a real job. I was too old to be washing golf clubs and picking up balls from the local driving range and needed something that would pay more than four bucks an hour. My dad, thank God, got me a job as a flag girl through one of his connections at work. He told me not to screw it up because it would reflect badly on him. I told him I would try not to but I couldn't actually guarantee anything.

It certainly wasn't my dream to work on a road crew, but I considered myself lucky to be working at all. I hated getting up at 5:30 in the morning. There couldn't possibly be anything worse on the planet than getting oneself up before the sun had even made an appearance. I had been going to bed at 5:30 in the morning, but those days were coming to an abrupt end.

My friend Patti got a job working on the road crew as well and so there we were, standing in the middle of a dusty construction site, directing cars back and forth all day long. We wore yellow hard hats and white jumpsuits that made us look like we were on some kind of a weird chain gang. We had signs that said "Stop" on one side, and "Slow" on the other. I am surprised both of us survived unscathed. I was almost run over a half-dozen times by graters and dump trucks. One woman actually ran over my foot one day in her Toyota Corolla. She just kept going, even after she heard me holler. Who would have thought that steel-toed boots actually served a purpose? Fashionable? No. Safe? Indeed!

It was a filthy existence. I came home with dirt in my belly button and gravel in my ears. It took me half an hour to shower the debris off my body. But none of that bothered me when I started getting my paycheques. For a minute or so, I pondered being a flag girl for the rest of my life. I was earning $900 every two weeks! I had never seen that much money in my life. My excitement wore off after about two months of standing on the side of that road, waiting for the hours to creep by. The weather was starting to get crappy as well. It was getting colder and raining a lot. It was fine standing out there when the sun was shining, but when it was cold and damp it was miserable. I couldn't wait much longer to figure out my life. I still had a few hurdles to jump over—and keep in mind, I was really short.

I went to a party in the city one Saturday night at my friend Cindy's house. (I didn't work Sundays at the construction site, so I could stay out a bit late.) I knew a lot of people there, some from school and some not. For the most part it was all the usual suspects, with the usual things going on. I can describe the scene with my eyes closed: there are bodies gathered around a kitchen table, shoving chips into their heads and guzzling beer. Music blasts from speakers that have long since seen their glory days. Lights flicker dimly or are off completely, depending on how late it's getting, and cigarette smoke billows into the air like small gathering storms. There are loud conversations in every corner of every room, and high-pitched drunken-girl laughs echo off the walls. Piles of shoes are kicked off at the front door, coats and scarves are strewn over chairs and couches, bottles and empty plastic cups litter every square foot of the carpeted floor. All the parties looked the same. Cindy's house was no different—it was a mess. Her parents weren't home, which was why these parties happened in the first place. Boys and girls visited the bedrooms upstairs and then came back downstairs twenty minutes later with huge grins on their faces.

I tried to convince myself that I was having fun, but it did cross my mind that I was bored and more or less on the outside looking in at something I didn't fit into. Part of me knew better than to be standing in the middle of a kitchen with a bunch of people I didn't care about and who didn't care about me. I had a funny weird feeling lingering in my chest. What was I doing there? Nothing, that's what.

My mom had dropped me off about 7:30, and it was almost 12:45 when it dawned on me to look at a clock. I was supposed to be home by 1 a.m. I had arranged a ride with a friend, but my ride was drunk and had been gnawing on a big, greasy piece of pizza and was now throwing it up into Cindy's mom's kitchen garbage can. I was pretty sure I wasn't going to be getting into a car with her. Cindy told me I could sleep over, but I didn't want my dad killing me before I found my true calling so I looked around for other options. I asked if anybody was driving anywhere near Springbank— well, I yelled it, actually. One guy in the living room said he was going out that way. I was saved. I sort of knew him, which made it even better.

Conrad lived in Calgary but I'd seen him at basketball games out at the high school, and I'd run into him at a little bar Theresa and I used to go to. I had talked to him at least half a dozen times, so he wasn't a stranger. He was always very nice to me. He called me at my parents' house a few times, inviting me to movies or to go bowling; it just never seemed to work out that I could go.

That night Conrad was going to drop off another girl, whom I also knew, before me, so I felt comfortable going with them. We dropped her off at her parents' house, she waved goodbye as she walked up her driveway, and then we headed out of town to Springbank. I asked him if he was sure it wasn't too far for him to go, and he insisted that it wasn't. I told him that I could call my parents to come and get me from the Co-op. I knew my mom would pick me up from there if I needed her to. Conrad told me not to be silly, that it was right on his way. I guess I believed him—

I didn't know where he lived, so I couldn't be sure if I was on his way or not. I was feeling uneasy, but what could I do? I was in the car and it was late and my options were very limited. There was no way I could walk home. It was miles. I was worried about the time. I didn't have a watch on, but I knew it was a lot later than one in the morning.

We chatted a little bit about the party and where he was going to go to school. It was just small talk to make the time go by. Everything seemed normal. When we were getting close to my house, Conrad made a sudden turn down an old gravel road. I felt sick to my stomach immediately. I knew whatever he was doing was not good. I told him that that wasn't my road and he said, "I know, I thought we could just park for a minute. It's all okay, I'll get you home."

I told him I was going to be in trouble if I was late, that my parents were expecting me.

"Come on, they won't mind," he said. "It'll just be a few minutes." He leaned into me and tried to kiss my mouth. His tongue jabbed at my lips like an eel. I pushed him back, or tried to. I was shocked; he was insistent. He just kept trying to kiss me and grab my breasts through my jacket. He started pulling at the buttons and trying to get himself up on top of me. I felt cramped and claustrophobic in his small car. I had nowhere to go.

I begged him to get off me. That was met with, "Aw, come on, let's fool around a bit, I really like you." If you really like me, I thought to myself, don't do this. As soon as he got around my jacket he began pulling at the clasps on my baby-blue overalls. Yes, I was wearing overalls, which you'd think would be boy-proof, but they weren't. Conrad grabbed the top clasps and ripped them off and in a split second had jammed his left hand down inside my pants. I started screaming and struggling to get him off. It was like he didn't hear me at all. Our bodies were tangled up and I didn't know where he began and I ended. I kept trying to force him back. I did fight, I did holler, I told him to *stop stop stop!* and then all at once I felt the most incredible piercing pain shoot through my stomach. He had somehow managed to shove his fingers into my vagina with such force that I felt like I was going to faint. It hurt so badly—as if he had torn me in two. I must have really screamed bloody murder because he stopped immediately. Just like that, he pulled his arm back and leapt to his side of the car.

He seemed surprised that he had really hurt me. I was crying so hard I couldn't see a foot in front of my face. It was so dark out. I managed to get my overalls back on and began looking for the missing clasp. I couldn't figure out what had just happened. I tried pulling on the door handle, but he'd started the car back up and turned on the headlights. We were beginning to roll back over the gravel towards the main road. I just cried and cried and begged him to take me home. We were about three miles from my house at this point.

"I didn't mean to hurt you," he said. "I was just fooling around." I was sobbing and I could feel blood trickling between my legs. I had so much snot coming out of my nose that I couldn't breathe. It was the kind of crying where you just suck gasps of air into your lungs like you're drowning. I could hardly speak.

"Are you a virgin?" he said. What an idiot.

I didn't answer him. I just cried. It was all I could do.

I *was* a virgin, I thought to myself. I'm pretty sure I'm not now.

"Please . . . just . . . take . . . me . . . me . . . me . . . home," I quietly murmured, snot pouring down my face.

"I'm really sorry. I didn't mean to . . . I didn't mean to." He kept repeating that as we drove the agonizing remaining miles to my house.

"Are you going to tell your parents?" he said to me.

"No, I'm not," was all I managed to say. And I never did.

Conrad pulled into the dark driveway and I nearly leapt out onto the ground before he'd come to a full stop. I didn't even close the door behind me, I just ran for the back door and never looked back. I watched his headlights go around the bend and then I stood by the washer and dryer and bawled. My overalls were destroyed. I had blood down the legs and my clasps were torn off. One of them was still in his car, I assumed, because I didn't have it. I was in so much pain it was hard to walk. The force of his fingers inside of me had ripped something, because I was still bleeding. I got a wad of toilet paper from the bathroom and placed it carefully between my legs. I was going to have to throw the overalls away. They were ruined, and I definitely didn't want my mom to see the blood or the torn fabric. I took them off and wrapped them into a ball and put them in a plastic bag. After I'd put my pyjamas on and got cleaned up, I went outside and put the whole works into the burning barrel, where we burned all our garbage. I picked up the shovel and covered the bag with ashes so no one would see it. The next day, it would just burn with everything else, and no one would ever know a thing about it.

I lay in bed that night, shaking and upset, and more or less whimpered until I finally fell asleep. I felt tears roll down the side of my face, most of them winding up in my eardrums. I went over the whole thing in my brain. Not one thing about it made any sense to me. He seemed like such a decent person. I knew him. What did he think he was doing? Why did he do it? What did I do to make him behave like that? I was so ashamed and so depressed. I was worried about my mom and dad finding out. I needed to take the whole night and put it away somewhere that nobody would be able to find it. Not even me.

chapter twelve

THE EXPANDING UNIVERSE

was glad to finally be starting at Mount Royal College in the drama program. I had to do something with my life. My mom told me that if I didn't like it I could just switch and take something else. She always put my mind at ease, even if she didn't mean to.

The first few days were a bit daunting. I had never seen so many crazy hairdos and strange outfits in my life. Everyone looked like they were going out of their way to be different from everyone else, which kind of made everyone look the same. It wasn't anything remotely like little old Springbank High School. The place was huge, and everybody rushed about with purpose and determination. I wondered where they were all going and why they were running to get there.

My classmates ranged from seventeen to forty-five years old. Clarice, who had two grown kids and a failed marriage, had decided to go back to school to become an actress. She spent all her time memorizing monologues and auditioning for plays. I was arriving mid-year and she had attended for a whole semester already, so she knew many important things, such as who I should and should not

hang out with and where to eat lunch. We became friends right
away, and I was grateful to have her showing me the ropes.

I hadn't ever thought about being an actress, but that's why
Clarice and most of these people were taking drama. They wanted
to act. I wanted to be a teacher. Oh well, I thought. I have to make
the best of it because my dad paid for six months' tuition and I can't
quit and take anything else until then or he'll see it as one more of
my flighty attempts to waste time.

I spent most of my days doing really bizarre things. Movement
class basically entailed my donning tights and leg warmers and
leaping around a large, mirrored room pretending to be a butterfly.
The class was all about being in touch with your body and, therefore,
the entire universe, or so said our instructor, Mrs. Grey. Part of me
wanted to light myself on fire. Another of my classes had me learning how to speak properly for the theatre. I likened it to controlled,
articulate yelling. Always concentrating on projection, diction and
enunciation, we basically made a lot of motorboat sounds and those
raspberries you blow on a baby's bare stomach. I was really glad my
dad wasn't sitting in the back of any of my classes. He would have
had me committed.

I don't know if I was learning anything but I was certainly
meeting some incredibly nutty people, many of whom I came to
adore. One girl named Dallas came to school every day in dresses
from the fifties. She had cat's-eye glasses and a wonderfully fluffy
hairdo. She must have gotten up at 5 a.m. to start combing it all into
place. Sheri D. was an incredible poet and writer. Everyone listened
when she spoke and heeded her every whim. She had a deep voice
that made me think of John Wayne if he had had a sex change and
was a lot prettier. Sheri showed me what confidence looked like.

I hadn't really met any gay people before, and there seemed to
be a heck of a lot of them in my college theatre course. The gay

fellows were so flamboyant and vocal and bold. They let you know exactly who they were and what they were all about. They dressed in scarves and hats and tight jeans and leg warmers and headbands. A few of them wore mascara and lip gloss. I thought they were marvellous. I am sure we had a few gay kids at Springbank, but they were in the closet so deep no one knew who they were. I'd see the lads holding hands in the hallways at Mount Royal. They taunted the straight boys by blowing kisses and patting bums. Nobody seemed to mind, not even the straight boys whose bums they were swatting.

I loved being exposed to so much diversity, but drama wasn't for me. I bought a guitar and brought it to school, playing it in the changing room whenever I could. I wrote a new song every day and made the best of my weird situation. At least I was learning about myself and how much was out there in the world. Springbank was looking smaller and smaller to me with every breath I took.

I was learning that college students drank a lot. On many occasions, seven or eight of us would stay after school to have a few drinks in one of the many lounges on campus. You could make an entire night out of drinking beer, chain-smoking and talking about nothing. Yes, I too was smoking now. It was hard at first but eventually you catch on and you're buying your own cigarettes in no time. It was beyond stupid.

One of the quirkiest girls I met at college was Leslie. I noticed her the first day Movement class. She was wearing an all-blue dance outfit that looked like she'd stepped right out of a Jane Fonda workout video. She was tall and pretty, and rumour had it that she was a part-time model with a local agency in Calgary. (I didn't know Calgary even had models, but I guess Leslie was one of them.) She was outspoken, even brash. When she walked into a room, she filled it up with her pure Leslie-ness. She flirted with the teachers, which I found unbelievable, but she pretty much flirted with anybody within arm's length. She and another girl named Wendy went out of their way to gather as much attention as humanly possible and hoarded it as if it was a drug. They couldn't get enough stares and glares. Wendy looked like a Playboy bunny in drag. She told everybody she had a sugar daddy named Floyd. I had heard about sugar daddies, but I didn't think for a minute they were real people. Wendy was only nineteen years old and she showed up at school in the middle of May in a full-length mink coat, so I guess she really did have a sugar daddy.

Leslie's parents were divorced, and she had one brother she was close to. She still lived with her mother and she had invited me over a few times. Her mom seemed like a really nice, albeit slightly off-kilter, lady. She always offered me a glass of wine out of a box she kept in the fridge. That made me feel grown-up. "Do I even need to ask if you'd like a glass of Chardonnay, Jann?" she'd enquire, with one eyebrow raised. No, she didn't need to ask. I always accepted.

Leslie and her mother were more like friends than they were mother and daughter, which I found odd. My mom was my mom, period, but Leslie talked to her mom like they were roommates and buddies. Some days I thought Leslie's mom was more like the child in the relationship than Leslie was. Leslie was always telling her mom what to do. They argued often and things became heated very quickly if they didn't go Leslie's way. Leslie had to have her way—end of story. Their house felt a bit like a three-ring circus, but I liked hanging out there. My own world was expanding, just like my dad had said the universe was.

Leslie had lots of boyfriends. I couldn't quite keep track of them all. She had a few guys she was stringing along at school. I watched them fall over themselves trying to woo her. She thought of it as a game more than anything else. I don't know where she learned all her little tricks, but she had a bag full of them. It was like watching an opera—they couldn't help but fall madly and hopelessly in love with her, only to have their hopes dashed and then they'd plummet to their deaths. I wanted to be able to do that to men. Yeah, right. Me? Not in a million and one years.

One day after class, Leslie had me and a few other girls over to her house. She was making lasagna and watching some show on TV. Her mom was going to be working until midnight so it was supposed to be a big girls' night in. Everyone she invited seemed so much more mature than I was. First we drank all of Leslie's mom's wine, and then we broke into her Grand Marnier. (That stuff could give a headache to a tree.) Around ten o'clock everybody started to head home. Leslie asked me what my rush was and told me to stay for awhile. I didn't see why I couldn't. For one thing, I needed to drink nine glasses of water and wait a little bit before I could drive home.

Leslie put on a Nina Simone record and fetched me a big glass of ice water. She had her Grand Marnier swirling about in a giant snifter and said that we could share it. I told her that I had had enough to drink, and she left it at that. She was singing along to the music with her eyes closed and her head swaying back and forth; she said she felt drunk. She started asking me all sorts of embarrassing questions about sex and what I had done and what I wanted to do. I was starting to feel like I was in some kind of foreign movie. My face was so red I thought it was going to melt off. Question after question, and each more intricate and personal. I felt like I didn't know anything. I wanted to tell her about my ride home with Conrad but I decided not to. I just blushed and answered no to almost everything she asked me. I felt very inexperienced and shy.

Leslie took a big sip of her drink and then leaned over and asked me if she could kiss me. Um . . . kiss me? She said she wanted to know what it was like to kiss a girl. By this time she was mere inches away from my mouth and before I had a chance to say anything, her lips were very gently covering mine. It wasn't a long kiss, it was just very sweet and kind. Leslie said, "Wow, that's so totally different." She took another sip of her Grand Marnier and kissed me again. Her lips tasted like oranges. I asked her if she was gay and she declared, "Oh God, *no!*"

Leslie told me she was "tri-sexual," which I thought was *very* Leslie. She told me that she'd try anything once, and if she liked it she'd try it twice. I will never forget that moment. She told me that she wanted to try everything in the world, as she swirled her Grand Marnier around. She asked me if she could kiss me again and I said yes. I didn't have to think about it. It seemed completely harmless. It was very easy to kiss her, although I didn't really know what I was doing. I felt like I was in a foreign movie for sure at this point.

We lay on the floor and listened to Nina Simone singing the saddest songs I'd ever heard in my life. After awhile Leslie made us some Kraft Dinner, which was odd because we still had half a giant pan of lasagna. We ate it silently and then I got up, said goodbye and drove back home to Springbank. Everything in my body was starting to tell me it was time to get out of that small town. I didn't want to wake up one day and discover I was forty years old with nothing to show for the time I'd been on the planet. It was my worst fear.

When I went to class the next day, Leslie was flirty and silly and friendly and acted like everything was as it had always been. I was relieved about that. She wasn't aloof and she didn't ignore me. This was definitely not like high school. We remained friends all through the rest of that year. I often remember her carefree spirit, her ability to just chase life and not worry about where it takes you. She was on to something.

One night near the end of term, Leslie and I were heading out on a date with two of her pals who were boxers from the Canadian Olympic team. For some unknown reason, my heart went completely bonkers. It was fine and then it wasn't. That was more or less how things were going for me at that point where my heart was concerned. Willie de Wit, one of the boxers, had to carry me to the emergency room at Colonel Belcher Hospital. I could not get my heart to slow down no matter what I tried. Willie picked me up like I was an empty milk carton and ran a few blocks down the street with me dangling from his giant arms. Had I not been so scared, I might have actually enjoyed the ride; he was after all, an Olympic heavyweight boxer . . .

Everybody thought I was dying, myself included. As things happen, my heart went back into rhythm as soon as we walked in the front door of the emergency room.

The intern who was on duty that night at the hospital ran lots of tests, and asked a whole bunch of questions that nobody else had asked me before. She was very interested in my odd heart health history, which took me ages to explain. But she listened patiently and was determined to figure out what was happening with me. Finally she said there were a couple of things she wanted to look into and that she'd be back in an hour or so; I was to "hang tight." Emergency rooms are not conducive to hanging tight, as far as I am concerned. On the contrary, they are breeding grounds for paranoia. But she did come back as promised and said there was one more test she wanted to perform, and that I would have to stay overnight. The test involved putting a wire inside my heart to assess some sort of electric waves. I had no idea what she meant, but I was willing to have the test done. By this point I was thinking that I should probably call my parents. I felt like I was finally being taken seriously by someone other than my mother. It's hard having something wrong with you that nobody believes you have. I didn't know what to believe anymore.

A few days later, another doctor performed my heart catheter test, and it came back showing some interesting results. Apparently they weren't good interesting results but, rather, bad ones. Everybody in the room looked at me like I was an old dog that was going to be put down. The nurses had expressions on their faces like they had just come from their grandmother's funeral. Thank God I was stoned out of my ever-loving mind or I would have started crying. Part of me was hoping they'd find something and the other part of me was praying they wouldn't. While I was being wheeled out down the hallway back to my room, the doctor leaned over to me and said he was sorry. I was so high on whatever they'd given me to relax that I had absolutely no idea what he was sorry about. I'm sorry too, I thought, sorry I'm feeling like I've been in a dentist's chair for sixty-seven hours straight.

When I finally came around from the sedatives they'd given me, the cardiologist told me that I would require a pacemaker. Just like that. He didn't decorate his words with anything the slightest bit flowery or delicate. He just blurted it out like a fart.

A pacemaker? What and why and when? That was for old people, wasn't it?

Dr. Wise explained that I had two unique heart conditions. I had alternately a very fast heartbeat and a very slow heartbeat—the fast heartbeat couldn't be treated with drugs because it would affect the slow heartbeat I experienced at night. My head was whirling around like one of those dervish people sans the white flowing outfit.

I had been diagnosed with something called sick sinus syndrome, which has nothing to do with your nose. My heart needed to be prompted to beat a little faster when I was sleeping. I was relieved somewhat that I would no longer have to be awake to keep my heart going in the wee hours of the morning. I would have a little machine doing that for me. They weren't exactly sure what to do about the fast heart rate, but they'd figure that out at a later date. That was comforting.

I checked into Foothills Hospital and was operated on the very next day. I was only twenty years old. I stayed in the hospital for about a week and then they sent me home armed with a user's manual for my new Medtronic pacemaker. The nurse told me to try not to stand in front of a microwave for too long.

Jesus.

Leslie and the two Olympic boxers had to go on to the party without me. It had, after all, been over a week since they'd dropped me off at the emergency ward. Four years after I had my pacemaker installed, Willie de Wit won a silver medal at the Los Angeles Summer Olympics. I had been carried across 12th Avenue to the hospital by the man the papers dubbed "the Great White Hope." Thanks for the lift, Willie.

I thought I was going to die within days of getting my pacemaker. My dad assured me that I wasn't. "You're not going to goddamn die, for Chrissake." He was very comforting. I was stupid enough to pull out my stitches because they were itchy and driving me bloody crazy. The scars became a lot bigger than they should have been. I used my mother's sewing scissors and a pair of tweezers to cut and yank the stitches out. It felt wonderful, but the whole area ended up looking pretty terrible. It was like pulling out giant black fly legs.

The pacemaker was the size of a hockey puck. I kept looking in the mirror at the bulge in my chest. It was visible through my T-shirts. I had so much to think about and I didn't know where to start. The first thing I had to do was drop out of college because, let's face it, I wasn't doing anything but learning how to smoke and pretend I was a dancing mushroom.

I got a job at a little restaurant in Calgary, where I was a singing waitress, of all things. I would wait tables and then go up to a small stage and sing a few songs. I was the worst waitress in the world, but I think my customers forgave me because I was somewhat entertaining. One of the men who owned the place was an alcoholic who wandered from table to table, spitting on people as he welcomed them to his establishment. It was a nightmare. I hated the job because I felt like I was actually going backwards and not forwards. I was twenty years old and still not doing anything.

One of the other girls who worked at the restaurant, Colette, said she had a place out in Vancouver that had an extra bedroom that I was welcome to rent if I wanted to. She was going to be driving out there in a few weeks. She had come to Calgary to look after her ailing dad and, since he was on the mend, she was ready to go back. I had to think about it. I had never been away from home. I didn't know what I would do for work. I was, as they say, unskilled. Colette seemed to think I would find a job right away. She said she knew people.

I didn't know Colette all that well; she seemed nice enough and was a hard worker. She was a real firecracker, that's for sure. She could talk the leg off the lamb of God. I had two weeks to decide if I was moving or not and I had no idea what I was going to say to my parents. I kind of felt like it was now or never, and if I thought about it for too long I wouldn't go anywhere, ever!

I am sure I waited until the last possible moment to tell my mother that I was moving. She was speechless at first. She looked at me with this terribly sad and disappointed face and told me I was making a mistake. She told me it was my decision, though. My dad didn't say much of anything. I think he was fed up with me flitting around and thought that moving out there would knock some sense into me. I felt so torn. I knew I had to do something to sort myself out, and moving to Vancouver seemed like something to me. My mom asked me what I was going to do out there; I told her I was going to get a job in a band. I realized how foolish I sounded, but I said the words anyway.

A few days later, I packed up my clothes and my guitar (which I was still paying off) and rolled out of our driveway in Colette's red-and-black station wagon. My mom stood there in the middle of the road as we drove off, but I couldn't bring myself to look back. I was crying and I knew that she would be crying too. Colette probably thought I was being a baby. I had borrowed money from my parents to get out there too, which made it all seem even more pathetic.

But the fourteen-hour drive through the Rocky Mountains was gorgeous. When we arrived in Vancouver the ocean was right there! I could jump in if I wanted to. Everything looked so green and lush. The sun was shining and it was warm and humid compared to Calgary. I had been to Vancouver a few times when I was a kid, but I didn't remember it being so lovely. This city looked like it was made of glass.

Colette's apartment overlooked the harbour, which was absolutely stunning at night. This whole thing might just turn out to be the best idea I'd ever had.

I needed to get a job. I didn't want to be a waitress and I sucked at it anyway. I didn't have a car, and I wasn't about to start taking buses anywhere, so I needed something I could walk to. I grabbed a newspaper and started circling things I might be able to do. I started walking around the neighbourhood every day to check out employment opportunities and get to know my way around.

I walked a few blocks down to the waterfront, where there were a bunch of shops and restaurants and a beautiful little harbour filled with boats of every description bobbing up and down in the water. There were signs in windows that said inspiring things like "Dishwasher wanted nights" and "Part-time sous-chef wanted mornings." I wasn't sure what a sous-chef was, but I was sure it involved some kind of cooking, which I was definitely not qualified to do. I had no clue how to land a job singing in a band. I thought that a rather lofty ambition. I hadn't ever been in a band before and I assumed one would need some experience. But how do you get experience? You have to get a job in a band. When I stopped long enough to think about what I was up against I was really scared. I wandered around for a few weeks until I finally found something that I felt like I could at least apply for. There was a distribution warehouse close to where we lived that had an ad in their window for a sales clerk. The job didn't seem to require any kind of prior experience, so I applied and somehow landed the job. (I think I may well have been the only person who came out for it.)

The owners of the business were each about 450 pounds. The woman had bleached-blond hair with jet-black roots, and looked like a villain in a Disney cartoon. She had a giant mole on her chin with three or four coarse, grey hairs sticking out of it that I couldn't help but stare at. Her husband was about four foot eleven and was completely bald except for nine hairs that he combed over the top of his greasy head. Their warehouse was filled to the brim with crap. They sold stuff that had either fallen off a truck or been acquired at some dead person's estate sale—everything from blue jeans to canned won ton soup. My job was to stand behind the cash register, ring up purchases and put whatever people had bought into a plastic bag.

I worked Monday, Wednesday, Friday and Sunday from 10 a.m. to 7 p.m. I was allowed to heat up my lunch—one of the eleven thousand dented cans of soup they had on the shelves—in a microwave in their office. Everything they sold out of that warehouse was generic. I had never heard of any of the brand names on any of the products we sold. I mean, Carter Klein underwear? What a rip-off.

I lasted two months. I was so bored out of my mind that I thought I would go crazy and start shooting customers with one of the eight hundred pellet guns we were trying to flog. They weren't happy when I handed in my resignation.

Sylvia asked me why I was leaving and I told her that I was moving back home to Calgary to go to school. Yes, I was lying. She said she was happy for me but she still wasn't thrilled to see me go. She told me I was the best employee they'd ever had. *I didn't do anything!* How would that make me a good employee? I had no idea. I got my last paycheque and wished I were going back home to go to school. I had to stay in Vancouver, though, because I had to make something of myself. I didn't want anybody saying I told you so, least of all myself.

I don't know if it was that I was so far away from my parents or that I had so little life experience or that I was depressed or what, but I started drinking more than I ever had in my life. It was a way to pass the time and have fun and feel like an adult. In Vancouver it just seemed like I was slipping away from who I was. Alcohol was creeping into my body an ounce at a time. I felt homesick and lost, but managed to bury it somewhere deep inside of my body.

Colette was a big drinker, perhaps because she worked at a bar. I didn't often see her without a drink in her hand. I was finding out things about her that were very surprising. Not just about the drinking. She was controlling and compulsive. She cleaned constantly. She vacuumed her carpets on her hands and knees using just the nozzle. Once a week she'd take everything out of the cupboards and wash it thoroughly—cups, plates, cutlery, pots, pans and ornaments—and then she moved on to walls and ceilings. It seemed completely crazy to me. She washed every leaf on every plant with soap and water. The whole process took hours. It turned out she was a pothead too. Duray smoked pot, but Colette made him look like a lightweight.

She was always rolling up joints, getting high and then cleaning like a madwoman.

Colette had a secret existence. I wasn't sure at first, but after a few weird incidents it dawned on me that she was having sex with men for money. Was Colette an actual hooker? She was some strange version of one, apparently. There was a giant Italian man who showed up at her apartment from time to time. After he'd leave, she'd have a surplus of cash, the fridge would be full of food and wine and beer and she'd act like she'd swallowed a canary. There were other men, one really old guy that she gave a bath to. I couldn't hear everything that was going on in the bathroom, but you didn't have to be a genius to figure it out. I wanted to run out of the apartment and just keep going.

I was pretty sure my time in her apartment was going to be coming to an end. Where else to live, I couldn't imagine. I didn't want to think about it. It was easier to drink a bottle of cheap wine. So I did.

After six months in Vancouver I was still spinning my wheels and wasting my time and not much else. I didn't have much money to contribute for the rent and the utilities and food. Colette told me that I could go down to the welfare office to apply for assistance. Why would I want to do that? She told me that it was easy—that she did it every month. So she was working at a nightclub, collecting social assistance and hooking on the side. She was a small corporation.

Finally I gave in. I felt terribly ashamed going down to the welfare office. Filling out those forms was one of the most humiliating things I'd ever done in my life. I felt so depressed. A few weeks later I received a cheque for $319. I signed the back of it and handed it over to Colette. I collected welfare for three months, and then I marched down to the office and had it cancelled. I told them I had a good job and the lady said to me, "Good for you. Glad we could help get you back on your feet." I was getting better and better at lying.

After that, I did manage to get a decent job selling women's clothing at a store called Designer Save. A wonderful forty-year-old English lady named Jean hired me to help her a few days a week, pricing and racking and doing up the display window. I don't think she even needed the help but she hired me anyway. Jean was married to an alcoholic named Chuck and had two kids whom she loved more than life itself. Though her mother was still alive, Jean told me she was a domineering matriarch who was practically impossible to reason with, so I think Jean felt motherless in many ways. She was convinced that her life was as good as it was going to get, and she would grin and bear it.

Jean was the first real friend I made in Vancouver. I liked working for her and she really looked out for me. She took me out for fancy dinners and let me borrow her car (it was a Ford Pinto, of all things). She had me over for sleepovers and movies at her house once in awhile. She was my little bit of sanity. Jean would ask me what the hell I was doing in Vancouver and I spent many hours trying to explain my hopes and goals to her. I told her all about my family and how much I wanted to go home. I told her all about my music and the songs I had written. She said she'd buy me a bus ticket whenever I wanted to go back to Calgary.

Jean didn't care for Colette, and told me she thought Colette was evil. She actually said "evil." And I do think that living with Colette was doing something to my soul. Not that it was at all her fault, but I was becoming more and more promiscuous. I'd drink too much at the nightclub where she worked, dance half the night with some guy I didn't know from a chair and then go with him and, well, have sex. It happened time and time again, and I didn't have a clue about why I was behaving in such a dangerous way.

I was doing things I didn't even want to do. I hated myself for it.

Every month I prayed that I wasn't pregnant. I actually had a prayer that I recited more times than you'd care to imagine. I would make a deal with God that if he could make me *not* pregnant that I would *never* have sex with anyone again. I often thought of my mom when I was in those precarious situations. I'd picture her there in the corner of some guy's cheap, messy apartment, watching me guzzle beer and smoke cigarettes and roll around in filthy sheets with a complete stranger. It made me cry all the way home. How had I gotten myself to this place? I had to get out and I had to get it together.

Jean kept telling me that I was going to find myself in a whole lot of trouble if I didn't start respecting myself. She was right. I didn't respect myself. I didn't think of myself at all, quite frankly. I didn't think I was worth anything good. I used to be so carefree and funny. Now I was one of the walking wounded, and it was my own doing.

I decided I was going to try as hard as I could to find a job singing in a band. If failure was the worst thing that could happen to me, I would surely be fine with that. People who were looking for a drummer or a keyboard player would place ads in the Help Wanted section of the *Georgia Straight*, and there was also a section for bands that were looking for singers. The ads would say something like, "Singer wanted for Top-40 cover band. Heart, Pat Benatar, Sheena Easton, Journey influenced." Some bands were looking for a jazz singer and some bands were looking for a blues singer. I thought I was more in the Bette Midler style, although nobody was looking for that. Top 40 was going to have to do.

The ad I circled said, "Must be willing to travel weekends." Well, that almost sounded like it could be fun—I could get out of Colette's apartment. I wrote down the address in the ad and discovered that the audition was three bus rides away. God forbid I should get the job and be facing ninety minutes on a bus every time we rehearsed.

Anyway, I took the three buses and ended up with the band in a tiny equipment-packed basement. There were cords everywhere, plugged into every possible outlet. The whole place looked like it could blow up at any second. I wanted to turn around and get back on the bus. Two other girls and I sat in the kitchen waiting to sing our songs. I had practised "Beast of Burden" by the Rolling Stones, as it was one of the songs on the list the band had provided for us.

To make a long story short, I sang. They all looked at me like I had eaten a baby. They had me sing it again. Then they had me try a Foreigner song and then a Journey song. I must have sung six songs in total and finally the drummer and band leader, who was named John, said, "You've got the job, sweet lady." *Sweet lady?* Sweet mother of God, I thought to myself. I had been called many things in my life but never did I expect to be called that. I think John was stuck firmly in 1967. Whatever, it didn't matter—I was in a band. My very first band! It was called Executive Sweet and I had no idea what in the world that meant.

We practised twice a week and I faithfully took buses across town and back again each time. I learned about thirty songs over the next month. It was a lot of fun, actually. I felt like I was moving forward; even if it was a crap band that sounded like its four members had just gotten out of prison, it was a band just the same. Jean said she'd come and see me sing if we ever played anywhere decent. I wasn't sure that was ever going to happen. We were terrible and I am not exaggerating. I think the guys thought that if they just played as loud as they could no one would notice they were complete shite.

Still, John got us quite a few jobs in little logging towns around British Columbia. We played B-circuit hotels, whose patrons were mainly guys who drank for a living. It was dismal. We would usually play a forty-minute set and then, during our breaks, a stripper with a name like Dusty Blossom would come out and swing around her brass pole to badly recorded music by Pink Floyd. I hadn't seen a lot of strippers in my life, but the ones that were on these hotel circuits were perhaps the worst in the world. They looked drugged out and lonesome. It made my heart hurt watching them. They were about my age, too, and I would always think about their parents and what they must think of their daughters out there flashing their bits.

The drunken men would whistle and holler and spew out the most vile things at them and stuff a handful of one-dollar bills into their G-strings and then the song would end and the strippers would slink off to the back room to put their clothes back on. They'd have to go out there three or four times a night because there were so few of them to dance. No wonder they drank and did drugs—who wouldn't?

The patrons always seemed sad when the band would start up again. They would have rather seen the peelers all night long. Nobody wanted to hear "I've Been Waiting for a Girl Like You" by Foreigner or "Jump" by Van Halen. Especially the versions we did. Those people wanted to hear "Cocaine" or "The Gambler" or "Tush" by ZZ Top.

Every weekend we played in some new crummy hotel that looked exactly the same as the last crummy hotel. I hardly ever made any money. After we paid for gas and our hotel rooms and our meals, it was eaten up. I was still drinking a lot. You'd kind of have to drink in self-defence around the people who'd come to see us play. Some plastered logger was always sending a round of shooters up onto the stage. It wasn't uncommon for me to have ten drinks a night; in fact it was the norm. Alcohol seemed to lower my intelligence to the point where I could communicate with pretty much anybody in the joint.

I got sick of working in awful places. But when I told John that I couldn't do it anymore, he was devastated. He asked me to stay long enough for them to find someone to replace me. That could have been an entire year for all I knew. I told him that I would finish out the month and then I was moving back home to go back to school. (That was one of my favourite lies.) I felt bad about leaving the band in the lurch, so of course I got drunk and had sex with John just to show him how sorry I was. I cried all the way on the long bus ride back to Colette's apartment. For the life of me, I could not figure out what the hell I was doing. I kept repeating *slut slut slut slut* in my head.

In what was perhaps my best move ever, I found, with Jean's help, a little one-bedroom apartment just a few blocks from the clothing store where Jean, bless her heart, still let me take some shifts around my unpredictable band schedule. I was nervous, but happy to be moving into my own place, though I didn't have a thing of my own. Jean collected all sorts of things for my big move: tea towels and plates and pots and a frying pan. She got me a few bath towels and forks and knives and a tea kettle. I couldn't believe the huge hampers she hauled into the apartment from her car.

Jean also gave me an ironing board, which I used as a kitchen table for several months. I never did own an iron. I had a cassette deck and my guitar and a couple of table lamps that looked like baskets of lemons. I felt like I was set, though I didn't have a bed. I slept on the floor on a big quilt until I could come up with something better, like a mattress. I found one of those one day in a dumpster. It had a few stains on it, nothing I couldn't scrub out with a little elbow grease and some Comet cleaner. I dragged it up to my apartment and put it into the bathtub. I worked on getting those stains out for two days. I used three gallons of bleach and a heck of a lot of scorching hot water and I got them all to disappear. It took a few days to dry, but when it did it looked like new. I was thrilled to be sleeping on a real bed.

The building I'd moved into was really old. My door could have been smashed down by a two-year-old with a plastic Fisher Price hammer. There was always somebody screaming in the hallways. There were loud footsteps constantly running up and down the stairs, fists pounding on doors and thumping walls wildly. It was a scary place in a sketchy part of town, but the rent was incredibly cheap.

I wanted to find a job where I could sing my own songs, but I didn't know how to go about it. I needed to find a gig in a lounge somewhere, but how? I met a young woman named Marion at a café and she told me that a person could make really good money busking in Gastown. *Busking?* I could probably do that. All I would have to do is stand there with my guitar case open and sing songs for a few hours. It couldn't be that hard. Marion had told me that she'd done it quite a few times and made some pretty good cash. Gastown was a really touristy area and it had a lot of pedestrian traffic going through it. It was full of shops and bars and restaurants and, presumably, folks with spare change to throw at me. It was right on the water in a beautiful part of town, so I assumed it was fairly safe.

The first day was the hardest. I took the Seabus across the harbour from my apartment and found a little niche to set myself up in. There seemed to be quite a few people milling about, and it looked bright and sunny. I would execute Operation Sing for Your Supper and see what happened.

I stood there alone in the sun and started playing my songs. It felt really strange. I felt very exposed and vulnerable. Everybody simply walked by as if I was invisible. Once in awhile somebody would dig into their pocket, toss two quarters into my case and keep right on going. That wasn't so bad, I thought to myself. I could build up a fairly good stash if I stayed out there long enough.

That first day I made about forty bucks in five hours. My fingers were ready to fall off my hands and I couldn't feel my fingertips. They were completely numb from strumming so long. I went home and soaked them in warm water and salt.

I counted the money out on the bed. It was mostly quarters, so it took me awhile to sort. I thought it was marvellous. I went back to my spot almost every day for two months. It was summertime and the entire area was bustling with people shopping and drinking beer on outdoor patios. I had regulars who came and sat in front of me to eat lunch while I sang. I was even getting applause once in awhile. Some people dropped five-dollar bills into my case and told me how much they loved the music. Busking was so much easier than lurching around in hotel bars in the BC interior with a bunch of stinky guys in a van. I was glad to have that behind me.

All I wanted to do was perform my own material and I was more or less doing that now. It wasn't the perfect situation but in my mind it was an improvement. I was writing new songs while I stood out there. In eight weeks I must have written about thirty of them. And I thought they were getting a lot better—they were more economical and straightforward. My confidence had grown noticeably. It was getting a lot easier to stand in front of people and sing. I pretended they weren't there at all; that helped. I didn't think anyone would notice me singing my own stuff. People came and went by me so quickly they'd never figure it out. I was making my rent money and writing new material. Things were looking up.

One Saturday afternoon I went over to Gastown, as I had been for months, and started playing. I might have been standing there maybe a half-hour and had a whopping three or four dollars in my case. It had been raining a fair amount, and so there weren't a lot of people around. They were inside somewhere keeping themselves warm and dry, right where I should have been. I was thinking about quitting and just calling it a day. I was gathering up my stuff when all of a sudden, I turned to see a very large person was rushing towards me. Before I could react he punched me in the side of the face so hard that I saw not only stars, but planets.

All I could make out was a large man hovering over me, picking the money out of my case and cramming it into his jacket pockets as fast as he could. I would gladly have given him all my money and spared myself the fist in the head. He didn't say anything to me. When he had every penny fished out, he walked off as if nothing had happened. I just stayed down on the ground and watched him disappear down an alley.

I felt like bawling, but I was too upset to shed a single tear. I could hardly pull a breath into my lungs. Maybe I was in shock. I was soaked from being on the ground, and freezing, and by now I was shaking so hard I could barely latch up my guitar case. I had a forty-five minute ferry ride across the harbour to where I lived, but the guy had taken all my money so I didn't have the fare to get me there. I would have to sneak on and hope I didn't get caught.

What kind of person can just punch you in the head and steal your money? My face started to swell up into a bruised and bloody mess. The blood vessels had been broken in my right eye and it looked awful. All night I felt like throwing up. I thought that maybe I had a concussion or a blood clot. I hardly slept, fearing that I might never wake up again. I would have called my mother, but my phone had been cut off. I didn't want her to know what had happened anyway so it was just as well. I should have gone to a walk-in clinic but decided not to. I didn't quite know what I was going to say about what had happened. I was embarrassed and very shaken up.

My career as a street performer was over. I didn't ever go busking again. I was too scared. I kept thinking that, had he hit me any harder, he could have actually killed me.

I laid low for at least a week. I stayed in and read books and slept and ate Kraft Dinner, which had become a staple at this point. I could buy three boxes for a dollar, so it was an affordable meal. I didn't want anyone to see me with my head banged up so I didn't go anywhere except to 7-Eleven to buy more Kraft Dinner. One half of my face turned green and yellow and my blood-filled eyeball took two weeks to clear up.

In every letter my mom sent to me—and she wrote every week—she begged me to come home. She knew I was miserable and she knew I was stubborn. She tucked twenty dollars in each letter and I was so grateful to get it and so sad at the same time. Sometimes it was all the money I had to last me until the next letter came. I had to find a way to make ends meet.

A girl named Janice, who used to come into Jean's store, told me that there was sometimes part-time work down at one of the piers. She wasn't specific and I couldn't imagine what kind of work was available, but I wandered down there anyway.

The pier turned out to be a commercial dock where the fishing trawlers tied up and unloaded their catch. I walked around for half an hour, watching the boats come and go and the giant fish being unloaded. I wasn't sure where to start. The whole place stank of something that smelled like a combination of bad breath and dog crap. I didn't know how everybody seemed to be ignoring it so successfully. There was a sign nailed up on a post that said "Deckhand required—no experience needed." The small print on the bottom of the sign read "See Norman Earl for details."

I didn't know what a deckhand was, but I figured that it wouldn't hurt to find out, I didn't have anything to lose. There was no phone number. I guessed I would just have to ask around as to the whereabouts of Norman Earl. What happened next was so crazy that not even I could fathom what I had gotten myself into.

chapter thirteen

NORMAN EARL AND THE REHAB BOAT

Norman Earl was the captain of a forty-two-foot salmon trawler, and he needed a deckhand to go out with him for at least a month to help him gut the salmon he caught and to cook his meals. His son, who normally worked with him on the boat, had sliced his Achilles tendon with a rather large knife and had had to bow out of the season's last run.

Norman was at least seventy-five years old; if I agreed to take the job, I would be in the middle of the Pacific Ocean alone with him. I thought that was really weird and fairly creepy but, considering what had just happened to me, I didn't think things could possibly get any worse. He eyed me up and down and, honest to God, after a good, long look, asked me if I was a girl or a boy. (I did have very short hair at the time.) I told him that I was a girl and felt stupid about it, for whatever reason. I had never been asked that question in my life, not even when I chummed around with Leonard and Dale. Norm asked me how old I was and if I got seasick. I told him that I had no idea if I got seasick because I had never been at sea.

"It can git pretty bad on them swells," he mumbled. "I can't have nobody out there throwing up all day and night with the fish coming in." I didn't know where he was from; he talked as if he was from somewhere in Europe, but I couldn't tell where. Turned out, though, he was just a local fella.

Maybe this isn't such a good idea, I thought. The idea of throwing up for weeks on end scared the crap out of me. He told me he was leaving in the morning—like, 4:30 in the morning—and he needed to know if I was coming or not. He said he'd pay me three percent of the catch, but I had no idea what that meant in dollars. It could have been anything from ten bucks to two hundred thousand. (A girl can dream, can't she?) I needed a job where nobody would be punching me out so I told Norman Earl that I would be there bright and early the next day and that's just what I did. I stuffed three pairs of jeans and some T-shirts into an old knapsack along with my toothbrush and my deodorant and my plastic hairbrush, hopped onto Norman Earl's fishing boat and we headed towards Vancouver Island.

I still couldn't believe that I was on a boat, sailing for a little city called Port Hardy on the far northern end of Vancouver Island, where we would stop for provisions. "We're gonna need to get you a fishing licence," he said. I told him I didn't have any money and he said that he'd pay for it, that I wasn't to worry. I hadn't thought about needing money where I was going. Norm told me that all the meals would be provided for me while we were out fishing. At least I would be eating three times a day and not have to worry about paying for all the food. I had found my dream job, I thought. We were going to stop in Port Hardy for a day or two—long enough to get my licence and buy enough groceries and supplies to allow us to stay out at sea for at least three or four weeks.

Three or four weeks? I suddenly felt sick, not seasick, just plain old thinking-I-was-crazy with a touch of job-remorse sick. There would be no going back now, though; I was a certified deckhand with a fishing licence on an old wooden boat with an ancient dude named Norman.

After we'd been sailing a few hours, I began to realize how wonderful the air felt blowing through my hair. Every breath I took in and released back up into the sky filled me with a sense of peace I hadn't felt in a long, long time. The water was quite simply gorgeous. I felt like we were floating through a sea of diamonds. I saw Vancouver disappear into the horizon. After an hour or so it was nothing more than a faint line of grey and white sinking into the water. The white-crested waves crashed into the bow of the boat and I felt my stomach flip over itself and fall straight down into my wobbling legs. It was the best ride I had ever been on in my life. I didn't feel nauseous at all. Maybe I would be a good sailor. Norman told me I wouldn't know if I was going to be seasick for a few days. I prayed hard to God and Jesus that I wouldn't be sick. He also told me that there was no smoking on his boat, and I told him that that was fine because I didn't smoke. (Big lie.) It was a dumb habit I wanted to quit anyway and I figured this was as good a time as any.

We arrived in Port Hardy after hours of cutting through the waves and, once we were tied up for the night, we set off to get my fishing licence. I forget how much it cost, but Norm paid for it with one-dollar bills. I remember him counting them out one by one on the counter for at least an hour. (I am lying again. It was at least two minutes.)

After I had my licence, which was just a plain old piece of paper with my name written on it, we headed over to the Overwaitea food store to stock up on our "provisions," as Norm called them. He grabbed a cart and told me to grab one too. "Are we going to need two carts?" I asked him. He told me that we might need three, but we'd start there. Norm bought more groceries than I had ever seen in my life. He bought about a dozen cans of salmon, which I thought was crazy because we were going to be catching a million pounds of the stuff. He bought pasta and beans and all sorts of meat and poultry. He bought fifteen loaves of bread and package after package of bologna. He bought canned tomatoes and frozen vegetables of every kind and colour, jars of peanut butter and three or four different kinds of jams and jellies, and ten pounds of maple-cured bacon. He bought chocolate bars and potato chips and salted mixed nuts. It was fun shopping with Norman Earl. He told me to pick out whatever I fancied, but the only things I ended up grabbing and putting into the cart were four boxes of Kraft Dinner. Our giant shopping excursion cost Norm almost a thousand dollars. It took three guys to help us put it all into a taxi. We headed back to the boat and spent the next hour and a half putting all the food away. I was tired out and I hadn't done a single day's work yet.

We set off on our fishing journey at sunrise the next day. Norm said we'd be sailing about six hours to get to the grounds where all the salmon supposedly were. He had his nautical maps spread out before him in the wheelhouse, but I don't think he even needed them. I'm pretty sure he knew the part of the Pacific Ocean we were floating in like the back of his hand. He told me that he came from a long line of fishermen, and that there was a cove, aptly known as "Earl's Cove," named after his grandfather. He showed me where it was on the map. I thought it was amazing that his grandfather had a place on the planet that was named in his honour. Norm told me that he and his father had built the very boat we were fishing in, that it was almost sixty years old. I hoped it was going to see sixty-one years and not sink somewhere in the middle of the great, unknown deep.

It dawned at me after the third or fourth day at sea that my parents didn't have a clue about where I was. I should have called from Port Hardy, but it hadn't crossed my mind. I was probably in shock from everything that had happened to me in the past few weeks. Norm told me we could call them from the boat on his two-way radio later that day, so that was a relief. I wanted someone to know where I was and who I was with. I wasn't afraid of Norm at all, don't get me wrong. He was such a decent man. He had kids of his own, a daughter in fact, and grandchildren. I didn't think I needed to be afraid of anything, apart from possibly drowning or being eaten by a killer whale.

I found the ocean inspiring. The sensation of the water splashing against my face and the sound of the seagulls that circled the boat like squawking clouds made for a wonderful day on the water. There were thousands of birds, all different kinds, that followed the boat, waiting for me to throw the salmon guts overboard. They were with us until the sun sank into the water at night. I always wondered where they went when they left us. Was there a sandy shore within flying distance? If only I could fly . . .

My first and main job was to gut the salmon as Norm hauled them onboard with the hydraulic lines. There were multiple lines in the water with multiple hooks on them, so when he started bringing them in there could be dozens of large salmon dangling on those hooks.

I learned to gut a salmon in mere seconds. I had to work quickly, as they were coming at me like the chocolates on the conveyor belt in that famous Lucille Ball skit. I was very mindful not to cut any of my fingers off. The boat was always bobbing up and down wildly, so I had to be very careful at all times.

I think I probably gutted five or six hundred fish a day. We stopped for half an hour for lunch around 10:30 in the morning and then carried on until the sun set. I cried the first day I saw the sun set. It looked like a giant ball of fire being sliced in half and then in half again. It was unforgettable. I could honestly feel myself waking up.

Fishing was hard, exhausting work. Norm was seventy-five, so it must have been extremely taxing on his body. He made it look easy, though. I couldn't believe how much the guy could eat. Another part of my job was to cook all the meals, which entailed opening a lot of cans and heating them in a big pot on the two-burner stove. I would dump two cans of Alpha-Getti into a pot with a can of beans and a can of corn and voilà! Dinner. Norm thought I was a good cook. I told him I was a good can-opener.

After we ate dinner, we'd have to go back out onto the deck and get the fish ready to put in the freezer. That was the hardest part of the day. Norm showed me how to dip the gutted and cleaned salmon into a big plastic barrel full of salty sea water in order to put a layer of ice on them, which would protect them from freezer burn. You'd have to repeat the process about three or four times for it to work properly. My fingers were frozen by the time we finished dipping all the fish in the barrels and throwing them into the hold.

We did the same thing every day. We'd get up at 4:30 in the morning and I'd toast half a loaf of bread, boil a dozen eggs and fry up a pound of bacon to eat between the two of us. It seems impossible that two people could eat so much, but we had to in order to keep up our energy. We'd drink two pots of coffee and then head out to catch the salmon. Some of them weighed over fifty pounds. They were as long as I was. I had never seen anything like it in my life. Norm would have to help me gut the big ones because I could not, for the life of me, cut their heads off. We'd save them for the end of the day. These giant, delicious fish had teeth! I couldn't help but think about the movie *Jaws*, which my dad had taken us to see at the drive-in a few years before. The giant salmon were so powerful and so wilful. When Norm hauled them into the boat with a gigantic, bloody steel hook, you could tell by looking in their black eyes that they were saying "fuck you!"

I slept on the kitchen table, which conveniently converted into a bed. On my first nights on board, I found it hard to go to sleep. The constant motion of the boat rocking on the water kept me awake for hours. I tried to read to help myself nod off, but the only books Norman had on board were written by Stephen King and they weren't conducive to falling asleep. I got halfway through *Cujo*, the novel about the St. Bernard that goes crazy after contracting rabies and eats everyone he comes across, and thought I was going to have a heart attack right there. I pictured the frozen salmon crawling up from their icy graves and throwing me overboard for having cut their innards out. I vowed to never read a Stephen King book again.

I could hear the sea whispering to me as I lay there in that pitch-black, tiny cabin. The salty, muffled voices made my mind wander off to the strangest places. They made me think about home. They made me think about mom and dad and Pat and Duray. I wondered how Duray was doing. I worried about him. I hadn't seen him much in two or three years. He would have loved being on Norm's fishing boat. I wondered if he'd ever get a chance to go on an adventure like the one I found myself on.

I had been on the boat three weeks before I realized I hadn't had so much as a beer or a single cigarette. My head felt as clear as it had been in a long time. I could see myself again. I knew how I felt! (I felt wonderful.) The boat turned out to be the world's best and most inexpensive detox program. The ocean had taken me back from the evil forces of the world, and I was beyond grateful.

For the longest time I hadn't known how I felt. I thought that if I didn't think about how I felt, all would be fine. I had my head and my heart so deeply buried in the sand that I couldn't see or hear what I was doing. But I was rediscovering who I was, and it was all because of Norman Earl and his mystical, magical salmon trawler.

Only a week into the trip I had begun to feel happy for no reason at all. I woke up on the fifth or sixth morning and felt as light as a seagull. I felt free and hopeful. I was tired of feeling guilty about all my mistakes. I had to get past them and move forward. An Emily Dickinson poem I had memorized in college came into my head like a bolt of lightning.

> *Pain has an element of blank;*
> *It cannot recollect*
> *When it began, or if there were*
> *A day when it was not.*
>
> *It has no future but itself,*
> *Its infinite realms contain*
> *Its past, enlightened to perceive*
> *New periods of pain.*

I didn't feel pain anymore. I didn't know when it had even begun to go, but it was gone.

I saw so many amazing things that month on the ocean. Pods of orcas swam beside us for miles. Their beguiling eyes would look right through you as if to say, "We know who you are and we know what you're thinking." It was so lovely having them glide beside the boat, watching over us. I couldn't believe how gentle and quiet they were. I had a hard time picturing any one of them chewing on a baby seal. At one point there were nine or ten of the black-and-white whales skimming right alongside the boat. I know they were interested in the salmon more than anything, but it was still so flattering having them so close.

Norm had so many amazing stories to tell about his youth and all the adventures he'd been on. He'd lived a good life but a hard one. He didn't know how many millions of fish he'd caught over the years but he said he often dreamed about them. He was humbled by nature and the beauty it provided. I loved listening to Norm. He was one of the most interesting people I'd ever met.

For the most part it was smooth sailing: clear skies and calm water. But somewhere in the middle of the fourth week we found ourselves in the middle of a pretty bad storm. I knew things were going sideways when Norman pulled up the lines and told me to put a life jacket on. He yelled it, in fact.

Within minutes the rain was pelting down so hard that it hurt the top of my head. The waves doubled and then tripled in size, throwing the boat around like it was nothing more than a wine cork. Norm pulled up the stabilizers, which were like wings that dragged through the water to keep the boat steady. They were so heavy he barely got them aboard. The wind was now blowing a million miles an hour and it sounded like hell was literally upon us.

I wanted to call my parents. But I wasn't scared, for some reason. Norm knew what to do. He told me not to worry. "Just hang onto something!" he yelled. He got behind the wooden steering wheel and said he was going to try to get us to a place called Bull Harbour to wait out the storm. We smashed our little boat through the fifteen-foot swells and the pelting rain and outrageously strong winds, but we did make it to Bull Harbour. I felt completely invigorated and totally alive. While Norman was busy steering us to safety and the waves were pounding on us, I was singing at the top of my lungs.

We spent the rest of that night tucked into the sheltering rocks of the harbour. We listened as we lay there while the wind ripped the sky apart above our heads. It was soothing and comforting. I can't explain it. All I knew was that at that moment I felt there was nothing I could do. I fell asleep as the boat rocked me side to side. "Goodnight, God," I whispered into the air.

The next morning, Norm rowed us ashore in the little dinghy he kept tied to the side of his boat, and let me wander around for a few hours on the rocky beach. It was so nice to have a break from gutting fish all day. We walked along the shoreline of Bull Harbour and talked about his family and my family. I realized that age wasn't such a big deal. Norm and I were more alike than I could have imagined. He told me he was really proud of the job I'd done and that he'd hire me back anytime. I was proud of myself too, actually. I had worked on a real live fishing boat and not killed myself by being eaten by a sixty-pound salmon or by falling overboard. I had weathered a huge storm and not cried once.

We fished for a few more days and then we headed back to Vancouver to unload our catch. It wasn't a huge amount, according to Norm. He didn't want me to be disappointed with the money I had earned. It was, after all, the last run of the season and the salmon stocks had begun to dwindle.

I helped to unload the fish and get them ashore. We hauled thousands of frozen-solid salmon out of the belly of Norm's boat and onto the docks. I couldn't believe that the two of us had done all that work. When it was all counted and weighed, I was paid fairly, just as Norm had promised me. Three percent of the gross catch. He wrote me a cheque for $390. I didn't care that it was so little. I would have paid to go on that trip. I knew in my heart that it had saved me. Norm the fisherman saved me.

chapter fourteen

THE SOUND OF SURRENDER

B ack on dry land in Vancouver, it took me three days to stop feeling like I was walking on water. (No Jesus reference here at all.) I felt like I was drunk and, believe it or not, for a change I wasn't! Even when I slept I felt like I was rocking on the ever-swaying waves. I slept for almost twenty hours when I got back to my crappy little apartment. Then I sat in front of my ironing board/table and contemplated what I was going to do next. I remember counting cracks in the ceiling of my bedroom. I got up to 371 and had to quit counting. I had salt in my blood and hope in my heart, and I had already made up my mind. I didn't belong here. This wasn't me. I was bigger than all of this. It felt so good to have a giant ball of faith in my body for a change.

I thought about my grandma Richards and her telling me that God could see me no matter what I did. Well, for the first time that didn't bother me. I was starting to see what God himself saw every day, all day long.

My face had completely healed up from having been slugged in Gastown. My skin was windburned and full of freckles but I looked pretty healthy and young and, if I dare say so, relaxed. I recognized somebody I actually liked when I looked in the mirror. And I wanted to take the face that was staring back at me . . . *home!* I missed being around my old friends and my family. I packed up all my meagre possessions and called my mom to tell her I was headed back to Alberta.

I can't even remember how I got home. I don't know if it was by bus or if I flew or if somebody drove me. I don't remember—I just got home. I didn't even stop long enough to say goodbye to my lovely friend Jean. I moved back into my mom and dad's basement and vowed to find my own place over the next few months. I just wanted to get back on my feet and gather myself up after my two-year voyage to nowhere. I was so relieved to be back home. I felt like I could breathe.

It took me longer than a few months to move out, but my parents didn't seem to mind me being there; in fact, they were very grateful that I had finally had the good sense to return from the west coast. I knew I was going to keep writing songs and at some point try to figure out what to do with them. In the meantime I needed to find a job again.

I am not sure what possessed my parents, but they decided they were going to buy some sort of small business so that I could work there. They told me they wanted to invest in something but, more than that, I think they just wanted to help me get back on track. I don't think I truly understood and appreciated that at the time. I certainly do now. They bought a small video store, of all things. I was glad it wasn't a bottle depot or a vacuum-repair shop. One thing I did like doing was watching movies. The store was aptly named Fairview Video because it was on Fairview Road. That made sense to my mother: she said it would help customers find us.

The store was in a strip mall across the street from a 7-Eleven so I knew where I was going to be eating every day. There was nothing else around but a bakery and a bowling alley. Our video store was open seven days a week from 10 a.m. to 10 p.m. and I worked every one of those days. Well, maybe not every one, but quite a few. I was late for work a *lot*, but I always did eventually show up. My mother tells me I was the worst employee they ever hired. I probably was. It was just us: mom and dad and Patrick and me. We ran the entire operation. Maybe mom hired one teenage girl to work a few hours a week but most of the time we were it.

I took my guitar with me every day and wrote songs like a madwoman. Most of them were terrible, but I was figuring out a truly original style. I was starting to sound more like myself than the singers I had admired so much. You start out emulating the artists you love and eventually, by process of elimination, you wind up sounding like your own self. That, at least, is the hope and the goal. I wrote hundreds of songs while I worked behind the desk at our video store. Our customers were very used to seeing me there, propped up on my stool, strumming away on my guitar.

I watched eighteen hundred movies the first year I worked there. I was like Roger Ebert on crack. Whenever I didn't know what to watch, I'd put on *The Goonies*: best movie of all time as far as I was concerned. It wasn't my dream job, but I didn't feel as hopeless as I had. For some reason I saw a very dim light at the end of my tunnel and I was determined to keep marching towards it.

One day my mom handed me a tiny little scrap of paper, maybe an inch long and the ends on it hardly legible. She told me she'd cut it out of the newspaper that morning. It was about a country show band looking for a backup singer.

"I think it would be good for you to get out and sing a little bit," she said. "You could make some pocket money." I thought I was already making some pocket money working at the video store. I had never once told her I wanted a singing job—I was through with all of that nonsense. But secretly I was kind of interested.

I didn't know if I wanted to sing in a country show band. I had never been a backup singer and I wasn't sure what backup singers did. My mom told me it that it wouldn't hurt to try out. She told me the experience would be a good thing to have. "Those things always look good on a resumé," she said. *A resumé for what?* What the hell, I would go and try out for a country show band. It wouldn't kill me.

The following weekend I drove to the other side of town, I mean the very *edge* of the other side of town, and, finally, after many wrong turns and missed signs, I managed to find the building where they were holding the auditions. I got lost twice and kept having to stop at a pay phone to call some guy and ask directions. He was getting tired of me bugging him, I could tell. Every time I called him he talked louder and faster.

When I finally arrived, there were about twenty girls lined up against the wall, all waiting for their turn. I brought my guitar and thought I would just sing something by the Carpenters. They were about as country as I got. Of course, I had been the last person to show up so I was going to be the last to audition. I didn't think I had any hope of making the cut, but I was there so I didn't see what harm it would do. When my name was finally called out, I grabbed my guitar and walked into a room that looked like the gymnasium of a Mormon church. (You'd have to have seen one to know what I mean.) It was very well lit; in fact, it was more or less blindingly lit. Maybe it was all part of a psychological game they were playing, but perhaps not . . . It took me a few seconds to see just what I had wandered into.

There was a big fat guy with a beard sitting in a chair whose name, I found out, was Larry. Perfect. He looked like a Larry. Larry was the band's lead singer and namesake. I was soon to find out that I was auditioning for the Larry Michaels Country Show Band. I had never heard of them or him but I was told by one of the other girls in the waiting room that he was a big deal and this was a very important job I was trying out for. Larry, so I was told, played the A circuit, which included casinos, country fairs and large weddings. Larry also played the Calgary Stampede every year. I guess I was supposed to be in awe, but I wasn't.

Larry's brother was there in the very well-lit, Mormon-looking gymnasium too. He was apparently the band's sound man and was operating the mics and getting all the girls set up. He looked like Elvis with his oily, jet-black hair, only this Elvis had eaten a Buick. I thought the whole audition thing was odd, but it had a car accident type quality to it that was really addicting to be around.

I went up to the mic and waited for instructions from fat Larry. I assumed he was the guy running the show. He didn't instruct me to do anything, though; he just looked me over like I was a sandwich. Larry's piano player asked me if I had any sheet music and I said that, no, I didn't and was that going to be a problem? I told him I was planning to play a song on my guitar.

The piano player, whose name turned out to be David Hart, looked at me for a long time and then casually told me that it wasn't going to be a problem. I felt relieved. David was the band leader and Big Elvis told me that he was the guy who was going to be doing all the hiring. Thank God, because Larry seemed to be lacking the sense Jesus gave a fish. I wanted to sing my song and get it over with. All this looking me over was making me anxious. I wondered if Larry could sing a note himself. I hoped in my heart that he could at least do a decent rendition of "Islands in the Stream." I could picture it as plain as toast: if I got the job he would be Kenny and I would be Dolly and we'd be on stage at the Calgary Stampede with thousands of people cheering us on . . . What a scary thought. I had to snap myself back into the present moment. Part of me hoped I wouldn't get the job. Maybe I thought that way so the rejection wouldn't hurt quite as much when they sent me packing.

"How did you hear about us?" David inquired.

"My mom cut an ad out of the paper."

"Oh," David replied, "I see." He rolled his eyes at fat Larry. Meanwhile Elvis was saying "check, check, check" into the mic.

I thought telling him about my mother cutting the ad out of the paper might have been a mistake. It probably wasn't the coolest thing I could have come up with. I thought by this point they must have already picked one of the cute girls I had seen in the hallway for the job.

I stood there for another few minutes while the three of them whispered among themselves. I felt my face burning. Finally David said, "You don't need to sing for us today." I was so disappointed and hurt. I immediately thought that I must not have looked the part.

"I'm good, I've got what I need," he said, very matter-of-factly. My heart sank. I swallowed hard and stood there like an idiot, looking out at everybody looking at me.

Nobody said a word. Not Larry, not his Elvis impersonator brother, not even David. They all sat there staring at me like my hair was on fire. It was really weird. Larry said something to David under his breath, and David whispered "Later" to him and sort of waved him off.

I asked them if they were sure I couldn't at least sing a little something, and David said he didn't think he needed to hear a single note.

"Don't worry, I've heard you before," David said, as I packed up my guitar. I didn't really think about what that implied, I just wanted to get out of there. "Thanks for coming out today, Jann, is it?" Larry looked over the brim of his thick reading glasses as he said my name.

"Yes. Jann Richards."

"Well, we'll get back to you in the next few days, Jann Richards."

I was pretty sure I wasn't going to be getting a call from Larry Michaels or David Hart. I threw my guitar into the back seat of my car and headed home.

Not two hours after I got home that night, our phone rang; it was David from the Larry Michaels Country Show Band. He told me that I had unanimously been chosen for the job as backup singer. I couldn't believe my ears. My mom asked me if everything was all right, and I told her that I had gotten the job in the band. My mom said, "See what happens when you try?" If only she'd known that I actually hadn't tried at all.

The Larry Michaels Band was a step up from Executive Sweet. They were very talented, actually, and gave me a really fun opportunity to learn and grow as a performer. Singing harmonies wasn't my strong suit, but I did get better at it as the weeks went by.

David spent extra time making sure my parts sounded perfect. I knew he could tell I was struggling a little bit, and he was extremely patient with me. Of all the band members, he and I especially hit it off. I probably spent three or four months doing weekend gigs with them, travelling around southern Alberta in a packed van, so we got to know each other quite well.

On one of the road trips I finally got around to asking him why they'd hired me and not one of the tall, pretty, country-looking girls who had shown up for the audition. I told David that I was quite sure I didn't fit the ideal physical type everybody was looking for. He looked me in the eye and said, "When I saw you walk in, I didn't even need to hear you sing. Like I told you, I had heard you sing before. I loved your voice back then and I was sure that I'd love what you were going to sing that day."

I hadn't really sung anywhere but in the middle of nowhere in British Columbia, so I couldn't imagine where he'd heard me. I was curious so I asked him exactly where he'd seen me sing. I wasn't prepared in any way for his answer.

David told me that he'd heard me sing on a ship sailing from England to the "new world, three hundred or so years ago." I wasn't sure how to respond.

"I know you think I'm crazy," he said candidly, "but I'm not kidding. It was you, as sure I'm standing here. It was you on that boat."

I started laughing because I didn't know what else to do. He'd heard me sing three hundred years earlier? What the hell? He explained to me that he was into something called Eckankar. Eckists, he told me, enjoyed many levels of existence and consciousness. He believed he had lived many other lives on this planet and had shared a few of those lives with me. I thought David was crazy but I humoured him anyway.

I asked him what I looked like on the boat and he told me that I looked the same—same eyes, same skin, same hair—only I was really fat! He told me that I was always singing. I apparently looked after all the men on the boat, and they all looked up to me like a mother. Good God, I thought, a mother to a bunch of toothless rum-drinkers looking for the new world. No wonder I had issues. I was smiling at this point. Part of me believed him even though it was so bizarre. I mean, who would make something like that up? A crazy person, that's who.

David and I talked about the girl on the boat once in awhile. He was always happy to answer my questions no matter how nutty they were. He never changed his story. David told me I was the best singer he'd ever heard, then and now. It made me blush.

David and I ended up leaving the Larry Michaels Band and going off to do our own little lounge gigs. Larry was probably mad but David thought it best to move on to other things. I think when David met me, he saw his chance to get somewhere and took it. I was kind of nervous about working as a duo in lounges, but David assured me that we could make some really good money and work in some really nice places. Both of those things sounded promising to me.

The first year we worked together was one of the most educational years of my musical life. David was a lot older than me, probably twenty plus years. He had fought in Vietnam (so he told me) and had come up to Canada from California to escape the "political bullshit" that he said haunted his every move. He was such an interesting man. For one thing, he had no front teeth. I never asked him how he lost them. I always figured he'd bring it up if he wanted to. I imagined his teeth being knocked out by the end of a machine gun in Vietnam although I was quite sure that's not at all what had happened. I think it was more a case of bad dental hygiene. I'd have to beg him to put his dentures in when we played in public because I was sure he was scaring some of our patrons away. He looked so weird without teeth. His cheeks were sunken and it made him look eighty-five years old. He hated his dentures and I couldn't blame him. I would have hated wearing them too. David smoked two packs of cigarettes a day, if not more. The fingers on his right hand were brown and yellow. Back then everybody smoked in bars so he could have a cigarette burning the entire time we played. He had an ashtray on his piano, and he lit one cigarette after another.

We both drank too much. People were forever buying us drinks and sending them over to the piano. Who could say no? It was free, after all, and free was good. David loved it when people bought us drinks. It meant that they were drinking too and that our tips might be higher. Sometimes we could make an extra few hundred dollars a night, and that made a huge difference to each of us.

My mom and dad were a bit leery of my new singing job, but I felt like I was living the dream. I was singing full-time now and making a wage as an honest-to-God singer! If somebody wanted to send me a drink, so be it. My parents liked David, although my mom said she felt sorry for him. I didn't feel sorry for him ever. He was so strong and so certain. He had two great kids and a really nice girlfriend, so I was very comfortable staying at his house to rehearse when we weren't working the circuit. I guess my mom saw something in him that I didn't. She was intuitive that way. My mom could see right through people's intentions. She still can. Not that David's intentions were ever bad, she just saw how troubled he was, and how broken. He never let on to me or anybody else how hard his life had been. There were a lot of secrets kept inside his heart.

Before meeting David I hadn't really been exposed to great music. I knew nothing of Motown, Detroit, and the brilliant black divas that carved a path so wide that every other singer in the world ran right through it after them. There was so much music he played to me, and all of it just about made my heart stop. It was all so good! I couldn't believe the new sounds I was hearing. I couldn't believe the soul and the depth of the singers he was introducing me to. For the first time in my life I could feel the heartache and hurt they were singing about. It was tangible.

He spun Nancy Wilson and Ella Fitzgerald and Nina Simone records. (Nina made me think about Leslie.) He would play DJ for hours on end. He would put on Tom Waits and Frank Sinatra, the Staple Singers, Aretha Franklin, Marvin Gaye, Otis Redding, Ray Charles and Mary Wells. It was a long list of amazing vocalists and hearing them changed the way I thought about songs and songwriting. Where had I been? Fishing, apparently.

He loved turning me on to new things: new grooves, new melodies. He told me I could sound just like them if I wanted to, or at least incorporate some of that soul into my own music. By this time, David had also talked me into putting some of my original songs into our act. I was reluctant at first but he told me that I needed to start singing my own songs and wondered why I hadn't been singing my own songs to begin with. He made me feel like they were really good, even great. I trusted his opinion and I didn't think he'd tell me my songs were good unless he meant it. He would quite often tell me that he didn't like a new song when I played it to him. He'd say "You need to work on the bridge" or "The melody could use some work." He was always honest.

After just a few months we had quite the eclectic crowd following us around the Calgary nightclubs. Most of the clubs were holes in the wall but we'd always manage to pack the people in. David had us earning about $1,200 a week, which I thought was fantastic. I was used to making maybe a hundred bucks a week, if that. Playing the nightclubs was like winning the lottery. I was happy to not be working full-time at the video store. I think my folks missed the manpower, but they were happy for me to be doing what I loved just the same. (Keep in mind, I was a terrible employee.)

I don't think David and I had more than two up-tempo songs in our entire set list. All our songs were dirges, including the ones I'd written. That's what I liked to sing and that's what David liked to play. We were a perfect team. People would sit around their little candlelit tables, drinking wine and puffing away on cigarettes with their eyes closed, and be lulled to near death by our sombre, depressing tunes. In between songs, I'd tell funny stories and jokes just to let everybody off the hook. Nobody can stay in the dirge zone for four straight hours, not even me. We'd start around 9 p.m. and finish at one in the morning. Most people stayed the entire night.

After that first year, David realized that we didn't really have a band name. We were David and Jann. Not all that original. One night when he was introducing us, he said, "Hello, guys and dolls, we are Hart and Soul . . . I'm Mr. D. Hart, and *this* (he pointed at me) is

Ms. R. Soul . . ." Everybody laughed hysterically. They got the joke, I guess. The name stuck.

Hart and Soul had eight or nine lounges that we played on a regular basis. We would rotate from one room to the next, playing a week at a time. Our calendar was booked for months ahead. It felt good to know what I was going to be doing. I wasn't used to that.

One of our regular gigs was at Marty's Diner. A five-hundred-pound guy named Marty (surprise, surprise) owned it. He and his eighty-pound wife, who looked like Olive Oyl, ran the joint. I know it's horrible, but I always wondered how in heaven's name they had sex. I tried hard not to think about it but once in awhile a disturbing vision crept into my head and I'd have to shake it out onto the floor as quickly as I could or go straight to hell for conjuring up such a dirty scenario.

Marty's was a quaint place, warm and woody. They had a rustic menu of sandwiches and soups and a few deep-fried delights. For the most part they served specialty coffees and an assortment of wine and beer. It seated thirty-five or forty people comfortably. On a good night Marty might be able to squeeze in another ten but it would be cramped. David and I played there every few months to a sold-out house. I loved being able to sing in front of people, but even more than that, I loved making them laugh.

I had no grandiose ideas about taking what we were doing to a professional level. David used to go on about how old he was and that no one in their right mind would ever want to work with an "old ugly fart" like him. I knew he was right but I never said so. I simply stayed the course and felt glad to be working, period.

Since I'd moved home from Vancouver I hadn't seen my brother Duray all that much. It was the norm for him to be in jail for some sort of minor offence. He'd serve a few months here and get out and do something all over again and serve a few months there. It was hard on our entire family. He was drinking all the time, smoking a lot of pot and hash. He would take any kind of pill he could get his hands on too, and not worry about the consequences to his body and soul.

My parents dreaded the phone calls that would inevitably come in the middle of the night from the police asking if they knew a Duray Richards. They'd hear that he'd been pulled over for drunk driving or that he'd threatened somebody or that he had assaulted some poor prostitute.

One night Duray found himself in a horrible fight at a house party. The house apparently belonged to a friend of a friend of a friend. Duray was always looking for a party to go to. It didn't matter where it was, or even if he knew anybody there. He'd simply show up. Duray told us later he'd been having an okay time. He was having a beer and a cigarette and talking shit to the drunk people around him. It was nothing out of the ordinary. Around midnight, he noticed that the guy who lived in the house was making a huge commotion in the kitchen. He was wrenching the arm of his little boy, shaking him and yelling at him to get to bed. Duray said it went on for a long time. Everybody at the party was noticeably uncomfortable but didn't make any attempt to do anything about it. The little boy was crying his eyes out and was obviously very upset. Finally Duray couldn't take it. He told the guy calmly to back off and take it easy. He told him he shouldn't be doing that to a kid, that it wasn't right. That didn't go over very well at all, and the guy got very aggressive very quickly, telling Duray, "Get the fuck out of my face and get the fuck outta my house!"

The guy started dragging his son towards the hallway. The little boy was hysterical. Duray told the man again to leave the kid alone. They exchanged a few more heated words in the crowded kitchen and then all hell broke loose. The guy grabbed a seven-inch kitchen knife and thrust it at Duray. Duray can't remember exactly what happened next, but he said that he managed to grab a big plant and get it between the knife and himself. There was dirt and leaves flying everywhere. Duray threw the plant at the guy and then started throwing punches. People were yelling and screaming and freaking out. By the time things calmed down, Duray realized he'd been stabbed in the stomach and was bleeding profusely. He said he didn't feel a thing, he just noticed the blood.

Someone at the party had the sense to get him to the emergency room. My brother had to undergo surgery that removed several feet of his small intestine and part of his colon and they took out a chunk of his stomach as well. He was in the hospital for several weeks. The doctor told Duray that the blade came within a quarter of an inch of severing a major artery and if it had done that he'd have bled to death in minutes.

Not even a near-death experience slowed Duray. We thought it might change him and get him back on track, but it didn't. He got worse.

David and I kept gigging around town. Once in awhile we'd play in Banff, which was lovely, more like a holiday than a job. We had the days to ourselves to walk around town and take in the sights. I was still going nowhere, but I didn't dare think about that for long.

I am not sure at what point this man started showing up at our gigs, but one night I took notice of a very tall, bearded fellow at the back of the room. He had thick, round glasses, and I thought he looked familiar. I remember David saying, "That dude's been following us around."

Night after night, for weeks, if not months, he'd come to see us play. No matter where we went, there he was. He sat with his back against a wall, drinking coffee and listening to every note I sang. I thought he was a weirdo, but he seemed harmless and it wasn't like he came up and harassed me. I had never spoken so much as a word to him. Just as the night was ending he always seemed to disappear. I'd look for him and he'd be gone. David was cautious about him. Although he had never even met him, he didn't like him. It was like he was jealous.

One night on a break the man—Neil, it turned out, was his name—came up to me and said hello. David looked on from the bar. Neil asked me if some of the songs I performed that night were original, and I told him that they all were. Then he said, "If you're serious about music, call me," and handed me his card. It wasn't a long conversation. Neil wasn't the first person who had talked to me about the music business, so I didn't understand why it bothered David so much. He was furious about the whole thing. "That guy is trying to fucking steal you from me. I know it." I thought David was being dramatic.

"Steal me from what?" I said to him.

"From this! *Us!* The *act!*" I tried to put his mind at ease. I told him that I doubted that very much. Neil seemed interested in my songwriting, I said. I didn't know that for sure, but I wanted to make David feel confident about our present situation. In my heart, I was intrigued by Neil's interest in me. What if he could do something for me? I felt like Neil was very sincere and legitimate. I went home that night and put Neil's business card on my nightstand. I kept picking it up and looking at it.

"If you're serious about music," he had said to me. I fell asleep thinking about the possibilities.

I *was* serious about music but I didn't know what to do about it. David and I were now fighting about this guy we didn't know from

Adam, and it was wearing me down. He kept going on about how Neil was trying to split us up, and I thought that was ridiculous. But David started wearing his teeth every night without my having to remind him. Then I knew for sure that he was worried about losing me.

After about a week or so of staring at Neil's business card, I called up a friend of mine who was a lawyer and asked her if she'd come with me to meet this "music guy." I told my lawyer friend, Karen, that I didn't know what he wanted. I was stupid to think I needed a lawyer with me, but I really didn't know any better. She told me that she'd be happy to go, and so I made the phone call and set up my first meeting with Neil MacGonigill. I didn't tell David. I felt bad about that but obviously not bad enough to not go.

Neil turned out to be anything but a weirdo. I knew in my heart I had found a true champion. He had such a kind face and gentle spirit. Neil could have passed for a clean-looking lumberjack; he was a big man with a big presence but soft-spoken and peaceful. He had had a lot of experience in the music business and had worked with the likes of Ian Tyson and k.d. lang. He was a music junkie of sorts; he knew a heck of a lot of useless facts about obscure recordings from the fifties, sixties and seventies. I'd never met anybody who could drop so many names in a single sentence—and I would seldom, if ever, recognize any of them. He knew a nerdy amount about songwriters and publishing and marketing and everything else that had to do with the recording industry.

We met several times over the next few weeks. Each time I got to know him a little better. He told me all about himself, where he'd worked and who he'd worked with. He was honest and straightforward. He didn't sit in front of me and make me a million promises. He knew how tough it was to get anywhere in the music business. He said he'd been watching me over the months and that he was completely impressed and amazed by my music and my voice. He also told me he had been very disappointed from time to time when he had come to see me sing and I had drunk too much. He told me I had sounded terrible on those occasions. I knew he was right.

"I think you could be so much better than you are," he said to me very firmly. "You're not anywhere near reaching your potential. You don't do any more than you have to. You're lazy."

It made me feel ashamed because he was right. I never worked harder than I had to, and that was a problem. He wanted me to think about the magnitude of the commitment I was going to have to make if I really wanted to pursue music as a career. He was serious about working with me and teaching me the ropes, but I was going to have to show up for my own party.

Neil wasn't talking about working with Hart and Soul; he was talking about working with me. I knew I was going to have to make a decision, and I knew that that would mean having to break things off with David. He would have to cancel jobs and lose money, and that made me feel sick. I didn't want anything bad to happen to him. He had a family to feed and bills to pay. I was torn. I didn't know how to go about telling him that I had to leave.

I kept hearing David's voice in my head saying, "I'm too old and too ugly, Neil's gonna split us apart. He doesn't want an old fart like me, I'll drag you down and you know it as well as I do." It was like he had predicted exactly what was about to happen. Maybe it was his Eckankar background kicking in. Neil told me that he would talk to David if I wanted, but I thought that I should be the one to explain what was going on.

Neil felt that my time would best be spent writing as much and as often as I could, and that meant removing myself from the lounge scene for the time being. He told me that I needed to think beyond the Calgary city limits. He said that if I was willing to trust him and commit myself to my music, he'd be able to get me a record deal within five years. I was twenty-five years old at the time, and I thought five years seemed like forever, but I was willing to give Neil the benefit of all my doubts.

When I finally did tell David that Neil had offered to work with me and that I had accepted, David was very good about it all. He sat at his kitchen table and listened to me go on about all the things that Neil wanted to do with my songs and what the possibilities could be. I could tell that David was trying his best to be supportive and had the generosity to tell me he knew our parting was inevitable.

"You deserve better than me," he said. "You have a chance to do something in this world, Jann. I don't." I felt like bawling. He said that he couldn't wait to see what I was going to do in this life and he felt lucky to have worked with me as long as he had. I asked him what he was going to do about the gigs and he said that he would try and find somebody to take my place. "They won't be anything like you, though. I'll never find a *you* again."

And then he laughed that crazy, cigarette-coughing, wet laugh that almost made me think he was choking.

"You want a beer before you go?" he said. I said sure. We sat there and had a beer and a cigarette and didn't talk much. We'd already said everything. I got up from the table and went outside to my car. David walked me out past the door and gave me a hug.

"It's been good, kid," he said quietly. He hung onto me a few extra seconds and then said, "Go on and get outta here. Say hi to your mom and dad for me." I started backing out of his driveway, holding in the urge to cry. I rolled down the window and told him that I would, and then waved goodbye. I never saw him again.

Neil started working on a plan for me almost immediately. He told me that, first off, we would need to get me out of my parents' basement and into a proper apartment. He had seen a "For rent" sign about a block away from where he lived and thought that it would be a perfect spot for me to settle so I could start "power-writing." He could keep an eye on me there, being so close and all, is what I was thinking to myself.

It was a basement apartment, so I wasn't technically moving up in the world. I was still a subterranean being. My parents helped me move all my stuff into the tiny 500-square-foot space. I was more or less living in the furnace room of a giant house. It was so bloody hot down there. (Too bad the world didn't know about hot yoga yet because I could have sublet my little place out to somebody named Bikram for some extra cash.)

Thankfully I was short, so the six-and-a-half-foot ceilings weren't a huge problem. The rent was $325 a month, and I was almost always late paying it. Thank God my parents still had the video store so I was able to work there and spend the rest of my time writing songs for Neil. He told me that I would have to hone my craft in order to get the attention of a label. "You can't just be a good songwriter, Jann, you have to be a great songwriter," he said. All he wanted me to do was write, write, write. So that's essentially what I did in that little apartment for the next few years.

I'd sit at my desk with a pile of blank paper in front of me and a box of black pens and wait for the words to fall into my head. And they did fall, fast and furious. I opened myself up to the ever-expanding universe and let it do its thing. I wrote for nine or ten hours at a time. It was probably the most creative time in my life. I was piling up songs as the days passed. Some were good and there were even a few that were great. As soon as Neil felt we had enough great songs, we'd go into the studio and do some demos.

chapter fifteen

WRITING FOR MY LIFE

The old three-storey brick house I had moved into was owned by a woman named June. She was in her sixties and as cranky as you could possibly imagine. To say she was stern would be a grave understatement. June lived in the lovely, spacious suite on the main floor, right above my head, so I knew her comings and goings very well. It always sounded like she was having six pirates over for dinner and as if each of them had a wooden leg and a talking parrot. I slept many a night with earplugs stuffed into my head. They didn't help much.

June, for whatever reason, had no time for me whatsoever. I tried so hard to get her to like me but nothing worked. I said a big happy "hello" whenever I saw her. I felt like I was a Walmart greeter, but she barely managed to grunt a "hi" back. Maybe she was tired, or lonely. I knew she was a divorcee and maybe that was a good part of her problem.

The way June acted towards me, you'd have thought I was the worst tenant in the world. I had a five-inch television in my tiny kitchen that I'd watch from time to time, and she'd always come pound on my door and tell me to turn it down. A five-inch television set with a half-inch speaker—how could it possibly be too loud? It was a good thing I still had my lip-reading skills from my parents' illegal satellite signal days because most of the time I watched TV with the sound off. When I sang I did it *very* quietly—June made a point of telling me that the floors were thin and she could hear everything I did down there. (How comforting.) She also told me I did too much laundry and used too much water. She didn't like that I came home late and that I had people over on occasion. She didn't want me burning candles or cooking things that might possibly stink up the rest of the house. She basically hated me. That's how I felt, anyway. She threatened to kick me out every month. But every month I managed to get her the $325 to keep the locks from being changed. If I didn't have the money, my parents or Neil would lend it to me, thank God. I was very lucky.

One night as I sat at my wooden desk eating curried goat and burning a dozen candles with the TV on really loud, lo and behold I came up with a song about what it was like living under June. It was a big hit with Neil. (I'm kidding about the curried goat, it was actually llama.)

I loved having my own place; even though it was crummy, it was mine. I had a poster tacked up in my tiny bathroom that said, "Great spirits have always encountered violent opposition from mediocre minds"—an Albert Einstein quote that became my mantra. I worked at the video store and played my guitar. That's what I did day in and day out. I felt like a mushroom down there in the dark most days (minus the shit). There wasn't much light that came in through the tiny windows. Some days I'd write three songs and then go a week without a single thought in my head. Still, I'd never worked so hard at anything. I was learning about passion and bliss and goals. I'd never had a goal in my life until that point. (I'd never even scored a goal when I played hockey.) Meeting Neil changed everything. Not only did he open a door, he took the hinges right off the thing and threw it into the ditch. I felt like something big was happening.

My parents, in the meantime, kept buying me used furniture at yard sales. They hauled all of it into my apartment, piece by horrible piece. After I'd lived there a few months, my quaint little space started to look like some bizarre furniture emporium. Nothing matched. The last straw was when they brought in a fluorescent, psychedelic, puffy armchair they'd bought at an auction. My mom thought that it would look "cute" in my living room. My dad, of course, mumbled "Goddamn this goddamn chair, Jesus Christ!" as he carried it awkwardly down my little staircase. I was officially out of space.

I would meet Neil a few times a week and play him the songs I'd written. He'd have lots of notes and make suggestions about what I should change or work on. It was the first time I had ever had that kind of constructive input. We talked structure and content and how I could be economical with my lyrics. Most of my songs were simply too long. I had to learn to say what I wanted to say but preferably in under sixteen verses. Neil was hard on me sometimes, but he wasn't trying to be mean; he was trying to get me a record deal.

At some point Neil decided it was time to reintroduce me to the live music scene. He got busy making calls and asking favours, determined to put together the best band he possibly could for me. He knew many musicians and had a firm grasp on how he wanted to put it all together. I was relieved to be working with someone who knew what he was doing. We would need to have extensive rehearsals because I was going to be playing some covers alongside my own songs, and Neil wanted the whole set to make sense. He definitely had a vision. He wanted it to be not just a regular bar gig, but a showcase where he could bring in important label people to hear me sing. He wanted to have hype surrounding the show, so he was very particular about when and where he had me play. He thought that the best way to get my name out there would be to create the illusion of success. He wanted people to think that I was much bigger than I was. Neil was a clever man with a plan.

A few nights before the first gig with the new band, I was over at his apartment going over some last-minute details. Neil was going through his yellow legal pad of notes and checking off the things that he wanted to address. As he neared the end of his list he cocked his head to one side and thoughtfully asked me what my middle name was. I told him that it was Arden.

"How do you feel about being Jann Arden?" he said.

I wasn't sure how I felt about it at all. I had been Jann Richards all my life. Arden sounded really weird to me.

"I think you should be Jann Arden because it puts you in good alphabetical order," he said. "Plus it kinda sounds like Ted Nugent." I had no idea what the hell he was talking about, but we both laughed. Neil and I laughed a lot. I had so many great times with him. We worked hard and we laughed even harder.

Before my first official gig with the band, I became Jann Arden. Neil was going to get posters printed up and do a fair amount of advertising for my future gigs, and I was beside myself. I was going to have *posters* with *my* name on them! I had to figure out how I was going to sign my new name. I practised signing "Jann Arden" for at least fifteen minutes and then I got completely bored and figured it would have to sort itself out. Besides, I had to go and pull a shift at Fairview Video. The universe had a way of keeping me humble at all times.

Neil had discovered a young photographer named Jeth Weinrich who he thought was a genius, and he was going to arrange a time with him to take some pictures of me. I had never had my picture taken professionally before, so I wasn't sure what I was supposed to do. I didn't have a lot of clothes. My stage outfits to that point had consisted of my friend Patti's dad's old suit jackets. That's what I'd always worn when I worked with David. I looked like a midget who'd had sex with a tuxedo.

I ended up borrowing some outfits from my friend Tia, whom I had met while I was involved in amateur women's boxing. (I really wish I was kidding, but I'm not. The boxing happened around the time I was hanging out with Leslie at college and was how I had met the Great White Hope. For two months I participated in a women's boxing league. Problem was, every other girl was a swimsuit model who didn't want to be punched in the face. Where else are you supposed to punch somebody when you're boxing? Like I said, it was a short-lived hobby.) My friend Tia was the best boxer of the lot of them, and she also happened to have beautiful taste in clothes. I was relieved to have her dress me up for my photo shoot with Jeth. The posters turned out beautifully, and I can't tell you how exciting it was to see my name plastered across the front of them. *Jann Arden*. I felt like I had suddenly become somebody.

I had a great time singing with the band Neil had put together. The few places he had me play in were always packed. If a club had a dance floor, Neil would make sure the owners put cocktail tables all over it to make the room more intimate. I would never have thought about that—few people would have. He'd make them put candles and tablecloths on all the tables, like you were in Paris somewhere listening to poetry. I performed in these big ugly bars, but Neil would somehow disguise them with his clever ideas.

After he and I had worked together for a year or so, he brought in his friend Rudy to work on our project. Rudy had worked for years with Sony Music and brought a wealth of experience with him. Rudy was generous to a fault and he and Neil were a good team. When they joined forces I felt like we were gaining momentum. The only negative thing I could say about either of them was that they smoked way too much pot. Neil said he was more creative when he was stoned, so perhaps that worked in my favour. I was never a pot smoker, so I didn't understand the attraction. After awhile it did get to me. If Neil wasn't stoned, he wasn't fun to be around. He could be a very dark person. I think he struggled a lot with depression. There were many times when he was unreachable for days. He'd hole up in his apartment and ignore the world completely. I always thought that pot was half of his problem. Mind you, Neil didn't drink at all and that had a profound effect on me. Ironically, he always encouraged me to live a healthy lifestyle. I eventually quit drinking altogether, and it had a lot to do with him. He also told me to never start smoking pot. I think he recognized it for what it was—a cop-out.

Neil and Rudy introduced me to some incredible musicians. One of my favourites was a piano player named Bob Foster. He was such a quirky, talented, funny person. He came to Canada from England to make a new life for himself, and in many ways he reminded me of one of the indelible characters in a Dickens novel. I loved the way he spoke. I loved his good humour and his extraordinarily good heart.

Bob had all the wacky computer gadgets you could possibly get back in those days. He loved to experiment with sounds and textures. He had such great instincts when we played my songs live. I loved how he played piano. His parts were always haunting and mysterious. One day he offered to have me come to his house to do some demos with him. Neil was all for it. He, too, was a fan of Bob's. Bob rarely if ever charged me for the demos we made, and if he did charge me anything, it was for the tape or mic rentals. I loved working with him. It was an adventure to flesh out some kind of original sound for me. I had written so many songs but had never really pro-duced them. I knew in my head what I wanted to hear, but I needed someone to help me get that sound out. Bob was that guy.

He was great at programming drums and could play not only keyboards but guitar and bass as well. I had my own one-man band. We spent hundreds of hours in his basement producing my songs. It was addicting. All I did was write songs, take them to Bob's place and record them. Between Bob and me and his wife, Astrid, we did everything. We sang everything and played everything and produced everything. We had developed a system that suited me to a T. I could feel the world turning in my favour. I couldn't wait to see what was in store.

Patrick was busy studying at the University of Calgary. He was up to his neck with the stress and anxiety of getting all of his work done. Pat had always been so easygoing, but university brought out the temper in him, which surprised us all. He would punch holes in the walls in his bedroom out of sheer frustration. (My parents were none too pleased about having holes in their walls, and who could blame them?) My mom said she didn't know what to do with him. I am sure there were days when she felt like the whole lot of us had lost our marbles. I didn't see Pat that much. He was five years younger than me and school was taking up most, if not all, of his time. I was busy writing music and playing in the bars, and Duray was working diligently on his criminal record. Maybe we had all lost our marbles.

My dad stayed on track. He continued going to AA meetings a few times a week and they, combined with his sheer determination, turned his life around. I can't imagine how hard it was to face his demons head on and come to terms with the changes he needed to make for himself and our entire family. It's incredible to me now how much both of my parents sacrificed to remain a committed team. They didn't give up, ever. They kept us all together no matter what that took. I am beyond grateful now as I look back on those difficult times.

Sobriety suited my dad for the most part, although he still yelled a lot. Still, the yelling came in fewer and shorter bursts. He had started his own concrete and construction company and was working harder than anyone I'd ever met. Fourteen- to sixteen-hour days had always been the norm for him and for my mom. When it came to work ethic, they set the bar high.

Neil and Rudy thought I had hit a wall and needed to expand my horizons a bit more. I knew they were right. Sometimes I felt limited in what I could do with Bob, although working together was completely wonderful. Neil had mentioned many times the possibility of going down to Nashville to record. He had a friend living down there, a producer named Miles Wilkenson. He thought Miles would be able to do a really professional job and provide us with demos good enough to shop to the labels. All we needed was the money to get down there.

I was excited about going anywhere. I hadn't travelled much other than my ill-fated trip to Vancouver. (I guess I should also mention my Hawaiian adventure with Theresa and a vacation to Disneyland that my parents took us on in the seventies.) Other than that, I had been stuck in Alberta.

I told my mom and dad about Neil's idea of recording some songs in Tennessee and they both seemed very excited for me. I didn't dare bring up how we were going to get there. I knew that my folks didn't have that kind of money lying around, so I didn't ask.

A few weeks went by, and I had more or less put Nashville out of my mind. I was going to meet my parents at Tony Roma's for dinner. We didn't go out that often to eat, but when we did, mom and dad would always split an entree. You could call them frugal, but they certainly weren't cheap. Near the end of our meal, my dad was rummaging around underneath the table. The waitress was in the middle of clearing away our rib bones when my dad placed an envelope on the table in front of me. He had the funniest look on his face. He said, "Your mom and I want you to have a chance." That's all he said. I knew what he meant. They wanted me to be able to go to Nashville and record my songs. He told me to open the envelope. It was sealed shut so I had to rip it open. My mom told me to be careful not to rip what was inside of it.

I pulled out five brand-new, crisp, one-thousand-dollar bills. I could not believe my eyes. I looked at my parents in disbelief. For one thing, I had never seen a one-thousand-dollar bill. I didn't know they existed. My mom said that maybe something good would come of it, and I wouldn't know unless I tried.

The lump in my throat was the size of a grapefruit. My parents could not afford to be giving me five thousand dollars. I didn't know what to say. I kept looking at it like it wasn't real, like I was dreaming. I was so grateful not only for the money, but because they actually believed that I could make something of myself. I am sure they were scared for me. They didn't want me to be hurt or rejected. Lord knows I didn't want to be hurt or rejected either.

So Neil and I went down to Nashville. We recorded four songs with Miles in the basement studio in the EMI building. I felt like I was on top of the world. I got to work with some brilliant musicians. I couldn't believe how my songs took shape. The sounds were so lush and so rich. Miles was an amazing engineer and a gifted producer. The five thousand dollars went a long way. Looking back, it was the best investment my dad ever made.

We flew home a week later with our treasured tapes in our hands. I knew that what we had done was really good—I didn't doubt it for a second. I played the songs over and over again in my little basement apartment. I am sure June was ready to kill me but I didn't care.

Neil had a plan. He sent my four-song cassette to Virgin Records. That was his number-one pick, so that's where we started our campaign. A guy named Doug Chappell was the president of the label at the time and he had a solid reputation for being a "song guy." I was excited about Virgin Records because a little band called U2 was signed there. I loved U2. Doug listened to the songs and wasn't too sure of what to make of them. He remarked about how personal they were. I think that made him a bit nervous. He was very constructive and positive with his criticism. He doled out the kindest rejection I ever received. He said he liked them but wasn't sure if the label was in a position to break a new artist. Unbeknownst to us, Doug sent the cassette along to a young A&R guy named Allan Reid, who had just started working at A&M Records in Toronto.

Allan was really set on signing a grunge band of some kind. The Seattle scene was exploding and he wanted to become a part of that. Doug told him to give my songs a listen. "She's got something there, and I'm not sure what that something is." Allan said he'd get to it eventually. I am pretty sure that signing a nearly thirty-year-old singer/songwriter from Springbank, Alberta, was nowhere near the top of his list.

Lucky for me, Allan's girlfriend had dumped him a few days after he got my cassette. Heartbroken and completely down in the dumps, he went for a drive to clear his head and listen to some tunes. The tunes he ended up listening to were mine. One song in particular, called "I Just Don't Love You Anymore," struck a nerve. He said he pulled his car over and "got it." He thought that if a twenty-six-year-old guy who liked grunge could understand this kind of music and be moved by it then he wanted to be a part of putting it out there.

Allan called Neil and set up an appointment to come see me sing in person. When Neil told me that there was some real interest coming from A&M Records, I nearly fell over. I didn't think it was possible. Everything we'd been working towards was coming together, and I was nearly breathless thinking about it.

Neil knew he had to present me in the right situation. He wanted it to be very simple. He didn't want the band backing me up; he didn't want a lot of people in the audience. He wanted me to sing five or six songs on my guitar in a stripped-down, almost bare setting. I hoped he knew what he was doing. I was beyond nervous—I was a wreck. Didn't I need the band behind me? But Neil was adamant: no band.

He rented a small space called the Pumphouse Theatre in Calgary. He told them he only needed it for a few hours one evening, but they told him in turn that they had a production going on at the time and it wasn't going to work. Neil begged. He arranged for us to go in the early afternoon so that we could be out of there before the play began. The Pumphouse people seemed okay with that. There was only one drawback. The stage I was set to perform on had a giant eight-foot papier mâché penis on it. They said they could move it to the side, but you'd still be able to see it from the audience. Good grief.

Neil didn't seem to think it was going to be a problem. He said that, if anything, it would be memorable. I mean, how could Allan forget a giant penis? So I stood beside the giant you-know-what and played my songs for an audience of three—Neil, Allan and Rudy. I could see the three of them sitting there, but just barely. The lights were in my eyes. Neil didn't want me to talk in between songs, he just wanted me to sing, so that's what I did.

I went home afterwards and waited on pins and more pins to hear back from Neil about what Allan thought. It was an eternity. It was longer than an eternity.

I found out later from Neil that Allan had listened carefully and hadn't commented at all. He'd just sat there looking at me and bobbing his head back and forth. At the end, as they made their way out of the theatre, Allan said to Neil, "Let's make a record."

Neil had done what he had told me he was going to do five years earlier—help me navigate the complex world of the music business. He called me later that night to tell me the good news.

"You just got a record deal, Jann. Congratulations."

I hung up the phone and cried for hours.

I was nearly thirty years old.

I was in a wonderful, beautiful, blissful state of shock. It took days, if not weeks, for the whole thing to settle in. I walked down the street with my feet barely touching the ground. My parents were beyond happy for me. My mom told me that she always knew I could do it. My dad was excited too. He wanted to know about the practical side of things, contracts and the like. I knew he would be looking out for me, and that he wouldn't take any crap from anybody. I was glad to have him on my side. Neil told me that we had a lot of challenges ahead of us, and that the real work was about to begin. I didn't care how much work it was going to be. I was willing to do whatever I needed to do to succeed.

But just as excitement and happiness swept over my entire family, pain and anguish were on their heels.

I had seen my brother Duray a few days before we got the call. He had decided to move to a little town in British Columbia a couple of months after getting out of jail, where he'd been for something minor. He phoned to tell us that he was coming back to Calgary to pick up some of the things that he'd left behind and wanted to meet us all for dinner. Patrick and mom and dad and I met him at Boston Pizza. We had a good visit. We laughed a lot. My mom and dad thought that maybe this would finally be the end of his problems. He was moving away and making a fresh start. He seemed in good spirits, happy to be free and moving forward. He was excited about his new job and his apartment. He was so happy and excited for me. He was so proud.

"You're gonna be a star, Jannie. You're gonna be rich!"

Duray explained he wanted to go somewhere where nobody knew him, and I can't say I blame him for that. He had so much baggage in Calgary. The police followed him around like a jilted lover. He couldn't do anything without them breathing down his neck. We ate our pizza, visited some more, and then we all went outside to say goodbye. Mom and dad and Pat and I stood and waved to him as he pulled out of the parking lot onto Sarcee Trail. He had no muffler on his car, and there was a huge plume of black smoke trailing behind him as he hit the gas.

It was the last time I saw him free.

A few days later the RCMP called my parents at home and told them that Duray had been arrested for the first-degree murder of a young woman named Carrie Marshall.

Our lives stopped. Everything stopped. I worried that my parents would die right then and there, but they didn't. They broke into a million tiny fragments of themselves, but they didn't die. They kept standing. They are still standing.

It hit the news the following day. We had thirty or forty calls to the house from people we hardly knew, all wanting the gory details. We wanted to disappear.

My brother has denied having anything to do with the murder since the day he was arrested. The RCMP had no other suspects but him. They didn't look for anybody else. They said they had their man.

—

Life is so random.

It picks you up and drops you off wherever it likes.

It breaks your heart into tiny shards of glass.

It humbles you.

You cling to love like it is the very last breath of air you will ever take.

I do.

For every line I have written down here, there are a thousand lines in between. There are so many moments that are floating through time and space that I will never be able to save or document. I don't think they're gone, I just don't think they're mine anymore. They belong to God. They belong to the incredible force of will that made me and made Duray and made Patrick and my mother and father.

My memories are strings of lights wrapped around everyone I have ever known and loved.

I know that all of this, all of what is around me, will be taken away, but also I know that what is truly important to our humanity is indelible and eternal. We may not be able to touch it, but it's there just the same.

What a journey.

To have been here at all has been remarkable.

To have lived.

To have lived.

My brother Duray has been in jail for twenty years. He is married with one son and three stepchildren. He continues to fight to prove his innocence.

Patrick is a successful businessman in the petroleum industry. He has two amazing sons, one who has cystic fibrosis and the other who suffers from severe autism. They are both doing well, despite their challenges.

My mom and dad live fifty feet from me on an acreage we share, five miles from where I grew up with Leonard and Dale. They are healthy and well and truly amazing souls. They are my heart. My dad has been sober for over thirty years.

I have been with Universal Records for twenty years. I have made eleven albums and am about to make my twelfth. I wrote a book called Falling Backwards, *and I am really proud of it.*

ACKNOWLEDGEMENTS

Thank you to my wonderful, kind-hearted, exceptionally brilliant editor, Michelle MacAleese, for making me feel like a real writer and making sense of my meanderings. And to Anne Collins and everyone at Random House of Canada for their hard work on this book.

To Michael Schellenberg, for starting this whole project off . . .

Thanks to my manager, Bruce Allen, to Jo Faloona and everyone at Bruce Allen Talent for their attention to detail, support, and enthusiasm for not only this, but everything I take on.

Thank you to my assistant, Chris Brunton, for making my life easy, organized and a lot of fun!

I would like to thank my family and my friends and everyone I have written about in this book . . . Thank you for being such a beautiful and inspirational part of my life.

Jann

Since releasing her debut album in 1993, Jann Arden has had seventeen top-ten singles from eight albums including "I Would Die for You," "Could I Be Your Girl" and "Insensitive." Winner of eight Junos and recipient of the National Achievement Award from SOCAN, Arden was also inducted into the Canadian Association of Broadcasters Hall of Fame and was the winner of the International Achievement Award at the 2007 Western Canadian Music Awards. She is the author of *If I Knew, Don't You Think I'd Tell You?* and *I'll Tell You One Damn Thing, and That's All I Know!*

A NOTE ABOUT THE TYPE

The body of *Falling Backwards* has been set in a digitized form of Bembo, a typeface based on an old-style Roman face that was used for Cardinal Bembo's tract De Aetna in 1495. Bembo was first cut by Francisco Griffo in the early sixteenth century. The Lanston Monotype Corporation of Philadelphia brought the well-proportioned letterforms of Bembo to North America in the 1930s.